COMPARATIVE WORLD POLITICS

edited by

COMPARATIVE
Readings in Western and

Wadsworth Publishing

Joel Larus, Brandeis University

WORLD POLITICS
Premodern Non-Western International Relations

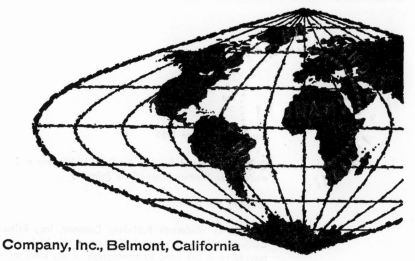

Company, Inc., Belmont, California

To J. B. L.

Third printing, June 1966

Comparative World Politics: Readings in Western and Pre-modern Non-Western International Relations

edited by Joel Larus

L. C. Cat. Card No.: 64-21773

Printed in the United States of America

The exclusive concentration in international relations courses today on the political theories and practices of the Western nation-states has compelled scholars and students to generalize about world politics without a sufficiently wide historical perspective. To help extend the current orientation, this book—something of an experiment—not only offers readings that emphasize the classical Western nation-state system and its modern, missile-age counterpart, but also provides a broadly conceived introduction to the premodern inter-state relations of (1) the Chinese Empire, (2) India before the Muslim ascendancy, and (3) the Islamic community.

No pioneering effort in any field springs into existence fully matured. This book, in due course, will be superseded by other works structured along similar lines because comparative world politics adds a new and provocative dimension to the study of international relations. As will be more fully developed in the introductory chapter, I believe that incorporating select material from the political systems of premodern, non-Western civilizations will benefit in a variety of ways a discipline long noted for its intellectual soul-searching. So the task that I have undertaken is to assemble a number of the leading concepts and ideas about the conduct of foreign affairs developed by China, India, and Arabia and to present them with the hope that the novel approach of the book will excite both the comment and the criticism of those who are interested in the further maturing of this field of study.

The format for arranging the chapters, as well as the articles themselves, requires a word of explanation. Each chapter was planned according to a threefold division of material. A selection that describes or analyzes a topic from a pre-1945 point of view introduces each group of essays. A number of these lead pieces have become classics. Each one emphasizes a number of provocative ideas concerning the classical political behavior formulated by the Western states. Following the initial selection are readings that concentrate on the premodern, non-Western states. (The original plan was to include essays from all three areas—China, India, and the Middle East—in each chapter, but it soon became apparent that considerable variation would be necessary. In some instances, no material was available because the chapter's topic was unknown in the older state-craft, and some readings were so specialized that they could not be appreciated by beginners.) The final article of each chapter returns to the contemporary scene and deals with the chapter topic from the vantage of the Age of Missiles. This arrangement of the selections, I believe, provides the most stimulating approach to comparative world politics.

Admittedly, this book of readings is broadly conceived. It has been planned to supplement, not to replace, any standard, Western-oriented international relations text. It intends to provoke thinking about the inter-state systems of a select number of non-Western empires and to present evidence of the patterns of continuity and change that exist between the Western nation-state system and its non-Western antecedents.

Many people have aided in bringing this book to completion. No author could ask for a more candid associate than James Barros of Dartmouth College. Originally a coeditor of these readings, Professor Barros was awarded a Fulbright at a critical stage of the book's early development and forced to withdraw. He remained an invaluable source of ideas and served as a model for intellectual integrity. Others who have read all or part of the text are Professors Donald Hindley of Brandeis and William T. R. Fox of Columbia. Each provided his valued judgment without incurring any responsibility for the format used or the views expressed. For their perceptive criticism and helpful comments, I wish to thank Stanley Anderson of the University of California, Santa Barbara; A. A. Castagno, Jr., of Queens College, New York; E. B. Haas of the University of California, Berkeley; John H. Herz of the City College of New York; K. J. Holsti of the University of British Columbia; Morton A. Kaplan of the Center of International Studies, Princeton University; Gerard J. Mangone of Syracuse University; Charles A. McClelland of San Francisco State College; and Walter L. Riley of the University of Washington. Finally, I am indebted to my students at Columbia and at Brandeis. Numerous improvements in the book resulted from their criticisms and suggestions.

Joel Larus

CONTENTS

INTRODUCTION

I

It is a poorly kept secret among social scientists that professors of international relations are unable to agree on the general assumptions and guiding principles of their area of study. The continual outpouring of new textbooks and annotated readers is testimony to the heterogeneity of the field as well as to the fertility of academic pens. The chairman of a discussion group consisting of a number of political scientists was probably more accurate than he realized when he introduced one of the participants as "an international relations professor distinguished for not having written a text in his field."

The struggle to establish international relations as an autonomous branch of political science has been described in some detail.[1] Those who have piloted this movement have repeatedly emphasized the need to develop a discipline distinguished both for its systematic reasoning and for its practical application to the current political scene. Because of the diverse intellectual commitments of international relations professors, a number of approaches have emerged concerning the relations of political communities. One scholar lists four ways to organize a course: the institutional, the historical, the philosophical, and the behavioral.[2] Another

---

[1] See Kenneth W. Thompson, "The Study of International Politics: A Survey of Trends and Developments," *Review of Politics*, XIV, No. 4 (October 1952), 433–457; William T. R. Fox and Annette Baker Fox, "The Teaching of International Relations in the United States," *World Politics*, XIII, No. 3 (April 1961), 339–359; Grayson Kirk, *The Study of International Relations in American Colleges and Universities* (New York: Council on Foreign Relations, Inc., 1947); Richard N. Swift, *World Affairs and the College Curriculum* (Washington, D.C.: American Council on Education, 1959); and Quincy Wright, *Study of International Relations* (New York: Appleton-Century-Crofts, Inc., 1955).

[2] Vernon Van Dyke, ed., *Some Approaches and Concepts Used in the Teaching of International Politics* (Iowa City: State University of Iowa, 1957), p. 5.

1

believes that a threefold grouping is more accurate and useful. These are the "states as actors," the "minds of men," and "corporate actors."[3] Others have stated that a more suitable arrangement is "the principle approach," "the country-by-country approach," or "the transformation approach."[4] One text declares that "roughly speaking, there have been two fundamental approaches to the problems of international politics": "general explanatory concepts" and "detailed empirical analysis."[5]

Regardless of their particular schools of analysis in the study of international relations, the leading textbooks utilize the same source materials. Scholars who are historically inclined, as well as those who are power oriented or concerned with the behavioral aspects of the field, concentrate their investigations almost exclusively on the foreign policies and diplomatic activities of the Western states. The Western nation-state system has thus become almost the sole source of empirical data in the field. This orientation has caused international relations (and international law) to become an exceedingly parochial discipline. A more academically precise title for the course that is typically offered in American colleges and universities could well be *The Western State in World Politics: 1648 to the Present.*

As a result of this self-imposed restriction, almost no attention has been given to the political patterns of non-Western states before they became the victims of European power. Their inter-state relations—their distinctive systems of fighting wars and maintaining peace—have been all but ignored in the field. It is indeed rare when international relations publicists depict Asia or the Middle East as areas in which, prior to the arrival of the Europeans, there were political communities that had distinctive modes of handling external affairs.[6] There have been many learned studies of the art, music, and religions of these regions, but the American-European community of political scientists has yet to examine with any degree of thoroughness the precolonial statecraft of China, India, or regions controlled by the Arabs.[7] Such self-imposed academic isolation is not difficult

[3] Arnold Wolfers, "The Actors in International Politics," in William T. R. Fox, ed., *Theoretical Aspects of International Relations* (Notre Dame, Ind.: University of Notre Dame Press, 1959), pp. 83–106.

[4] Fox and Fox, p. 350.

[5] Richard N. Rosecrance, *Action and Reaction in World Politics* (Boston: Little, Brown and Co., 1963), pp. 1–2. The author introduces a third approach, which he calls "systematic empirical analysis" (pp. 5ff.).

[6] Two books that analyze and examine non-Western inter-state systems are Frank M. Russell's *Theories of International Relations* (New York: Appleton-Century-Crofts, Inc., 1936), and Adda B. Bozeman, *Politics and Culture in International History* (Princeton, N.J.: Princeton University Press, 1960).

[7] In the introduction to a collection of essays that he edited, Professor Fairbank notes: "In penetrating the neglected field of Chinese political thought, these papers deal less with the formulations of classical texts than with the use of Confucian ideas in

to explain. An assumption is commonly made that the ancient Far East is unfathomable and the premodern Near East unintelligible to anyone but the area expert. Large gaps exist in the training and in the background of the academic generalists who normally teach the basic course in international affairs. Familiar events, pronounceable names, and a recognizable geography are not present when one moves away from the political experiences of the principal Western states. Competence in Chinese, Arabic, or Hindu and Sanskrit is not so easily acquired as is a working knowledge of French or German. Furthermore, some professors do not believe that it is prudent to attempt to transcend one's own culture. The result is that many students have the impression that these non-Western regions were unacquainted with the problems of power politics before the first European traders and settlers arrived.

There is no need to question the major emphasis placed on the external affairs of the Western powers in courses dealing with world affairs: one has but to consider the impact of the Western nation-states around the globe during the past three hundred years. The political activities of Great Britain, France, Germany, Italy, Russia, and the United States unquestionably support the position of those who concentrate on the Western nation-state system and its principal tenets, assumptions, and theoretical structure for the conduct of international relations. However, *the political record of the non-Western state systems has been cast aside in much too arbitrary a manner.*

II

Consider briefly the inter-state system of the Chinese Empire, the earliest Hindu polity of India, or the Muslim community before each became a victim of the West's superiority in arms and technology. Centuries before the age of the nation-state, each in its own way had become a great power, dominated a significant area of the world, and developed a distinctive pattern of state behavior that reflected its own unique civilization, its geo-

---

political struggles and sociopolitical institutions. Rather surprisingly, these studies have been produced by historians, with some sociological assistance, rather than by political scientists. The latter, though in a discipline which seems not to be moribund, have generally succeeded thus far in avoiding the challenge of the Chinese political record— in spite of the fact that it is not only easily accessible in our libraries, but represents, after all, the most long-continued experience of government, in the most populous of states, in human history." John K. Fairbank, ed., *Chinese Thought and Institutions* (Chicago: University of Chicago Press, 1957), p. 1.

At another point in the same work Professor Fairbank states: "It is a commentary on political science studies of China in the West that the most thorough work in English on the Ch'ing administration is now thirty years old . . ." (p. 382).

graphical conditions, and the political pressures to which it was exposed. The complex of techniques that these states employed in their respective external affairs represent the three most important non-Western systems of statecraft that can be examined. For this reason, they have been selected for discussion in this book.

What do we know of these societies? Sinologists generally agree that the recorded history of the Chinese civilization is the longest known to man. As early as the Shang dynasty (c. 1500–1100 B.C.) the Chinese began to develop a scheme for conducting relations with adjacent tribes and states. The institutional framework and philosophical doctrines of the Chinese system of inter-state relations came from the writings of Confucius and his disciples, the most notable of whom was Mencius. In looking beyond their country, the early Chinese were greatly impressed with their own cultural superiority. They decided that the inhabitants of the areas surrounding the Middle Kingdom were barbarians, men whose culture and ethics were markedly inferior to their own. Furthermore, they believed that the Confucian principles of government—which included suasion, courtesy, ruling by virtuous example, and avoidance of the use of military power to resolve political conflicts—was so irresistible that no barbarian state could withstand the attraction of Chinese preeminence. Leaders in Korea, Annam, Laos, Nepal, Burma, and Siam could not help but recognize the superiority of Confucian society and "would naturally seek to 'come and be transformed' (lai-hua) and so participate in its benefits."[8]

These ideas formed the basis of China's famed tributary system, an inter-state arrangement that lasted with varying degrees of success approximately twenty-five hundred years. During these centuries, the court at Peking expected barbarian states to accept their designated role and periodically to send representatives and gifts to the Emperor. "The formalities of the tributary system," according to one distinguished expert, "constituted a mechanism by which formerly barbarous regions outside the empire were given their place in the all-embracing Sinocentric cosmos."[9]

The typical introductory course in international relations fails to discuss the Chinese empire before the onset of Western imperialism. This omission denies the importance of a truly remarkable political organization. Professor Paul M. A. Linebarger rightly chides Western scholars for neglecting "a working international system—the Confucian Family of Nations—which antedated the Western community of nations by some

[8] John K. Fairbank, "Tributary Trade and China's Relations with the West," *Far Eastern Quarterly*, I, No. 2 (1942), 132.

[9] Fairbank, p. 133.

centuries and which had functioned as well as, if not better than, its Western counterpart."[10]

Equally disturbing is the lack of attention given to the Hindu system of inter-state relations before the ascendancy of the Muslim invaders. To most Westerners, the Hindu civilization probably is the least familiar of those examined here; but even a cursory recital of early Indian history reveals that Hindu statecraft is far from being the least politically sophisticated.

Two great empires existed in ancient India. Chandragupta Maurya, in the early part of the fourth century B.C., succeeded in unifying all of the country north of the Narbada River and established the first centralized state in Indic history. Undoubtedly the most illustrious Mauryan king was Chandragupta's grandson, Asoka, who reigned from 273 to 232 B.C. At the peak of his military career, and with his armies triumphant, Asoka decided to devote the remainder of his life to championing the humanitarian ethics of his new Buddhist faith. He renounced war as an instrument of Mauryan policy and pledged never to fight again except to repel an invader. In his *Outline of History*, H. G. Wells says of Asoka:

Amidst the tens of thousands of names of monarchs that crowd the columns of history, their majesties and graciousnesses and serenities and royal highnesses and the like, the name of Asoka shines, and shines almost alone, a star. From the Volga to Japan his name is still honoured. China, Tibet, and even India, though it has left his doctrine, preserve the tradition of his greatness. More living men cherish his memory today than have ever heard the names of Constantine or Charlemagne.[11]

The second important Hindu dynasty was the Gupta, which ruled India from approximately 300 A.D. to the middle of the sixth century. This period is still remembered as the Golden Age of Hindu civilization: art flourished; the Gupta kings ruled skillfully and were militarily successful. The Gupta capital city of Pataliputra was known throughout much of Asia.

Although a number of impressive political treatises were written during these many centuries, the one generally ascribed to Kautilya, the political adviser and personal confidant of Chandragupta, is the masterpiece of ancient Hindu statecraft. He described and analyzed in considerable detail a wide assortment of political problems that confronted the Hindu

[10] Paul M. A. Linebarger, Djang Chu, and Ardath W. Burks, *Far Eastern Governments and Politics* (New York: D. Van Nostrand Co., Inc., 1954), p. 88.

[11] H. G. Wells, *Outline of History* (New York: Triangle Books, 1940), I, 404; quoted in Jawaharlal Nehru, *The Discovery of India* (New York: Doubleday & Co., Inc., 1959), p. 126.

state, but we are concerned only with the advice he offered concerning inter-state relations.

What were the distinguishing characteristics of this system that differed in so many respects from both the Chinese and the Muslim? A study of the principles which Kautilya expounded in the *Arthaśāstra* reveals a striking analysis of foreign affairs and power politics. In the sections devoted to inter-state relations, he established his reputation for being "the greatest Indian exponent of the art of government, the duties of kings, ministers, and officials, and the methods of diplomacy."[12] His philosophy of statecraft is based on a code in which moral considerations, religious beliefs, and legal norms did not play a significant part. Hindu inter-state relations, Kautilya maintained, are invariably marked by perpetual strife and constant intrigue. Every ruler is expected to dedicate himself unceasingly to the acquisition, preservation, and unlimited aggrandizement of his kingdom, even as he plots and conspires for the disintegration of his enemy's power. What components of state power did the early Hindu kings consider of primary importance? Did these monarchs have any appreciation whatsoever of such concepts as balance of power or international law? Was the Buddhist emphasis on nonviolence, so dramatically evinced by Asoka, a permanent influence in the formulation of the foreign policies of later Indian kings?

These questions concerning the inter-state relations of the Hindu state are not unimportant to students who attempt to understand India's foreign policies in the Missile Age. "Undoubtedly the most distinctive and in all probability the most significant part of Indian political thought," Professor Norman D. Palmer has noted, "is the political thought of ancient India, chiefly Hindu polity."[13] Most of today's international relations publicists, however, write about the India that was under British control or that existed after the subcontinent achieved independence. Unquestionably, the tragedy that took place at the Black Hole of Calcutta in 1756 deeply affected Asia's relations with the major European powers; Mahatma Gandhi's campaign of nonviolence and noncooperation helped bring about an end to Western imperialism. Furthermore, India's boundary dispute with Pakistan over the Kashmir, its mercurial relations with the Chinese Communists, even the demographic problems of the country are current topics that do affect world politics. But students of international relations should not be reluctant to turn back to the Mauryan and Gupta dynasties to investigate their inter-state system, because "If Indian administration

---

[12] *Arthaśāstra*, trans. R. Shamasastry (Mysore, India: Mysore Printing and Publishing House, 1961), p. v.

[13] "Indian and Western Political Thought: Coalescence or Clash?" *American Political Science Review*, XLIX, No. 3 (September 1955), 753.

of today is analysed to its bases," the distinguished Asian historian K. M. Panikkar notes, "the doctrines and practices of Chanakya [Kautilya] will be found to be still in force."[14]

The classical Islamic system of inter-state relations has received as little attention from contemporary scholars as either the Chinese or the Hindu system. After the death of the Prophet Muḥammad in 632 A.D., his followers initiated a century of unprecedented religious and political activity. From its origin in Arabia, the Muslim community of the Middle East envisioned a universal Islamic state and attempted to defeat those who refused to accept the theological and institutional ideas set out in the Koran. In their quest for empire, the various caliphs (literally, successor to the Prophet) sent their armies to conquer the world for their faith. Arab troops raced westward across North Africa into Spain and France, and for a time it appeared that their drive for European hegemony could not be stopped. But at Tours, in 732 A.D., Charles Martel permanently ended their military advances in this area. During the same period, the banner of Islam was carried eastward into Asia. In 712 A.D., it reached the Sind area of the lower Indus valley; by the middle of the sixteenth century, Muslim armies had destroyed the Hindu empire.

The political and military activity of the Muslims represents the third major non-Western system of inter-state relations to be discussed. Students of politics will be interested in learning how Islamic foreign policy during the zenith of Muslim power was influenced by the Koran. Were Muslim leaders concerned with problems of ethics in their drive to win supremacy? If not, why not? What role did the Islamic community assign to war? Did the Muslims formulate any diplomatic procedures before they came into frequent contact with the great European powers of the sixteenth century? One would look in vain for the answers to such questions in a standard international relations text.

III

What advantages—if any—does a comparative approach to the field of international relations offer to students and teachers? To answer the question, we must know in what specific ways those who are interested in world politics will better appreciate this complex area of human relations by reading selected material from the non-Western states' political heritage along with the customary matter dealing with the foreign policies of the Western powers. Two multifaceted main questions must be answered affirmatively. First, will an even more meaningful discipline of inter-

[14] A Survey of Indian History (Bombay: Asia Publishing House, 1954), p. 29.

national relations emerge if the sources of empirical data are broadened to include non-Western, inter-state political systems? After examining a group of readings pertaining to the statecraft of precolonial China, India, and the Islamic community, will political analysts be better able to evaluate the foreign relations of European states? Will the student gain an enriched appreciation of the Western world's political experiences since the Treaty of Westphalia of 1648, the date when it is generally agreed that the nation-state system began to assume its modern form? Will a comparative approach be significant and practical for research scholars who are vigorously attempting to construct a theory of international relations?

The second basic question deals with the contemporary value of comparative world politics. Is it reasonable to expect that the current foreign policies of Peking, Cairo, Rawalpindi, Riyadh, or New Delhi will be more intelligible to students who have had some exposure to the classical inter-state patterns and beliefs of the predecessor governments of these non-Western capitals? Will there be a strengthened discipline if the sources of empirical data are broadened?

The comparative approach adds a decidedly worthwhile dimension to the political perspective of the academic community, students and teachers alike. Much in the West's political experience during the last three hundred years is not unique. Not all the political concepts, forms, and institutions used by European powers and the United States are peculiar to Western civilization. Many ideas and instrumentalities that are associated with Great Britain, France, or the United States have an Asian counterpart or a Middle Eastern equivalent that often antedates the Treaty of Westphalia.

Niccolò Machiavelli, for example, is the tutelary hero of many Western-trained students of international affairs. His chapters in *The Prince* have provided countless generations with a powerful explanation of the mainsprings of state action. Political realism, the school of statecraft that Machiavelli epitomizes, has equally illustrious Asian supporters. A section of the *Mahābhārata*, one of the two epic poems of ancient India, is part of the same tradition. It deserves to be more widely known. In one section, Kanika, who is described as the "foremost of ministers—well-versed in the science of politics and expert in counsels," offers his king advice on how best to deal with his allies and enemies. "Kings," he says, "should sometimes feign blindness and deafness, for if impotent to chastise they should pretend not to notice the faults that call for chastisement." In the same speech, Kanika cautions that "in speech thou shouldst ever be humble, but let thy heart be ever sharp as the razor. And when thou art engaged in doing even a very cruel and terrible act, thou shouldst talk with smiles on thy lips."[15]

As these quotations indicate, the student who reads and considers *The Prince,* the *Mahābhārata,* and the *Arthaśāstra* will gain the opportunity to enlarge his political perspective. Subtle policies that formerly might have escaped his notice may take on a new importance, and he may see more clearly the justification for political realism. The comparative approach to international relations reveals a number of such East-West parallels.

Since many incidents in the history of the Western nation-state system are novel, a comparative approach to the field may result in a sharper understanding of these events, too. The confrontation between the imperial Chinese court and the major European powers in the eighteenth, nineteenth, and twentieth centuries was an unprecedented clash of dissimilar state systems. Students of Far Eastern politics are probably familiar with the more dramatic incidents of the Sino-European confrontation. Great Britain's dispute concerning the performance of the kowtow—the traditional ceremonial act of three kneelings and nine prostrations—has been widely commented upon.[16] But was Peking's insistence that Western diplomats perform the kowtow before the Emperor simply an arrogant desire to humiliate foreigners who disturbed Chinese isolation or was it an essential aspect of Chinese inter-state relations? The famous letter that the Emperor of China wrote to George III in 1793 illustrates how ill-prepared the Manchu dynasty was to meet the West. Unable to compete with Britain's military and technological superiority, and unwilling to engage in Western-type state intercourse, China attempted to deal with Europeans in the same manner that it had employed in handling the barbarian peoples living on its periphery. This time the results were disastrous. Rejecting King George's requests to begin traditional Western-style diplomatic representation with his country, the emperor of the Celestial Dynasty wrote in part:

Swaying the wide world, I have but one aim in view, namely, to maintain a perfect governance and to fulfil the duties of the State. . . . Our dynasty's majestic virtue has penetrated unto every country under Heaven, and Kings of

[15] *Mahābhārata,* trans. Protap Chandra Roy (Calcutta: Bharata Press, 1883), I, 416–417, 421.
[16] Almost all studies of the foreign impact on China during the early nineteenth century deal with the kowtow dispute. See such standard texts as Harold M. Vinacke, *A History of the Far East in Modern Times,* 6th ed. (New York: Appleton-Century-Crofts, Inc., 1961), p. 56; Hosea Ballou Morse, *The International Relations of the Chinese Empire* (Shanghai: Kelly & Walsh, Ltd., 1910), pp. 48ff.; Kenneth Scott Latourette, *The Chinese: Their History and Culture* (New York: Macmillan Co., 1942), pp. 347ff.

all nations have offered their costly tribute by land and sea. As your Ambassador can see for himself, we possess all things . . . It behoves you, O King, to respect my sentiments and to display even greater devotion and loyalty in future, so that, by perpetual submission to our Throne, you may secure peace and prosperity for your country hereafter . . .[17]

His letter was not the foolhardy message of an arrogant and condescending emperor. Its significance and its meaning, along with the kowtow dispute, can be understood only after an examination of the classical pattern of inter-state relations of the Chinese court, including the regulations for tributary intercourse. Such incidents, involving a collision of differing political orientations, take on a new interpretation when this particular non-Western theory of the state has been examined.

A second benefit of the comparative approach to international relations concerns the present. Perhaps the influences hardest to isolate and evaluate in the formulation of the foreign policy of any government are (a) the force of tradition and culture, (b) the impact of historical experience, (c) religious attitudes, and (d) philosophical convictions. To assess with any great precision the extent to which the current foreign policies of Communist China, India, or of the various Arab states of the Middle East are the direct or indirect result of their respective political heritages is, of course, the assignment for an area expert. It is well beyond the scope of a general international relations course. It is possible, on the other hand, to make the student more aware of the effect of the past on the present. For serious students of international politics, a healthy sense of historical perspective means considerably more than merely understanding our Western tradition.

It is an irrefutable fact that the non-Western states have adopted the leading Western ideas and characteristics concerning the conduct of international relations. The nation-state system that originated and developed in the West has become a worldwide phenomenon. Sovereignty, nationalism, permanent diplomatic representation, and the norms of international law are but a few of the political ideas of the West that now give international politics a considerable degree of standardization. Nonetheless, many area specialists believe that the foreign policies of a number of the leading non-Western states cannot be fully understood if attention is paid exclusively to the political traditions which they share with the West. A more enlightened interpretation of non-Western statecraft, they maintain, is possible only after some attention has been given to the premodern systems of inter-state intercourse of these regions. Two of this country's leading Sinologists hold this position. Professor Fairbank has

[17] Edict of Ch'ien-lung to George III of England, quoted in Derk Bodde, *China's Cultural Tradition* (New York: Holt, Rinehart and Winston, Inc., 1959), pp. 62–63.

written that "no one can understand Chiang Kai-shek or even Mao Tse-
tung without knowing something of the Confucian tradition."[18] Professor
Linebarger is even more emphatic in stressing the continuing importance
of China's classical political patterns. He states that

the problem of the concentric structuring of an old Chinese Empire . . . would
be important only in the eyes of historians if the political habits, the semantic
drives, and the sense of appropriateness bequeathed to the Chinese past were
not communicated to the present. If there were any expectation among Western
observers that modern China would behave in colonial, frontier, and foreign
matters different from its Imperial predecessors, these doubts should have been
dispelled by the spectacle of Nationalist China, weak and war-ridden as it was,
attempting to raise a boundary issue with British Burma over a slice of un-
inhabited and uninhabitable jungle territory in the very midst of World War II,
or the sight of Communist China acting as the patron state for a necessarily
dependent Communist North Korea.[19]

Islamicists and Indianists, with varying degrees of enthusiasm, hold a
similar belief about the current significance of the political traditions of
their respective areas of scholarship. Professor Zeine N. Zeine of the
American University of Beirut leaves no doubts concerning his point of
view. He writes that

many students of contemporary Arab history are either uninformed or, looking
through the coloured glasses of modern political and secular nationalism, deliberately ignore and therefore fail to comprehend the religious background
of the forces which for centuries influenced and moulded the Arab Near East—
Islam.
    Hence for a correct understanding and appraisal of the Arab Near East, to-
day, a study of Islam, Muslim institutions and Muslim psychology is imperative.
Lacking this basic inquiry, other studies will touch only the surface and not the
heart of the matter.[20]

The importance of the political past to India's foreign policy today is
more arguable. Prime Minister Nehru repeatedly has said that "the most
important thing about our foreign policy is that it is part of our great

---

[18] John King Fairbank, *The United States and China*, rev. ed., (Cambridge, Mass.:
Harvard University Press, 1958), p. 52.
[19] Linebarger, Chu, and Burks, *Far Eastern Government*, p. 76.
[20] *Arab-Turkish Relations and the Emergence of Arab Nationalism* (Lebanon:
Khayat's Publishers, 1958), p. 118.
    In a less precise way, Professor George E. Kirk suggests the same conclusion. He
has written of the region, "clearly, there is a semantic double-standard between Middle
Eastern nationalists and Western governments. Does this double standard arise, as our
liberal critics suggest, from the sense of Middle Eastern physical inferiority and its
accompanying frustrations? Or does it have a deeper derivation in the time-honoured
concept of a double standard as between the Islamic world (*Dār ul-Islam*) and the
outer darkness of the unbelievers (*Dār ul-ḥarb*)?" George E. Kirk, *A Short History of
the Middle East* (London: Methuen & Co., Ltd., 1959), p. 316.

historical tradition"; his country has "evolved a foreign policy in keeping with the traditional background and temper of the country."[21] Distinguished Indian scholars agree. Dr. C. P. Ramaswami Aiyar of Annamalai University states:

Throughout the rich heritage of Indian literature . . . there are innumerable passages illustrating every known theory of government and temporal power. But it should not be forgotten that political thought is an integral aspect of Indian philosophy . . . Except in relation to such doctrines as rebirth and Karma, the meaning of the Indian heritage and the traditional Indian approach to world problems cannot be understood.[22]

Not all of today's political disputes can be explained by references to a nation's political history. Facile but unfounded comparisons between heterogeneous political systems are always a temptation to historians and political scientists. Frequent appeals to history to justify policy decisions are often made too casually. However, the principal governments of Asia and the Middle East to some degree have been influenced by their early views concerning inter-state relations, and academic concentration on the Western state system has barred beginning students of international relations even from considering the effects of these views.

Another reason supports a comparative approach to the field. In recent years, considerable activity has been devoted to postulating a theory of international relations that will analyze the discipline systematically.[23] Models and patterns of behavior have been constructed that attempt to anticipate the responses of states in a variety of hypothetical situations. A number of experimental techniques have been introduced, many of which are borrowed from allied disciplines. It is still too early to determine

[21] R. G. Neale, "Tradition and Foreign Policy in India" (unpublished essay, University of Queensland, Australia, n.d.), p. 3. Dr. Neale concludes: "All the principles of India's foreign policy . . . are not so much the outcome of a cultural heritage as [due] to the peculiar circumstances of the period in which they were developed."

[22] "Foreword," in D. Mackenzie Brown, The White Umbrella (Berkeley: University of California Press, 1953), p. v.

One of the leading American experts on India who disagree with this premise, Professor Norman D. Palmer, has written: "For all the efforts of the revivalists of Hindu traditions during the Hindu Renaissance of the late nineteenth and early twentieth centuries, and for all the present emphasis on the rediscovery of India's past, it is difficult to find any continuity between ancient Hindu political thought and the political ideas that move modern India, or to appraise the relative influence of the many streams of thought that have influenced modern India." The Indian Political System (Boston: Houghton Mifflin Co., 1962), p. 3.

[23] See, for example, Stanley H. Hoffmann, Contemporary Theory in International Relations (Englewood Cliffs, N.J.: Prentice-Hall, Inc., 1960); Morton A. Kaplan, System and Process in International Politics (New York: John Wiley & Sons, Inc., 1957); Klaus E. Knorr and Sidney Verba, eds., The International System: Theoretical Essays (Princeton, N.J.: Princeton University Press, 1961).

with any assurance whether scholars concerned with theory building will produce worthwhile results, but one general observation concerning their research is in order.

The experiences of a single state model are too narrow a base on which to theorize or even to establish a framework of ideas from which to speculate. Those undertaking such investigations should consider as broad a range of data as possible, but they have concentrated their research almost exclusively on the Western nation-state system. The political heritage of Asia and the Middle East, though, should not be discounted. A total field can never be grasped in a scientific manner if the selection of material is made in a restricted and rigid way.

Balance of power, to mention just one topic that is almost always considered in international relations, is among the most frequently analyzed doctrines in world politics. Exponents of a theory of international relations, as well as those more concerned with a descriptive analysis of the field, seek to explore its innermost determinants.[24] But the balance-of-power concepts that were developed by non-Western states in their pre-colonial histories are seldom considered in such explorations. Source material is certainly not lacking. Chandragupta determined Mauryan foreign policy according to a balance-of-power arrangement that the ancient Hindus called the *maṇḍala* system, and its operation is carefully recorded in Kautilya's *Arthaśāstra*. This "principal Hindu formula for the arrangement of foreign alliances and coalitions"[25] is as politically intuitive as the frequently cited 1907 Memorandum on the balance of power by Sir Eyre Crowe. There is evidence that Chinese statesmen also appreciated the im-

[24] See such significant studies of the balance of power as Inis L. Claude Jr., *Power and International Relations* (New York: Random House, Inc., 1962), pp. 11–149; Frederick H. Gareau, ed., *The Balance of Power and Nuclear Deterrence* (Boston: Houghton Mifflin Co., 1962); Edward Vose Gulick, *Europe's Classical Balance of Power* (Ithaca, N.Y.: Cornell University Press, 1955); Ernest B. Haas, "The Balance of Power as a Guide to Policy Making," *The Journal of Politics*, XV, No. 3 (August 1953), 370–398, and "The Balance of Power: Concept, Prescription or Propaganda," *World Politics*, V, No. 4 (July 1953), 459–474; Morton A. Kaplan, "Balance of Power, Bipolarity and Other Models of International Systems," *The American Political Science Review*, LI, No. 3 (September 1957), 684–695; Hans J. Morgenthau, *Politics among Nations: The Struggle for Power and Peace*, 3rd ed. (New York: Alfred A. Knopf, Inc., 1960; Richard N. Rosecrance, *Action and Reaction in World Politics* (Boston: Little, Brown and Co., 1963).

[25] Heinrich Zimmer, *Philosophies of India*, ed. Joseph Campbell (Cleveland: World Publishing Co., 1956), p. 114.

Concerning the *maṇḍala*, the late Professor Zimmer said, "This somewhat formal pattern...reflects the geographical conditions of the Indian subcontinent. Also it is amply warranted by the modern history of Europe. It is the basic figure of a kind of political geometry that can be applied with few adjustments to the practical reckoning of the stresses in almost any historical sense..." pp. 115–116.

portance of balancing power with power.[26] A systematic exploration of these early non-Western concepts, along with the balance-of-power systems formulated in the West, might conceivably lead to worthwhile conclusions concerning the central validity of the doctrine.

A final reason supporting a comparative approach to the study of international relations is to offer a measure of hope for the future. A bipolar world replete with nuclear and thermonuclear weapons is a new feature of world politics, and this book of readings attempts to illustrate the momentous changes this feature brings by offering essays that illustrate the nature of international affairs before and after World War II. The West's experiences in the Nuclear Age can be characterized as years of unprecedented international crises and unique political dilemmas.

Concurrent with the new problems of bipolar politics are many international issues that were as troublesome to the leaders of the ancient non-Western states as they have been to post-1945 European governments. The development and maintenance of regional alliances, disarmament, diplomacy, and the formulation of inter-state legal codes are but a sampling of the timeless nature of international affairs. Recognition that non-Western civilizations have attempted to deal with these topics—and with a fair degree of success—is not without importance. Not infrequently, today's students of world affairs are overly anxious to beat the swords into plowshares *immediately*. But they may have to accept an imperfect political universe; they may have to admit that the establishment of a stable world order is an elusive goal, one that will require constant improvisation involving many failures. Learning that early non-Western statesmen did not find lasting solutions to inter-state power conflicts and that international politics is an art rather than a science is not the least important benefit to be gained from a comparative approach.

[26] See Ssu-yü Têng and John K. Fairbank, *China's Response to the West* (Cambridge, Mass.: Harvard University Press, 1954), pp. 29–33.

THE WESTERN STATE SYSTEM AND
ITS NON-WESTERN ANTECEDENTS

PART ONE

THE WESTERN STATE SYSTEM AND
ITS NON-WESTERN ANTECEDENTS

CHAPTER ONE

The State and Its Foreign Relations: Orientation and Perspective

The study of international relations demands a knowledge of the origin, meaning, and functioning of the Western nation-state system as well as an appreciation of the twentieth-century factors that have so decisively altered that system's structure. Such background material has been cogently provided by John H. Herz in his now famous essay "Rise and Demise of the Territorial State."

Herz begins his analysis by determining the basic features that characterized the nation-state in the pre-nuclear age. According to the author, until fairly recent times a "hard shell of fortifications" afforded those within a state's boundaries a desired measure of protection from foreign invasions. This salient advantage Professor Herz designates as the state's impermeability, impenetrability, or simply its territoriality. Each resident of the West's various political communities willingly recognized his state as "the ultimate unit" because "people, in the long run, will recognize that authority, any authority, which possesses the power of protection."

The durability of the nation-state system began to be questioned only after the technical and scientific inventions of the last fifty years lessened its military adaptability. Until that time it was considered an unalterable political arrangement. The marriage of nuclear physics to aerodynamics accelerated the decline of the nation-state, however, so that today the system no longer can be considered exclusively in traditional terms—according to the author—because "now that power can destroy from center to center, everything is different." Students of world politics, striving to gain competence concerning the interactions and relations of political communities and not seeking a survey of current problems and events, must examine and be deeply concerned with the "transformation in the 'statehood' of nations." To appreciate how such dramatic changes

17

occurred, and their long-range political significance, "we must study more closely the origin and nature of the classical system itself." Professor Herz's selection has become a classic study of the reasons for these alterations.

Following the introductory essay, we turn to the Chinese, Hindu, and Muslim patterns of inter-state behavior. Each of the three selections offers a panoramic description of these political communities vis-à-vis their neighbors, as well as some general information concerning the cultural past of these respective civilizations.

Through centuries-old contact with the people in the surrounding area, the Chinese became convinced of the overwhelming superiority of their culture, ethics, and governmental organization. This Chinese ethnocentrism, reinforced by a complicated code of Confucian principles and goals, gave rise to a system of inter-state relations unlike anything ever known in Western history. China considered itself the Middle Kingdom, the center around which the political life of the world revolved. The Chinese believed that they had an obligation to civilize their chronically inferior neighbors by righteous example and teaching. M. Frederick Nelson explains the complicated mechanics that helped determine China's premodern foreign policies, including the tributary system that they originated. His article "The World Outlook of the Chinese Empire" introduces the principal features of a political arrangement that "became altogether dominant in China as the ethics of its people and as the guide for governmental policy."

The second non-Western example that is presented is the state system of the ancient Hindus of India. Although the kingdom of the Mauryan emperors and its successors abutted China, the original Indian philosophy for conducting inter-state relations did not resemble in the least the one formulated in the Middle Kingdom. To use today's terminology, the early Hindus advocated political realism; their leading political writers have often been compared to Machiavelli. All states, they believed, were engaged in a constant struggle to prevail, and the basis of a successful foreign policy was the possession of dominant military power. A ruler, for the most part, was not concerned with ethical considerations in deciding the affairs of state, but sought to "arrange all his affairs that no ally, neutral prince or enemy may obtain any advantage over him; this in a few words is the sum of [Hindu] political wisdom."[1]

A. L. Basham's article "Some Fundamentals of Hindu Statecraft" offers a wide-ranging view of a civilization that is considered exotic by most

---

[1] From the *Institutes of Manu*, quoted in M. N. Nawaz, "The Law of Nations in Ancient India," *Indian Year Book of International Affairs*, VI (1957), 177.

Westerners. Ancient Indian political life certainly had its distinctive features, but today's student will also discover much that is familiar among Hindu ideas of war and peace. The author, a leading British scholar of Indian history, culture, and institutions, also discusses the writings of a number of the country's outstanding legal and political commentators, who examined the same kinds of problems that interested subsequent European political theorists. Yet the Hindus, as Professor Basham points out, failed to develop a formal political philosophy although they did "much cultivate the science of statecraft."

Why were the classical Hindu writers able to produce such distinguished epics as the *Arthaśāstra* and the *Mahābhārata*, but not speculate on the ends of political action or the obligations inherent in the political process? One explanation for the contradiction has been provided by a modern Indian author, who notes that

after the days of Kautilya the conditions were, in a sense, unfavorable to the advance of political speculation. The extraordinary thoroughness of Kautilya's work, its eminent inductiveness and political character, its unflinching logic and heedlessness of adventitious moral or religious standards, and its wide range of subjects and interests—which give it a unique combination of features that, in European literature, we find only separately in an Aristotle, a Machiavelli, and a Bacon—must have cooperated with the rise of a well-knit empire of unprecedented dimensions, under the Mauryan and succeeding dynasties, to depress creative political thought in the centuries after Kautilya.[2]

The third non-Western political system to be presented originated with the Muslims of Arabia during the seventh century A.D. Its founder and first leader, Muḥammad the Prophet of Allah, conceived of his mission as having a dual purpose. Not only did he set out to establish a new religious faith that offered its believers salvation within the House of Islam, but also to create a universal ecclesiastical state whose legal, social, and governmental practices would be regulated by the Koran and the *sunna* (the customs or traditions of the Community). Warning his followers that "Ye are one Community over against Mankind," Muḥammad imposed on them a duty to spread their religion throughout the world. The early political leaders of the kingdom of Allah were admonished never to recognize the coexistence of any non-Muslim state as a permanent political arrangement. In the centuries following Muḥammad's death, the caliphs of Islam aggressively carried out their religio-political goals, and they ultimately developed a pattern of inter-state behavior that is distinctive of their civilization. The world was divided into two distinct and mutually antagonistic parts. One was the *dār ul Islam,* or world of Islam; and the other

[2] Rangaswami Aiyangar, *Considerations on Some Aspects of Ancient Indian Polity* (Madras: University of Madras, 1916), p. 35; quoted in D. Mackenzie Brown, *The White Umbrella* (Berkeley: University of California Press, 1959), p. 52.

was the *dār ul ḥarb,* or world of the unbeliever. The obligation of all Muslims, early in their ascendancy, was to work for the progressive conversion of all non-Muslim states. This policy helped determine the world outlook of their political leaders.

"Muslim Universalism" is the theme of Costi K. Zurayk's essay. His remarks, originally presented to a 1948 UNESCO Conference in Lebanon when the author was Vice-President of the American University of Beirut, provide the background material necessary to an appreciation of the complexity of Muslim inter-state relations.

The final article in this chapter returns us to the contemporary scene. Not all sovereign states are experiencing the complicated problems that Professor Herz describes in the introductory essay. Many newly independent nations of the Far East, the Middle East, and Africa are confronted with political phenomena of a different sort. Robert Montagne, in his inaugural lecture in the Collège de France on December 1, 1948, discussed some of the uncertainties that arise when the Western nation-state system is exported to non-Western civilizations. His selection, "The Nation-State System in Modern Africa and Asia," is concerned specifically with the political communities that have emerged since the end of World War II. "Is the world . . . giving birth to entirely new societies," he asks, "or is it that what we see are only ephemeral structures, mere juristic phantoms, which only hide from us the obstinate survival of ancient ways of life able to resist indefinitely the influence of the West?" It is too early to determine the answer to Professor Montagne's question, but his article brilliantly describes the forceful impact of the Western state system after it was imposed on the clans and tribes of these continents.

RISE AND DEMISE OF THE TERRITORIAL STATE*

John H. Herz

Basic Features of the Modern State System

Traditionally, the classical system of international relations, or the modern state system, has been considered "anarchic," because it was based

* John H. Herz, "Rise and Demise of the Territorial State," *World Politics,* IX, No. 4 (July 1957), 473–493. Reprinted by permission. Mr. Herz is Professor of Government, City College of New York, and author of *Political Realism and Political Idealism* (1951) and *International Politics in the Atomic Age* (1959).

on unequally distributed power and was deficient in higher—that is, supranational—authority. Its units, the independent, sovereign nation-states, were forever threatened by stronger power and survived precariously through the balance-of-power system. Customarily, then, the modern state system has been contrasted with the medieval system, on the one hand, where units of international relations were under higher law and higher authority, and with those more recent international trends, on the other, which seemed to point toward a greater, "collective" security of nations and a "rule of law" that would protect them from the indiscriminate use of force characteristic of the age of power politics.

From the vantage point of the atomic age, we can probe deeper into the basic characteristics of the classical system. What is it that ultimately accounted for the peculiar unity, compactness, coherence of the modern nation-state, setting it off from other nation-states as a separate, independent, and sovereign power? It would seem that this underlying factor is to be found neither in the sphere of law nor in that of politics, but rather in that substratum of statehood where the state unit confronts us, as it were, in its physical, corporeal capacity: as an expanse of territory encircled for its identification and its defense by a "hard shell" of fortifications. In this lies what will here be referred to as the "impermeability," or "impenetrability," or simply the "territoriality," of the modern state. The fact that it was surrounded by a hard shell rendered it to some extent secure from foreign penetration, and thus made it an ultimate unit of protection for those within its boundaries. Throughout history, that unit which affords protection and security to human beings has tended to become the basic political unit; people, in the long run, will recognize that authority, any authority, which possesses the power of protection.

Some similarity perhaps prevails between an international structure consisting of impenetrable units with an ensuing measurability of power and comparability of power relations, and the system of classical physics with its measurable forces and the (then) impenetrable atom as its basic unit. And as that system has given way to relativity and to what nuclear science has uncovered, the impenetrability of the political atom, the nation-state, is giving way to a permeability which tends to obliterate the very meaning of unit and unity, power and power relations, sovereignty and independence. The possibility of "hydrogenization" merely represents the culmination of a development which has rendered the traditional defense structure of nations obsolete through the power to by-pass the shell protecting a two-dimensional territory and thus to destroy—vertically, as it were—even the most powerful ones. Paradoxically, utmost strength now coincides in the same unit with utmost vulnerability, absolute power with utter impotence.

This development must inevitably affect traditional power concepts. Considering power units as politically independent and legally sovereign made sense when power, measurable, graded, calculable, served as a standard of comparison between units which, in the sense indicated above, could be described as impermeable. Under those conditions, then, power indicated the strategic aspect, independence the political aspect, sovereignty the legal aspect of this selfsame impermeability. With the passing of the age of territoriality, the usefulness of these concepts must now be questioned.

Thus the Great Divide does not separate "international anarchy," or "balance of power," or "power politics," from incipient international interdependence, or from "collective security"; all these remain within the realm of the territorial structure of states and can therefore be considered as trends or stages *within* the classical system of "hard shell" power units. Rather, the Divide occurs where the basis of territorial power and defensibility vanishes. It is here and now. But in order to understand the present, we must study more closely the origin and nature of the classical system itself.

The Rise of the Territorial State

The rise of the modern territorial state meant that, within countries, "feudal anarchy" of jurisdictions yielded to the ordered centralism of the absolute monarchy, which ruled over a pacified area with the aid of a bureaucracy, a professional army, and the power to levy taxes, while in foreign relations, in place of the medieval hierachy of power and authority, there prevailed insecurity, a disorder only slightly attenuated by a power balance that was forever being threatened, disturbed, and then restored. Such has been the customary interpretation.

It is possible to view developments in a somewhat different light. Instead of contrasting the security of groups and individuals within the sovereign territoral state with conditions of insecurity outside, the establishment of territorial independence can be interpreted as an at least partially successful attempt to render the territorial group secure in its outward relations as well. Especially when contrasted with the age of anarchy and insecurity which immediately preceded it, the age of territoriality appears as one of relative order and safety.

Indeed, the transition from medieval hierarchism to modern compartmentalized sovereignties was neither easy, nor straight, nor short. Modern sovereignty arose out of the triangular struggle among emperors and popes, popes and kings, and kings and emperors. When the lawyers of Philip the Fair propounded the dual maxim according to which the king was to be "emperor in his realm" (*rex est imperator in regno suo*) and was no longer to "recognize any superior" (*superiorem non recognoscens*), it was the beginning of a development in the course of which, in McIlwain's words, "Independence *de facto* was ultimately translated into a sovereignty *de jure*." But centuries of disturbance and real anarchy ensued during which the problems or rulership and security remained unsettled. The relative protection which the sway of moral standards and the absence of highly destructive weapons had afforded groups and individuals in the earlier Middle Ages gave way to total insecurity when gunpowder was invented and common standards broke down. Out of the internal and external turmoil during the age of religious and civil wars, a "neutralist" central power eventually managed to establish itself in and for each of the different territories like so many *rochers de bronze*.

The idea that a territorial coexistence of states, based on the power of the territorial princes, might afford a better guarantee of peace than the Holy Roman Empire was already widespread at the height of the Middle Ages when the emperor proved incapable of enforcing the peace. But territoriality could hardly prevail so long as the knight in his castle (that medieval unit of impermeability) was relatively immune from attack, as was the medieval city within its walls. Only with a developing money economy were overlords able to free themselves from dependence on vassals and lay the foundations of their own power by establishing a professional army. Infantry and artillery now proved superior to old-style cavalry, firearms prevailed over the old weapons.

As in all cases of radically new developments in military technology, the "gunpowder revolution" caused a real revolution in the superstructure of economic, social, and political relationships because of its impact on the units of protection and security. A feeling of insecurity swept all Europe. Though a Machiavelli might establish new rules as to how to gain and maintain power, there still followed more than a century of unregulated, ideological "total" wars inside and among countries until the new units of power were clearly established. Before old or new sovereigns could claim to be recognized as rulers of large areas, it had to be determined how far, on the basis of their new military power, they were able to extend their control geographically.

The large-area state came finally to occupy the place that the castle or fortified town had previously held as a unit of impenetrability. But the new unit could not be considered consolidated until all independent fortifications within it had disappeared and, in their place, fortresses lining the circumference of the country had been built by the new central power and manned by its armed forces. If we contrast our present system of bases and similar outposts surrounding entire world regions with what are today small-scale nation-states, perhaps we can visualize what the hard shell of frontier fortifications consolidating the then large-scale territorial states meant by way of extending power units in the age of absolutism. They became, in the words of Frederick the Great, "mighty nails which hold a ruler's provinces together." There now was peace and protection within. War became a regularized military procedure; only the breaking of the shell permitted interference with what had now become the internal affairs of another country.

In this way was established the basic structure of the territorial state which was to last throughout the classical period of the modern state system. Upon this foundation a new system and new concepts of international relations could arise. . . .

The Territorial State in International Relations

From territoriality resulted the concepts and institutions which characterized the interrelations of sovereign units, the modern state system. Modern international law, for instance, could now develop. Like the international system that produced it, international law has often been considered inherently contradictory because of its claim to bind sovereign units. But whether or not we deny to it for this reason the name and character of genuine law, it is important to see it in its connection with the territorial nature of the state system that it served. Only then can it be understood as a system of rules not contrary to, but implementing, the sovereign independence of states. Only to the extent that it reflected their territoriality and took into account their sovereignty could international law develop in modern times. For its general rules and principles deal primarily with the delimitation of the jurisdiction of countries. It thus implements the *de facto* condition of territorial impenetrability by more closely defining unit, area, and conditions of impenetrability. Such a law must reflect, rather than regulate. As one author has rightly remarked, "International law really amounts to laying down the principle of national sovereignty and deducing the consequences." It is not for this reason superfluous, for sovereign units must know in some detail where their jurisdictions end and those of other units begin; without such standards, nations would be involved in constant strife over the implementation of their independence.

But it was not only this mutual legal accommodation which rendered possible a relatively peaceful coexistence of nations. War itself, the very phenomenon which reflected, not the strength, but the limitations of impermeability, was of such a nature as to maintain at least the principle of territoriality. War was limited not only in conduct but also in objectives.

It was not a process of physical or political annihilation but a contest of power and will in which the interests, but not the existence, of the contestants were at stake. Now that we approach the era of absolute exposure, without walls or moats, where penetration will mean not mere damage or change but utter annihilation of life and way of life, it may dawn on us that what has vanished with the age of sovereignty and "power politics" was not entirely adverse in nature and effects.

Among other "conservative" features of the classical system, we notice one only in passing: the balance of power. It is only recently that emphasis has shifted from a somewhat one-sided concern with the negative aspects of the balance—its uncertainty, its giving rise to unending conflicts and frequent wars, etc.—to its protective effect of preventing the expansionist capacity of power from destroying other power altogether. But at the time of its perfection in statecraft and diplomacy, there were even theories (not lived up to in practice, of course) about the *legal* obligations of nations to form barriers against hegemony power in the common interest.

More fundamental to the conservative structure of the old system was its character as a community. Forming a comparatively pacified whole, Europe was set off sharply against the world outside, a world beyond those lines which, by common agreement, separated a community based on territoriality and common heritage from anarchy, where the law of nature reigned and no standards of civilization applied. Only recently have the existence and role of so-called "amity lines" been rediscovered, lines which were drawn in the treaties of the early modern period and which separated European territories, where the rules of war and peace were to prevail, from overseas territories and areas. There was to be "no peace beyond the line"; that is, European powers, although possibly at peace in Europe, continued to be *homo homini lupus* abroad. This practice made it easier for the European family of nations to observe self-denying standards at home by providing them with an outlet in the vast realm discovered outside Europe. While the practice of drawing amity lines subsequently disappeared, one chief function of overseas expansion remained: a European balance of power could be maintained or adjusted because it was relatively easy to divert European conflicts into overseas directions and adjust them there. Thus the openness of the world contributed to the consolidation of the territorial system. The end of the "world frontier" and the resulting closedness of an interdependent world inevitably affected this system's effectiveness.

Another characteristic of the old system's protective nature may be seen in the almost complete absence of instances in which countries were wiped out in the course of wars or as a consequence of other power-political events. This, of course, refers to the territorial units at home only, not to the peoples and state units beyond the pale abroad; and to the complete destruction of a state's independent existence, not to mere loss of territory or similar changes, which obviously abounded in the age of power politics.

Evidence of this is to be found not only in a legal and political ideology that denied the permissibility of conquest at home while recognizing it as a title for the acquisition of territorial jurisdiction abroad. For such a doctrine had its non-ideological foundation in the actual difference between European and non-European politics so far as their territoriality was concerned. European states were impermeable in the sense here outlined, while most of those overseas were easily penetrable by Europeans. In accordance with these circumstances, international politics in Europe knew only rare and exceptional instances of actual annihilation through conquest or similar forceful means.

Prior to the twentieth century, there were indeed the Napoleonic conquests, but I submit that this is a case where the exception confirms the rule. The Napoleonic system, as a hegemonial one, was devised to destroy the established system of territoriality and balanced power as such. Consequently, Napoleon and his policies appeared "demonic" to contemporaries, as well as to a nineteenth century which experienced the restoration of the earlier system. During that century occurred Bismarck's annexations of some German units into Prussia in pursuance of German unification. As in Napoleon's case, they appeared abnormal to many of his contemporaries, although the issue of national unification tended to mitigate this impression. Besides these, there was indeed the partition of Poland, and considering the lamentable and lasting impression and the universal bad conscience it produced even among the ruling nations in a century used to quite a bit of international skulduggery, again one may well claim an exceptional character for that event.

What, in particular, accounts for this remarkable stability? Territoriality—the establishment of defensible units, internally pacified and hard-shell rimmed—may be called its foundation. On this foundation, two phenomena permitted the system to become more stable than might otherwise have been the case: the prevalence of the legitimacy principle and, subsequently, nationalism. Legitimacy implied that the dynasties ruling the territorial states of old Europe mutually recognized each other as rightful sovereigns. Depriving one sovereign of his rights by force could not but appear to destroy the very principle on which the rights of all of them rested.

With the rise of nationalism, we witness the personalization of the units as self-determining, national groups. Nationalism now made it appear as abhorrent to deprive a sovereign nation of its independence as to despoil a legitimate ruler had appeared before. States, of course, had first to become "nation-states," considering themselves as representing specific nationality groups, which explains why in the two regions of Europe where larger numbers of old units stood in the way of national unification their demise encountered little objection. In most instances, however, the rise of nationalism led to the emergence of *new* states, which split away from multinational or colonial empires. This meant the extension of the European principle of "non-obliteration" all over the world. It is perhaps significant that even in our century, and even after the turmoil of attempted world conquest and resulting world wars, a point has been made of restoring the most minute and inconsiderable of sovereignties, down to Luxembourg and Albania.

This hypertrophy of nation-states presented new problems—above all, that of an improved system of protection. For by now it had become clear that the protective function of the old system was only a relative blessing after all. Continued existence of states as such was perhaps more or less guaranteed. But power and influence, status, frontiers, economic interests —in short, everything that constituted the life and interests of nations beyond bare existence—were always at the mercy of what power politics wrought. Furthermore, much of the relative stability and political equilib- rium of the territorial states had been due to the extension of Western control over the world. When what could be penetrated had been sub- jugated, assimilated, or established as fellow "sovereign" states, the old units were thrown back upon themselves. Hence the demand for a new system which would offer more security to old and new nations: collective security.

I propose to view collective security not as the extreme opposite of power politics, but as an attempt to maintain, and render more secure, the impermeability of what were still territorial states. To an age which took territoriality for granted, replacing power politics with collective security would indeed appear to be a radical departure. From the vantage point of the nuclear age, however, a plan to protect individual sovereign- ties by collective guarantees for continuing sovereignty appears question- able not because of its innovating, but because of its conservative, nature. Its conservatism lies in its basic objective: the protection of the hard-shell territorial structure of its members, or, as the core article of the Covenant of the League of Nations put it, its guarantee of their "territorial integrity and political independence" against external aggression. The beginning of air war and the increasing economic interdependence of nations had indicated by the end of World War I that the old-style military barriers might be by-passed. If territorial units were to be preserved in the future, it would be accomplished less by reliance on individual defense potentials than by marshaling collective power in order to preserve individual powers.

But since the idea of organizing a genuine supranational force—an international police force—was rejected, the League had to cling to classical arrangements insofar as the procedures of protection were concerned. The guarantee to the individual states was to be the formation of the "Grand Coalition" of all against the isolated aggressor, which presupposed the maintenance of a certain level of armed strength by the member states. A member without that minimum of military strength would be a liability rather than an asset to the organization—in Geneva parlance, a "consumer" and not a "producer" of security. Thus classical concepts (the sovereignty and independence of nation-states) as well as classical institutions (in particular, hard-shell defensibility) were to be maintained under the new system.

Whether there ever was a chance for the system to be effective in practice is beside the point here. It is sufficient to realize how closely it was tied to the underlying structure as well as to the prevailing concepts and policies of the territorial age.

The Decline of the Territorial State

Beginning with the nineteenth century, certain trends became visible which tended to endanger the functioning of the classical system. Directly or indirectly, all of them had a bearing upon that feature of the territorial state which was the strongest guarantee of its independent coexistence with other states of like nature: its hard shell—that is, its defensibility in case of war.

Naturally, many of these trends concerned war itself and the way in which it was conducted. But they were not related to the shift from the limited, duel-type contests of the eighteenth century to the more or less unlimited wars that developed in the nineteenth century with conscription, "nations in arms," and increasing destructiveness of weapons. By themselves, these developments were not inconsistent with the classical function of war. Enhancing a nation's defensive capacity, instituting universal military service, putting the economy on a war footing, and similar measures tended to bolster the territorial state rather than to endanger it.

Total war in a quite different sense is tied up with developments in warfare which enable the belligerents to overleap or by-pass the traditional hard-shell defense of states. When this happens, the traditional relationship between war, on the one hand, and territorial power and sovereignty, on the other, is altered decisively. Arranged in order of increasing effectiveness, these new factors may be listed under the following headings:

(a) possibility of economic blockade; (b) ideological-political penetration; (c) air warfare; and (d) atomic warfare.

ECONOMIC WARFARE. It should be said from the outset that so far economic blockade has never enabled one belligerent to force another into surrender through starvation alone. Although in World War I Germany and her allies were seriously endangered when the Western allies cut them off from overseas supplies, a very real effort was still required to defeat them on the military fronts. The same thing applies to World War II. Blockade was an important contributing factor, however. Its importance for the present analysis lies in its unconventional nature, permitting belligerents to by-pass the hard shell of the enemy. Its effect is due to the changed economic status of industrialized nations.

Prior to the industrial age, the territorial state was largely self-contained economically. Although one of the customary means of conducting limited war was starving fortresses into surrender, this applied merely to these individual portions of the hard shell, and not to entire nations. Attempts to starve a belligerent nation in order to avoid having to breach the shell proved rather ineffective, as witness the Continental Blockade and its counterpart in the Napoleonic era. The Industrial Revolution made countries like Britain and Germany increasingly dependent on imports. In war, this meant that they could survive only by controlling areas larger than their own territory. In peacetime, economic dependency became one of the causes of a phenomenon which itself contributed to the transformation of the old state system: imperialism. Anticipating war, with its new danger of blockade, countries strove to become more self-sufficient through enlargement of their areas of control. To the extent that the industrialized nations lost self-sufficiency, they were driven into expansion in a (futile) effort to regain it. Today, if at all, only control of entire continents enables major nations to survive economically in major wars. This implies that hard-shell military defense must be a matter of defending more than a single nation; it must extend around half the world.

PSYCHOLOGICAL WARFARE. The attempt to undermine the morale of an enemy population, or to subvert its loyalty, shares with economic warfare a by-passing effect on old-style territorial defensibility. It was formerly practiced, and practicable, only under quite exceptional circumstances. Short periods of genuine world revolutionary propaganda, such as the early stages of the French Revolution, scarcely affected a general practice under which dynasties, and later governments, fought each other with little ideological involvement on the part of larger masses or classes. Only in rare cases—for instance, where national groups enclosed in and hostile to multinational empires could be appealed to—was there an opening wedge for "fifth column" strategies.

With the emergence of political belief-systems, however, nations became more susceptible to undermining from within. Although wars have not yet been won solely by subversion of loyalties, the threat involved has affected the inner coherence of the territorial state ever since the rise to power of a regime that claims to represent, not the cause of a particular nation, but that of mankind, or at least of its suppressed and exploited portions. Bolshevism from 1917 on has provided the second instance in modern history of world revolutionary propaganda. Communist penetration tactics subsequently were imitated by the Nazi and Fascist regimes and, eventually, by the democracies. In this way, new lines of division, cutting horizontally through state units instead of leaving them separated vertically from each other at their frontiers, have now become possible.

AIR WARFARE AND NUCLEAR WARFARE. Of all the new developments, air warfare, up to the atomic age, has been the one that affected the territoriality of nations most radically. With its coming, the bottom dropped out—or, rather, the roof blew off—the relative security of the territorial state. True, even this new kind of warfare, up to and including the Second World War, did not by itself account for the defeat of a belligerent, as some of the more enthusiastic prophets of the air age had predicted it would. Undoubtedly, however, it had a massive contributory effect. And this effect was due to strategic action in the *hinterland* rather than to tactical use at the front. It came at least close to defeating one side by direct action against the "soft" interior of the country, by-passing outer defenses and thus foreshadowing the end of the frontier—that is, the demise of the traditional impermeability of even the militarily most powerful states. Warfare now changed "from a fight to a process of devastation."

That air warfare was considered as something entirely unconventional is seen from the initial reaction to it. Revolutionary transition from an old to a new system has always affected moral standards. In the classical age of the modern state system, the "new morality" of shooting at human beings from a distance had finally come to be accepted, but the standards of the age clearly distinguished "lawful combatants" at the front or in fortifications from the civilian remainder of the population. When air war came, reactions thus differed significantly in the cases of air fighting at the front and of air war carried behind the front. City bombing was felt to constitute "illegitimate" warfare, and populations were inclined to treat airmen engaging in it as "war criminals." This feeling continued into World War II, with its large-scale area bombing. Such sentiments reflected the general feeling of helplessness in the face of a war which threatened to render obsolete the concept of territorial power, together with its ancient implication of protection.

The process has now been completed with the advent of nuclear weapons. For it is more than doubtful that the processes of scientific invention and technological discovery, which not only have created and perfected the fission and fusion weapons themselves but have brought in their wake guided missiles with nuclear warheads, jet aircraft with intercontinental range and supersonic speed, and the prospect of nuclear-powered planes or rockets with unlimited range and with automatic guidance to specific targets anywhere in the world, can in any meaningful way be likened to previous new inventions, however revolutionary. These processes add up to an uncanny absoluteness of effect which previous innovations could not achieve. The latter might render power units of a certain type (for instance, castles or cities) obsolete and enlarge the realm of defensible power units from city-state to territorial state or even large-area empire. They might involve destruction, in war, of entire populations. But there still remained the seemingly inexhaustible reservoir of the rest of mankind. Today, when not even two halves of the globe remain impermeable, it can no longer be a question of enlarging an area of protection and of substituting one unit of security for another. Since we are inhabitants of a planet of limited (and, as it now seems, insufficient) size, we have reached the limit within which the effect of the means of destruction has become absolute. Whatever remained of the impermeability of states seems to have gone for good.

What has been lost can be seen from two statements by thinkers separated by thousands of years and half the world; both reflect the condition of territorial security. Mencius, in ancient China, when asked for guidance in matters of defense and foreign policy by the ruler of a small state, is said to have counseled: "Dig deeper your moats; build higher your walls; guard them along with your people." This remained the classical posture up to our age, when a Western sage, Bertrand Russell, in the interwar period could still define power as something radiating from one center and growing less with distance from that center until it finds an equilibrium with that of similar geographically anchored units. Now that power can destroy power from center to center, everything is different.

THE WORLD OUTLOOK OF
THE CHINESE EMPIRE*

M. Frederick Nelson

Fundamentals of the Confucian System

Unfortunately, the Far East had little knowledge of the Western civilization which confronted it in the first half of the nineteenth century. Equally regrettable, however, was the lack of comprehension on the part of the Western peoples of the nature of society and government in the Far East. The application of Western terms to Asiatic institutions led only to misunderstanding and confusion when these institutions failed to act in the manner of their Western counterparts. Since the East Asiatic peoples possessed a world outlook altogether different from Western thought of the time, this confusion was particularly apparent in the field of international relations. Furthermore, the nature of government, the function of officialdom, and numerous other aspects of the social organization differed greatly from those of the West.

The Chinese, and the Koreans as well, had for centuries followed a philosophy and code of ethics which had been so general in their diffusion as to constitute the mores of the people. Based primarily upon the writings of the great sage Confucius (Kung Fu-tzǔ, 551–479 B.C.), there had been constructed a complete philosophy of civilization which may be termed Confucianism, though it was somewhat modified by the glosses of the followers of Confucius and by rival schools of thought. The Confucian dogma was incorporated in a series called *The Classics,* knowledge of which became the highest standard of intellectual attainment and of proficiency in government. Apt quotation of them would win an argument or determine a course of action. In fact, their principles governed all human relationships and conduct in the Sino-Korean area.

For any complete understanding of political action in the Far East it is necessary, therefore, to devote some attention to the background of Confucian thought. It is only against this background that the social conduct, the actions of government, relationships among the countries of

* M. Frederick Nelson, *Korea and the Old Orders in Eastern Asia* (Baton Rouge: Louisiana State University Press, 1945), pp. 3–20. Reprinted by permission.

the Far East, and the conflicts of the Far East with the Western states can be properly understood.

According to the Confucian theory, the world is a single unit, natural in organization, with a set of hierarchical relationships ascending from the lowest man up to Heaven itself. Heaven is viewed as the source and the ancestor of all things. But the Chinese do not view Heaven as a paradise even though they believe it to be the abode of the spirits of selected emperors and sages. To them it is rather a presiding spirit or principle which is fundamentally moral in its nature and, therefore, analogous to Western concepts of fate or providence. It punishes and rewards, and its commands repose in the hearts of the people. For at least the later Confucians, who were less influenced by superstition, Heaven corresponds very nearly to the English word "nature."

Confucianism makes all men subject to the will of Heaven, and even an emperor must conform to the natural ordering of this will or lose his right to rule under Heaven's mandate. Man, therefore, occupies the position of having as his main duty the obligation to conform with Heaven's will, to fit himself into its natural order and thus attain peace and happiness. . . . However, the fact that unreasonable actions often produce unfortunate results reminds us that one can never be certain that he is actually anticipating Heaven. This illustrates the tenet in Confucian theory that there can be no bending of nature to man's will, but rather, only the limited field of "appropriate" actions within an established natural order.

This concept of a preordained natural order suggested that a definite relationship existed between all material things and that, in every situation, proper conduct depended upon the status of the actors. In the structure of society five fundamental relationships were postulated, and man's entire existence was embraced within them. The first relation, male and female or husband and wife, evolved from the original existence of Heaven and earth. The second relation, derived from the first, is that of father and son; the third that of elder brother and younger brother. The fourth and fifth are those of friend and friend, and of sovereign and minister (or subject). These relationships are held to be as permanent as the universe. Peace and order exist automatically when the husband is truly a husband, the wife truly a wife, the sovereign truly a sovereign, and so on. By appropriately conforming to relationships which man finds in his social existence, one would follow Heaven's will and would receive Heaven's blessings.

But not all men are wise, or able to discern within their hearts the behavior true to each of the five relations. Furthermore, men are born with desires and are constantly seeking the satisfaction of them. Means for the satisfaction of desires are naturally scarce, while the craving for satisfaction is without measure or limits, hence contention between men. Contention leads to disorder and confusion, and disorder and confusion to poverty. Therefore, from their wisdom and knowledge of the true order of things, the ancient Sage-Kings interpreted and set down the rules of proper conduct or propriety known as *li*. *Li* is held to be more than a set of arbitrary rules conjured from men's minds; rather it is the natural rules which govern even the relation of Heaven and earth, and of the stars and the seasons as well. The rules of *li* were discovered, not made, by the ancient sages. *Li* is termed the greatest of all principles, for "He who follows it will be preserved; he who does not follow it will be destroyed."

The fundamental element in the rules of proper conduct (*li*) and, in fact, in the whole system of Confucian thought, is that of inequality. Because of the relation of the natural desires of each man "to be as honourable as the Emperor and so wealthy as to own the country," and the disorder which would result from man's attempt to achieve these rare satisfactions, nature has decreed inequalities or the distinctions of superior and inferior in all relations....

This theory, that everyone and everything should be under someone's direction, illustrates the hierarchical nature of the Confucian system. Within the extremes of the lowest and the highest, everyone has inferiors below him and superiors above. Responsibility and benevolence descend from above, and obedience and respect ascend from below—all emanating from or culminating in the emperor, or Son of Heaven, who, in turn, looks to Heaven as his superior and as the bestower of his mandate to rule. Banishment of inequality, according to Confucian theory, would mean a return to a state of barbarism and chaos wherein men's desires have no limits. Therefore, desire is subordinated to the distinctions of superior and inferior; and this subordination attains advantageous social relations under conditions imposed by innate nature. This does not mean that men are unequal in their original capacities. In fact, the Confucians democratically maintain the theory of equal capacities for all men. The aristocracy in which they believe is a moral one, based on equality in capacity but inequality in development.

With a natural order of society in which man's whole social duty is embraced in five great relationships, with a hierarchical scale of inferiors and superiors ascending to the emperor, with each inferior controlled by a superior, and with *li*, the rules of proper conduct, embracing all of these relations, the position of the emperor and the nature of government (in the Confucian sense) become apparent. Government is formally the indoctrination of inferiors by superiors with the rules of proper conduct. The downward flow from Heaven of these doctrines is conceived to be the force which will preserve natural order in society. Government is thus not an artificial creation based on the fiat of law, but is the entire ethics of society. Just as the seasons are natural to Heaven, and wealth is natural to the earth, so government is natural to man. Its sole object is to keep men within the natural rules of conduct, to prevent the disorder that will result when men stray from the "way." Or, as Confucius expressed it, "To govern is to rectify." . . .

The emperor is the apex of the Confucian system. As the supreme man, he is Heaven's substitute on earth, and his relation to his subjects is similar to that of Heaven to earth. All men are his children, and to protect them and prevent them from straying from the natural way is the purpose of his existence. Since the emperor views the people as a great family, the rules of proper conduct between parent and child are applied in the relation of sovereign and subject. But though Heaven creates the emperor, and though the emperor rules under Heaven's authority, the mandate of Heaven, through which a dynasty keeps the throne, is not unshakable. For "Imperial Heaven," states the *Book of History,* "has no predilections. It always allies itself to the virtuous." When disorder and calamities attest the disfavor of Heaven, the right of rebellion is recognized and asserted by those seeking to overthrow a dynasty.

The method whereby men are to be brought to observe the rules of *li* is in sharp contrast with Western methods of carrying out governmental policy. As the emperor deserves to be emperor only as long as he remains virtuous and in accord with Heaven's rules of propriety, so all officials of the empire are likewise to be models of proper conduct. Logically, then, no rigid, lifeless laws are needed to set the standard for the conduct of the people. Instead, the example of virtue in the official hierarchy which ascends to the all-virtuous Son of Heaven is to be so overwhelming as to compel acquiescence.

Here is a "government of men"—virtuous men—who are not respected and followed for the power they may possess as much as for the model they present. Each inferior views his superior as a model, and from the emperor down, government is not force but instruction. By proper example and instruction in the principles of *li*, all men are to cultivate a sense of shame which will cause them to comply with the proper rules. Only when they lack this sense of shame and cannot be swayed by reason and instruction, is punitive power to be exercised. In theory, the emperor is a teacher and model primarily and a ruler only in extreme cases.

Silence concerning the concept of law in Confucian theory is not the result of ignorance. Other Chinese advocated a regime wherein one impersonal standard is set by law, and obedience secured by force. Such a school existed in the third and fourth centuries B.C., and their theories became the basis for the government of the Ch'in dynasty (221–206 B.C.).

The tyranny possible under a rule of law designed for the benefit of the rulers rather than for the welfare of the people was well illustrated during this era. With the overthrow of the Ch'in dynasty by revolution, government by law and force was definitely replaced by theories of self-control through teaching and example.

The doctrine of control through example, of conquering through virtue, throws the problem of the control of society back upon the individual. If the empire is in disorder, the emperor is at fault; he has presumably failed to cultivate virtue within himself. If a family is disrupted, the parent is lacking in sufficient virtue and knowledge of the rules of proper conduct. Therefore, the man who would govern (i.e., enforce the rules of proper conduct) must first rectify himself with Heaven's way. An often quoted passage of Confucius illustrates this expanding nature of individual virtue.

Their hearts being rectified, their persons were cultivated. Their persons being cultivated, their families were regulated. Their families being regulated, their states were rightly governed. Their states being rightly governed, the whole empire was made tranquil and happy.

War is therefore incompatible with Confucian theory, which requires that an unsubmissive people should be conquered by a display of civil culture and virtue, not coerced by force. When a ruler invited Confucius to teach military tactics, the Sage refused and left the state of so unrighteous a monarch. Mencius also denounced offensive war, except for the punishing of unrighteousness. The fighting which occurred in the Spring and Autumn Epoch (770–473 B.C.) was all unrighteous; those who boasted of their military skill were termed "great criminals," and the ministers who advised the use of force were "robbers of the people."

In this renunciation of war the Confucian theory was supported by the theories of all the other major schools of thought in China, with the exception of the short-lived Legalists. . . . However, Confucian theory in one respect encouraged civil as opposed to international warfare by its doctrine of the Mandate of Heaven. Whenever a ruler's government decayed, some person felt justified in raising the standard of revolution. Though civil war was common in China, foreign conquest was viewed as being in a different category and was not justified by Confucian doctrine. Genuinely Confucian dynasties avoided foreign aggrandizement.

East Asiatic International Theories

The Confucian theory viewed the whole world as a single unit. As Confucius expressed it, "Within four seas" all men are brothers. Since the control exercised by the emperor was that of a teacher and a model of proper conduct, it inevitably diminished as the outlying areas were reached where the non-Chinese inhabitants, being semi-civilized, paid less heed to emperors who sought to conquer by virtue.

The area of China proper, where all men abided by the rules of propriety, was termed *Chung Kuo,* the "Middle Kingdom." Most who lived outside the area were termed barbarians. The latter term did not necessarily denote savagery; it meant rather those who had not acquired Chinese customs and dress, who did not observe the proprieties, and who were not amenable to reason. Such people actually possessed a lower degree of civilization, according to Confucian standards, and were therefore classed as rude. . . .

The surrounding tribes, not being civilized enough to enable their members to feel a voluntary sense of shame and to submit to the reason and teaching of the Middle Kingdom, presented a perplexing problem. No actual intergovernmental relations in the Confucian sense could exist between China and these people to whom government by benevolence and reason was not understandable. Consequently, these barbarians were looked upon as something less than men at their full stature, who had occasionally to be dealt with, to be sure, but who were to be treated in the kindly and benevolent spirit one would exercise toward lesser animals or young and unruly children. This attitude is expressed by an old saying that "When a *hsiu t'sai* (scholar of the first degree) meets a soldier eye to eye, although the former has reason, his arguments will not be clear."

As time passed, however, through immigration, social intercourse, and conquest, the once rude barbarians within the Far Eastern areas surrounding the Middle Kingdom were brought gradually within the Confucian realm of thought. Eventually they developed scholars who brought them the Classics, they adopted *li* as their rule of conduct, and they came to respect the civilization and might of China, thus exemplifying the fact that China's most enduring conquests have been cultural, not military. Confucius himself had said that it was desirable to treat those barbarians who had become Chinese in a Chinese manner, that is, with Government-by-Reason. No new theory needed to be evolved, therefore, for the intergovernmental relations of Confucian states. "All within the four seas" and the "Middle Kingdom" were rather vague terms, and with the whole world being in theory subject to the emperor, there was no definite point at which one passed from the confines of China into the periphery, from Confucianism into barbarism.

When civilized and Confucianized groups rose from the barbarians, the Confucian system was merely extended to them. The emperor would then attain the attitude described in the Classics, which was to view all in the Middle Kingdom as one man, as a *person* in that *family of persons* which comprised "all under Heaven." Here is the basic theory of Confucian international relations. The rules which were to govern this Far Eastern family were the same natural rules, the same code of *li*, that governed the individual family. Here, much more than ever existed in the West, was an international family in the true meaning of the word—natural, governed merely by a further extension of the principles which made up East Asiatic social existence. Since inequality was an essential element in the natural family, these principles were likewise projected into the international sphere. Consequently, China—the superior, the Middle Kingdom—was surrounded by inferior or lesser members who looked to her and were viewed by her as younger brothers or children in the international family.

The rules which governed the relation between the Confucian nations were not definite and uniform. Each situation as it arose was judged according to the principles of *li*. The control by China, the superior, was that of teaching and admonition, of presenting herself as the model for the lesser countries to follow. Chinese influence, and the relationship of the lesser states, varied from rather close supervision, such as China exercised over Korea, to occasional ceremonial contacts such as those with Siam and Burma. This distinction was recognized in Chinese theory by the classic conception of the various domains extending outward from the Central domain of the emperor, each varying in degree of civilization and in obligations to the imperial power according to the distance of the domain from China. . . . Varying treatment among the lesser nations, or at different times toward the same nation, was supported by the Confucian principle which held that the superior, under ordinary circumstances, should not exercise his utmost authority, but should reserve it for emergencies.

However, certain general rules were followed, which had for their purpose the preservation of the natural familial relation. One of the most important was the old theory of the extension of control and the maintenance of supervision by virtue and by the voluntary submission of the lesser nation. While it is true that this theory was often violated and that force was frequently used to compel submission or to restore order within a lesser nation, it is nevertheless important to notice that this force was used mainly either to secure recognition of some new Chinese dynasty as truly holding the mandate of Heaven, or to chastise an area which had strayed from the proper rules of conduct and had allowed disorder to rise among its people. The Classics are replete with examples of how ancient emperors had failed in bringing certain areas under their control by force, only to succeed when they rectified themselves, put their own area in order, and allowed the tales of their virtuous government to bring recalcitrant groups to voluntary submission.

The ruler of the lesser nation accepted investiture from the Chinese emperor in the form of a seal to be used as a badge of office. After the death of the lesser ruler of the inferior country, the Chinese emperor would bestow on him a posthumous title. In rare cases the succession to the throne might be interfered with and a more virtuous heir set up to rule. For use in dating all official documents, the lesser state would each year receive a calendar arranged in terms of the reigning dynasty of China, and the Chinese emperor would also send letters for the instruction and admonition of the lesser king.

Relations were maintained by periodic visits of a Chinese envoy and by return visits by a mission of the lesser nation. The unequal status in this interchange of envoys is particularly well brought out in the commentary of Tso-ch'iu Ming, a disciple of Confucius, who stated:

When a great state goes to a small one it (the smaller) rears a high structure (for the large state's reception). When a small state goes to a great one it (the great one) should construct a booth. . . . When a great state visits a small one it should do five good things: be indulgent to its offenses, pardon its errors and failures, relieve its calamities, reward it for its virtues and laws, and teach it where it is deficient. There is thus no pressure on the small state. It cherishes (the great) state's virtue, and submits to it, fondly as one goes home. On this account a high structure is reared, to display the merit (of the great state), and to make it known to posterity, that they may not be idle in the cultivation of virtue. When a small state goes to a great one, it has five bad things to do. It must explain its trespasses, beg forgiveness for its deficiencies, perform governmental services, and contribute its proper dues and attend to its seasonal commands . . . it has to double its various offerings, to felicitate (the great state) on its happiness, and show condolence with it in its misfortunes.

The envoys from China were no mere messengers. Their credentials were half of a set (the other half having been previously given to the lesser nation) which, when presented and matched, carried a restricted power of command over the lesser ruler. When the superior nation had decided on a military expedition for the purpose of "correction," the inferior nation could be required to furnish both men and supplies. Other practices were the custom of having for education at the Chinese court a son of each of the lesser nations' kings and, in rare cases and as a special favor, the granting to rulers of lesser countries women of the Imperial Household to be their wives.

The most obvious indication of the relationship between China and the lesser nations appeared in the so-called tribute missions periodically sent by the lesser states to China. The principle was an old one derived from the idea that all areas should contribute services and pay homage to the Son of Heaven in accordance with a gradation based on the concentric, ideal, classic arrangement. According to Confucian mythology, in the most ancient times the domains near-by offered slaughtered victims daily; the next distant domains offered monthly sacrifices; and the outposts of civilization offered thanks seasonally. Among the more civilized barbarians of the east and south tribute was offered yearly. Among the less cultured, and, consequently, the less dominated, tribes of the north and west, acknowledgment of the emperor's overlordship occurred only upon the ascension of a new ruler. All homage and gifts of areas outside of China proper, however, continued to be termed tribute, even after these one-time barbarians had taken over Chinese customs.

Aside from any religious base which the paying of this graded homage to the emperor may have contained, there was another element which leads to the conclusion that the tribute missions were also designed as an early form of interchange of goods between the vast reaches of the empire, and as an encouragement to the production of varied products throughout its breadth. It is recorded in the *Shu-ching* that when a large hound, a curiosity because of its size and training, was sent as tribute, the disapproval of the great guardian of the emperor was expressed in a memorial setting forth the correct subjects of tribute. Here the great guardian stated that tribute should be "the produce of their parts... clothing, food and implements of use." He admonished the emperor "not to deal in unprofitable things and not to neglect those that are worthy." Moreover, the emperor should "not set value on strange productions, nor belittle those that are useful. ... Dogs and horses, except in their natural countries, should not be reared. If rare birds and creatures are not bred in the country, and you do not set a false value on foreign products," the guardian warned, "then strangers will be admonished."

While it is true that this tribute came to consist of materials other than the usual products of the country, its contribution did not cease to resemble an economic transaction. China, the superior, generally gave in return presents of more worth than the offerings of the inferiors. Thus the system served as a subsidy to the lesser states and encouraged uncontrolled areas to come into the Chinese orbit.

Finally, the tributary mission was an act acknowledging the seniority of China in the Confucian family of nations, though China apparently had no desire to use this acknowledgment for the direct control of internal affairs. If a lesser ruler kept the peace, endeavored to live as the model for his people, and fulfilled the few duties which his subordinate position required, he was autonomous. Theoretically, Far Eastern government, both imperial and international, involved the enforcement of the rules for proper conduct (the doctrine of *li*) through passive example. Power politics, on the other hand, which employs force as a legitimate agent of diplomacy, was definitely rejected by Confucian thought. This attitude is explained by the fact that extinction of a country by conquest was considered akin to the murder of one individual by another. Thus Confucian theory was basically pacifistic.

It should be mentioned, however, that those who controlled the affairs of China under Confucian principles were not merely theorists, but often practical politicians as well. For Confucianism was a very flexible doctrine, and within its many volumes of Classics could be found precedent for a wide variety of conduct. Even though those in control of government acknowledged Confucian theory as their guiding principle, they were able to use it to accomplish their own ends instead of merely conforming passively to fixed tenets.

A second qualification which should be noted is the fact that the theory itself was rejected or ignored at times as a guide for the administration of government. At other times when the entire theory was not put aside, certain portions of it were not made effective. For instance, the Ch'in rulers (221–206 B.C.) based their government upon legalist theories, and the period of disorganization after the downfall of the Han dynasty also saw a decline in the authority of Confucianism. The first T'ang Emperor was not a Confucian, but a Taoist. Later in the T'ang dynasty, however, Confucian doctrines again came into prominence, and from the eleventh century on, this philosophy became altogether dominant in China as the ethics of its people and as the guide for governmental policy.

Followed as a guide for the preservation of the order decreed by Heaven in all affairs—personal, familial, national, and international—these principles of Confucianism constituted the source book for scholars and officials. Since governmental employment depended on scholarship, which in turn was determined by a knowledge of Confucian principles, it was inescapable that Confucianism practically guided governmental administration.

With its natural world order, its idea of government by indoctrination and example rather than by law and compulsion, and with its definite formula prescribing relations with peoples beyond the Middle Kingdom, Confucian theory should be viewed as the ideological background [for the inter-state relations of ancient China].

SOME FUNDAMENTALS OF HINDU STATECRAFT*

A. L. Basham

The Discovery of Ancient India

The ancient civilization of India differs from those of Egypt, Mesopotamia and Greece, in that its traditions have been preserved without a break down to the present day. Until the advent of the archæologist, the peasant of Egypt or Iraq had no knowledge of the culture of his forefathers, and it is doubtful whether his Greek counterpart had any but the vaguest ideas about the glory of Periclean Athens. In each case there had been an almost complete break with the past. On the other hand, the earliest Europeans to visit India found a culture fully conscious of its own antiquity—a culture which indeed exaggerated that antiquity, and claimed not to have fundamentally changed for many thousands of years. To this day legends known to the humblest Indian recall the names of shadowy chieftains who lived nearly a thousand years before Christ, and the orthodox brāhman in his daily worship repeats hymns composed even earlier. India and China have, in fact, the oldest continuous cultural traditions in the world.

Until the last half of the 18th century Europeans made no real attempt to study India's ancient past, and her early history was known only from brief passages in the works of Greek and Latin authors. A few devoted missionaries in the Peninsula gained a deep understanding of contemporary Indian life, and a brilliant mastery of the vernaculars, but they made no real attempt to understand the historical background of the culture of the people among whom they worked. They accepted that culture at its face value, as very ancient and unchanging, and their only studies of India's past were in the nature of speculations linking the Indians with the descendants of Noah and the vanished empires of the Bible. . . .

* From the book *The Wonder That Was India*, New and Revised Edition, by A. L. Basham, © 1963 by Hawthorn Books, Inc., 70 Fifth Ave., New York, N.Y. Mr. Basham is Professor of History of South Asia, University of London, and author of *History and Doctrine of the Ajivikas* (1951).

The Glory of Ancient India

At most periods of her history India, though a cultural unit, has been torn by internecine war. In statecraft her rulers were cunning and unscrupulous. Famine, flood and plague visited her from time to time, and killed millions of her people. Inequality of birth was given religious sanction, and the lot of the humble was generally hard. Yet our overall impression is that in no other part of the ancient world were the relations of man and man, and of man and the state, so fair and humane. In no other early civilization were slaves so few in number, and in no other ancient lawbook are their rights so well protected as in the *Arthaśāstra.* No other ancient lawgiver proclaimed such noble ideals of fair play in battle as did Manu. In all her history of warfare Hindu India has few tales to tell of cities put to the sword or of the massacre of non-combatants. The ghastly sadism of the kings of Assyria, who flayed their captives alive, is completely without parallel in ancient India. There was sporadic cruelty and oppression no doubt, but, in comparison with conditions in other early cultures, it was mild. To us the most striking feature of ancient Indian civilization is its humanity.

Some 19th-century missionaries, armed with passages from Hindu and Buddhist scriptures, often taken out of their context, and with tales of famine, disease, and the evils of the Hindu caste and family system, have helped to propagate the widespread fallacy that India is a land of lethargic gloom. The traveller landing at Bombay has only to watch the rush-hour crowds, and to compare them mentally with those of London, to realize that the Indian character is neither lethargic nor unhappy. This conclusion is borne out by a general acquaintance with the remains of India's past. Our second general impression of ancient India is that her people enjoyed life, passionately delighting both in the things of the senses and the things of the spirit.

The European student who concentrates on religious texts of a certain type may well gain the impression that ancient India was a land of "life-negating" ascetics, imposing their gloomy and sterile ideas upon the trusting millions who were their lay followers. The fallacy of this impression is quite evident from the secular literature, sculpture and painting of the time. The average Indian, though he might pay lip-service to the ascetic and respect his ideals, did not find life a vale of tears from which to escape at all costs; rather he was willing to accept the world as he found it, and to extract what happiness he could from it. . . . India was a cheerful land, whose people, each finding a niche in a complex and slowly evolving social system, reached a higher level of kindliness and gentleness in their mutual relationships than any other nation of antiquity. For this, as well as for her great achievements in religion, literature, art and mathematics, one European student at least would record his admiration of her ancient culture. . . .

Sources of Indian Political Philosophy

From the days of Plato and Aristotle European thought has turned its attention to such questions as the origin of the state, the ideal form of government, and the basis of law, and politics has long been looked on as a branch of philosophy. India also thought on such questions, but she had no schools of political philosophy in the Western sense. The problems which form the stock-in-trade of the European political philosopher are answered in Indian texts, but in a take-it-or-leave-it manner, with little discussion; often indeed the only argument in favour of a proposition is the citation of an old legend, used much as Plato's adaptations of older myths to reinforce his theories.

Though India had no formal political philosophy, the science of statecraft was much cultivated, and a number of important textbooks on this topic have survived. Daṇḍanīti, the administration of force, or rājanīti, the conduct of kings, was a severely practical science, and the texts cursorily dismiss the more philosophical aspect of politics, but give comparatively detailed advice on the organization of the state and the conduct of governmental affairs. The later Vedic literature tells us something, incidentally, about political life and thought in the pre-Buddhist period, and we can gather much from the Pāli scriptures of Buddhism; but the earliest and most important textbook specifically devoted to statecraft is the Kauṭilīya Arthaśāstra, which is attributed to Kauṭilya, the famous minister of Candragupta Maurya. Some authorities still maintain the full authenticity of the work, but there are grave objections to this view. The text refers to people and places (notably China) which do not seem to have been known to the Indians in the 4th century B.C. It does not use much of the official terminology employed in the Aśokan inscriptions or in the Pāli scriptures, but it contains many governmental terms which apparently did not become popular until post-Mauryan times. Yet it is certainly pre-Guptan, and is, we believe, the elaboration of a Mauryan original which was perhaps the work of Kauṭilya himself. Whatever its age, the Arthaśāstra gives very detailed instructions on the control of the state, the organization of the national economy, and the conduct of war, and it is a most precious source-book for many aspects of ancient Indian life.

The next important source, in chronological order, is the great epic, the Mahābhārata, of which the twelfth book, known as the Śānti Parvan, is a collection of many disparate passages on statecraft and human conduct, inserted into the body of the epic in the early centuries of the Christian era. Other passages on statecraft are found elsewhere in the *Mahābhārata*, and in the second of the great epics, the *Rāmāyaṇa*. The great body of literature generally called *Smṛti*, giving instruction in the Sacred Law, is very important in this connexion; especially significant is the seventh section of the lawbook ascribed to the primeval sage Manu, probably composed early in the Christian era.

From the Gupta period and the Middle Ages a number of political texts survive, the most important of which are the *Nītisāra* ("Essence of Politics") of Kāmandaka, perhaps written during the Gupta period, the *Nītivākyāmṛta* ("Nectar of Aphorisms on Politics") of Somadeva Sūri, a Jaina writer of the 10th century, and the *Nītiśāstra* ("Treatise on Politics") attributed to the ancient sage Śukra, but evidently of late medieval origin. These repeat much that has been said before, but here and there contain original ideas. Besides sources specifically dealing with political life and thought, ancient Indian literature as a whole, from the *Ṛg Veda* onwards, yields much information, and inscriptions of one kind and another are extremely valuable in this connexion.

The texts do not discuss wholly impossible utopias; their advice is often pedantic, but usually more or less feasible. However, it is not likely that any king conducted his affairs wholly on textbook lines, and there is ample evidence that the recommendations of the experts were not always put into effect. The reader must always bear in mind that in the texts on statecraft and Sacred Law the authors describe things not as they were in fact, but as they believed they ought to be. Probably in no kingdom of ancient India, not even in that of the Mauryas, was the influence of the state quite so all-pervading as in the system envisaged by the *Arthaśāstra*, though its author evidently based his precept upon current practice. Similarly the vicious punishments laid down by Manu for religious crimes (for example a śūdra who "arrogantly teaches brāhmans their duty" shall have boiling oil poured in his mouth and ears) are the suggestions of a fanatic and were rarely if ever put into pratice. Moreover the texts are permeated with pedantry, and show the passion for sterile classification to which the Indian pandit has often been prone. It is unlikely that the more energetic and self-reliant rulers worried overmuch about the *Arthaśāstara's* discussion of different schools of thought on such questions as whether it is better to acquire a wild and rebellious but prosperous country, or a pacific but poor one. Many errors have been made by historians through their uncritical acceptance of these political texts as giving an exact picture of things as they were. . . .

The Royal Function

The idea of a body politic, of the state as an organism transcending its component parts, though it appears in a rather vague form, does not seem to have taken any great hold on ancient Indian thought. A classification popular with the theorists enumerates seven elements of sovereignty, which are occasionally compared to the limbs and parts of the human body—the king to the head, the ministers to the eyes, the ally to the ear, the treasury to the mouth, the army to the mind, the fortifications to the arms, and the land and people to the legs. Such weak analogies carried little weight, however. Society, the age-old divinely ordained way of Indian life, transcended the state and was independent of it. The king's function was the protection of society, and the state was merely an extension of the king for the furtherance of that end.

The king's function involved the protection not only of his kingdom against external aggression, but also of life, property and traditional custom against internal foes. He protected the purity of class and caste by ensuring that those who broke caste custom were excommunicated; he protected the family system by punishing adultery, and ensuring the fair inheritance of family property; he protected widows and orphans by making them his wards; he protected the rich against the poor by suppressing robbery; and he protected the poor against the rich by punishing extortion and oppression. Religion was protected by liberal grants to learned brāhmans and temples, and frequently to heterodox sects also. The duty of protection was often little more than the preservation of the *status quo,* but it was nevertheless onerous, and involved positive duties, such as developing irrigation, relieving famine, and generally supervising the economic life of the realm.

The ideal set before the king was one of energetic beneficence. Aśoka was not the only king of India to proclaim that all men were his children, or to take pride in his ceaseless activity. The *Arthaśāstra,* despite its advocacy of every dishonest expedient for the acquisition and maintenance of power, puts the kingly duty in simple and forceful language, setting an ideal such as few ancient civilizations can boast of. Comparing the king and the ascetic it says:

> The king's pious vow is readiness in action,
> his sacrifice, the discharge of his duty.
>
> . . . .
>
> In the happiness of his subjects lies the king's happiness,
> in the welfare of his subjects, his welfare.
> The king's good is not that which pleases him,
> but that which pleases his subjects.

Therefore the king should be ever active,
and should strive for prosperity,
    for prosperity depends on effort,
and failure on the reverse.

Elsewhere the *Arthaśāstra* suggests a time-table for the king's day, which allows him only four and a half hours' sleep and three hours for eating and recreation, the rest of the day being spent in state affairs of one kind or another. No doubt such a programme was rarely kept in practice, but it at least shows the ideal at which the king was expected to aim. Candragupta Maurya is said by Megasthenes to have listened to the petitions of his subjects even while in the hands of his masseurs, while his grandson Aśoka ordered that important business was to be set before him at all times, even when he was in his harem. In all sources the king is told that he must be prompt in the administration of justice and always accessible to his people. The swarms of guards, ushers, and other officials who surrounded the king's person must often have demanded bribes, and otherwise have obstructed the access of the subject to his sovereign, but the best of Indian kings at all times have made the public audience, or *darbār*, an important instrument of government....

Hindu Militarism

The rule of law in personal, family and class relations was a fundamental element of ancient Indian thought, but in the sphere of international affairs there was no real conception of its possibility. A few enlightened people recognized the evil effects of the warfare which afflicted the Indian sub-continent during most of its history, but their message was generally unheard. Aśoka was possibly the only ancient Indian king who finally broke with the tradition of aggression, though his spirit can perhaps be heard in certain passages in Buddhist texts, and many ordinary people must have echoed his sentiments. Nevertheless, positive condemnations of war are rare in Indian literature.

In one story the Buddha himself is depicted as intervening in a tribal war between the Śākyas and their neighbours the Koliyas, and persuading the contestants to come to terms. In the beautiful *Dhammapada,* an early collection of Buddhist verse, we read:

Victory breeds hatred,
    for the conquered sleep in sorrow;
above victory or defeat
    the calm man dwells in peace.

Buddhism was specially popular with the mercantile classes, who stood to lose much from constant warfare, and the passing and rare references to the evils of war in Buddhist texts may in part represent the mild protest of the vaiśyas[1] against the continual campaigning which interfered with their trading ventures. In any case war was generally accepted as a normal activity of the state, even by Buddhist kings. The doctrine of non-violence, which in medieval India had become very influential, and had made most of the respectable classes vegetarian, was never at this time taken to forbid war or capital punishment. It was only in modern times that Mahātmā Gāndhī reinterpreted it in this sense.

The intense militarism of ancient India did not lead to the building of a permanent empire over the whole sub-continent. In this respect the early history of India contrasts strikingly with that of China, where, from the 3rd century B.C., a single empire was the rule, and division the exception. In India the Mauryas succeeded in creating a unified empire for a century, and in the heyday of the Guptas much of North India was under one hand, but with these exceptions numerous factors prevented the unification of the recognized cultural unit of Bhāratavarṣa, which so many ambitious monarchs desired.

One of these factors was the mere size of the land, but the Chinese emperors conquered equal difficulties. Another reason for the failure of Indian empire builders was that, for all the wise counsel of the *Arthaśāstra,* no king of India was able to develop a bureaucracy capable of functioning without a strong guiding hand; in China the examination system and the ethics of Confucius ensured that those in charge of affairs would usually be men of character and intellect, if rather pedantic and conservative. But the main factor which prevented the unification of India was the martial tradition itself.

For the post-Mauryan king the idea of empire was something very different from that to which the West is accustomed. According to the *Arthaśāstra* there are three types of conquest: righteous conquest, conquest for greed, and demoniac conquest. The first is conquest in which the defeated king is forced to render homage and tribute, after which he or a member of his family is reinstated as a vassal. The second is victory in which enormous booty is demanded and large portions of enemy territory annexed. The third involves the political annihilation of the conquered kingdom and its incorporation in that of the victor. The two latter types are generally disapproved of by all sources except the *Arthaśāstra.* Thus the *Mahābhārata* declares:

> A king should not attempt
> to gain the earth unrighteously,

[1] The vaiśyas were the mercantile class—Ed.

for who reveres the king
who wins unrighteous victory?
Unrighteous conquest is impermanent,
and does not lead to heaven.

The idea of "righteous conquest" or "conquest according to the Sacred Law" may have developed among the Aryans soon after their occupation of North India, as an expression of their solidarity against the dark-skinned natives. It is evident, though not explicitly stated, in later Vedic literature. The kings of Magadha ... ignored it, and annexed territory without compunction; but the doctrine that war should be waged for glory and homage rather than sordid aims such as wealth and power grew in importance with the fall of the Mauryas, and was accepted by the medieval quasi-feudal order. "Demoniac conquest" still took place from time to time, notably under the Guptas, but "righteous conquest" was the ideal which Hindu kings were expected to follow, and it is evident that they usually did. War became the sport of kings—a sport which was often very profitable and always very serious, in which the shame of defeat might well only be expunged by suicide, but a sport nevertheless. The Peninsula, inheriting a fierce Dravidian tradition never completely submerged by Aryan influence, had a more realistic approach; here conquest with annexation was more common, as well as ruthlessness towards captives and non-combatants, but even the South was not unaffected by the ideal of the "righteous conquest."

In most of the texts on statecraft we read of the "six instruments of policy" (*ṣāḍguṇya*): peace, war, waiting for the enemy to strike the first blow, attack, alliance, and "double policy" or making peace with one enemy and continuing war with another. The list is a stock one, and gives a further example of the delight of the Indian theorist in pedantic classification, but it is nevertheless significant. Peace is only one of the six categories; the others are aspects of war in all its branches. The *Arthaśāstra* quotes an earlier authority, Vātavyādhi, as disagreeing with the sixfold classification, and maintaining that statecraft involved only two aspects, peace and war. Of this view the text strongly disapproves; pacific relations are straightforward and obvious, while war is complex and highly developed. It is significant that one of the words commonly used for enemy, *para,* has the simple primary meaning of "other."

At all times conquest was the chief ambition of the Indian king. Even Aśoka, who abjured aggressive war, did not give up the hope of conquest. The position is succinctly put by the *Arthaśāstra:* "The king who is weaker than 'the other' should keep the peace; he who is stronger should make war." The same aphorism is repeated in many other sources, in slightly varying forms, but a difference of attitude is apparent as we leave the

Mauryan recollections of the *Arthaśāstra* for the later texts, the outlook of which reflects memories of the later Vedic age, adapted to the often anarchic conditions of the period between the Mauryas and Guptas.

For the earlier source war is a "continuation of policy by other means." Its purpose is not glory, but wealth and power, and the passage we have quoted, defining the three types of conquest, is, we believe, either a sop to conventional doctrine or a later interpolation, for it is inconsistent with the tenor of the book. The whole work is written for a king who aspires to become an emperor on the Mauryan model, and such a king is not advised to embark on war lightly. There are many other ways of gaining power, intrigue and assassination among them, and these should always be resorted to in preference to war, which should only be looked on as a last resort. If a king suffers decisive defeat he must submit, in the hope that he will be allowed to retain his throne as a vassal and ultimately again achieve independence and conquer his former overlord. The *Arthaśāstra* says nothing about fair play in battle, and evidently looks on conquest of the demoniac variety as the most profitable and advisable. Though in one passage, not in keeping with the main tenor of the work, it suggests allowing the conquered king to remain as a vassal, it ends on a note of humanitarian imperialism. The victor must do everything in his power to conciliate the conquered people; if their economy has suffered badly from the war, taxes must be remitted; ministers of the defeated king must be won round, and law and order restored as quickly as possible; when in the conquered country the king should wear local dress and follow local customs. Evidently, from the point of view of the *Arthaśāstra*, the main motive of war is gain and the building up of a great empire.

The more orthodox texts, however, take a different point of view. Here the major motive of war is glory, not gain. War is not merely a means to an end, but part of the warrior's *dharma*, and good for its own sake. As soon as a king has established himself on the throne he should, as a matter of course, attack his neighbours. Rules of fair fighting are laid down, which are not heard of in the *Arthaśāstra*. For the later sources, such as Manu, a battle was ideally a gigantic tournament with many rules: a warrior fighting from a chariot might not strike one on foot; an enemy in flight, wounded or asking quarter might not be slain; the lives of enemy soldiers who had lost their weapons were to be respected; poisoned weapons were not to be used. Homage and not annexation was the rightful fruit of victory.

These rules were not always kept. The heroes of the *Mahābhārata* infringe them many times, even at the behest of their mentor Kṛṣṇa, and the infringements are explained and pardoned by recourse to casuistical arguments of expediency and necessity. The rules of war could only be maintained strictly by a king certain of victory or certain of defeat. Where chances were narrow the claims of self-preservation inevitably made themselves felt. But the chivalrous rules of warfare, probably based on very old tradition, and codified in their present form among the martial peoples of Western India in post-Mauryan times, must have had some effect in mitigating the harshness of war for combatant and non-combatant alike. It is doubtful if any other ancient civilization set such humane ideals of warfare.

Together with these rules, the later texts introduce the conception of military honour, which is not found in the realistic *Arthaśāstra,* except in the form of propaganda to maintain the morale of the troops. Flight is the deepest of shames; the soldier slain in flight incurs the guilt of his lord, and suffers proportionately in the after-life, but the soldier slain while fighting to the last passes straight to heaven. Such ideals culminated in the *jauhar,* the final holocaust which was the fate of many a medieval Rājput king, with his family and bodyguard, the women and children burning alive in the inner chambers of the fort while the men fought to the last on the battlements.

The live dog was no longer thought to be better than the dead lion, in so far as the spirit of the Epics permeated Hindu life. But the *Arthaśāstra* was not wholly forgotten, and not every king of medieval India was willing to sacrifice himself and his family when defeat stared him in the face. As well as kings who resisted the Muslim invaders to the last there were many who tried to buy them off, and who retained diminished kingdoms under the suzerainty of the hated *Mleccha.*[2]

In this political climate it is not surprising that inter-state relations were of the most Machiavellian character. The basic concept which governed the relations of one king with another was the doctrine of the "circles" (*maṇḍala*), which, like many other concepts, was pedantically elaborated by the theorists on statecraft. The king on whose territory the circle is centred is known as "he who desires conquest" (*vijigīṣu*). The king whose territory adjoins that of the would-be conqueror is "the enemy" (*ari*)— "when he is in trouble he must be attacked, when he has little or no help he may be uprooted, otherwise he must be harassed and weakened." Beyond the enemy lies "the friend" (*mitra*) the natural ally of the conqueror. So far the system of circles is simple and obvious, but the theorists enlarged it further. Beyond the friend is "the enemy's friend" (*arimitra*), and beyond him "the friend's friend" (*mitramitra*). The opposite frontier of the conqueror's kingdom provides a further series of potential foes and allies, the "heelseizer" (*pārṣṇigraha*), who is an ally of the conqueror's enemy and

[2] A *mleccha* is a non-Indian—Ed.

is liable to attack him in the rear, the "defender" or rearward friend (ākranda), the heelseizer's ally (pārṣṇigrahāsāra), and the rearward friend's friend (ākrandāsāra). The main purport of this enumeration is clear—a king's neighbour is his natural enemy, while the king beyond his neighbour is his natural ally. The working of this principle can be seen throughout the history of Hindu India in the temporary alliances of two kingdoms to accomplish the encirclement and destruction of the kingdoms between them.

In such conditions diplomatic relations were not thoroughly organized, and there is no evidence of a system of permanent ambassadors. Relations between one court and another were maintained by envoys (dūta), who resided at the court to which they were sent only while transacting the business in hand. As in most civilizations, the person of the envoy was inviolable, and a king slaying an envoy was thought to be reborn in hell with all his councillors....

Conditions in Hindu India were not unlike those in medieval Europe, where there was a broad and recognized cultural unity accompanied by inter-state anarchy resulting in perpetual warfare. In Europe, however, the well-organized and centralized Roman Church often acted as a pacifying element in the situation; in India Hinduism, which had no all-embracing super-national organization, rather encouraged inter-state anarchy by incorporating many martial traditions into the Sacred Law.

MUSLIM UNIVERSALISM*

Costi K. Zurayk

In the turmoil of the present age, we are prone to be so distracted by the political and economic aspects of our national and international problems as to lose sight of their origin and meaning. We tend to forget that these problems can be understood only within the context of the particular civilization in which they arise. For this reason, students and thinkers can

* Costi K. Zurayk, "The Essence of Arab Civilization," reprinted by permission from the Middle East Journal, III:2 (Spring 1949), 125–132. Costi K. Zurayk (Constantine Kaysar Zurayk), former Minister of Syria to the United States, is Distinguished Professor of History, American University of Beirut, Lebanon; and author of Al-Wa'y al Qawmi (National Consciousness), Ayyu Ghadin (Whither Tomorrow), and Ma'na al-Nakbah (The Meaning of the Tragedy).

do no greater service in the present critical situation of the world than to bring out the fundamental implications of these problems in terms of the civilization in which they occur as well as in terms of modern Western civilization, which is fast weaving its web over the whole of human society.

This paper is an attempt to analyze the nature of Arab civilization—a civilization which was growing and creative during the Middle Ages and contributed its share to human culture and progress, but which, after a period of decline, is now seeking to protect its existence and to reinterpret its meaning *vis à vis* the advancing aggressive Western civilization. Such a study is necessary for a true understanding of the present problems of the Arab world. Readers may not agree completely with the particular conclusions here reached; what is more important is that those who are truly concerned with the destiny of the Arabs think out the present problems of the Arab world in their true setting, and with particular attention to the moral values involved.

The birth of Arabic civilization was attended, or rather caused, by a great spiritual revival of the Arab people. Stirrings of this revival were felt in the latter half of the sixth century A.D., and perhaps earlier, but it was left to the Prophet Muḥammad in the 7th century to gather together the streams of spiritual consciousness and to drive them forth in one mighty current. His essential message was the unity of God and the apostleship of His prophets, he—Muḥammad—being the last of them and God's revelation to him the perfect and ultimate revelation. His personality kindled the spirit of his followers, and transformed them from ordinary men into great leaders. Under their brilliant guidance, the Arabs set out to establish one of the greatest empires of history, and to carry the banner of a religious movement which today commands the loyalty of about 250 million of the world's population.

Attempts to explain the birth of Arab civilization by exclusively material factors have not met with complete success. Scholars following such a theory have looked upon the Arab expansion from Arabia as one in a series of outbursts of Semitic migration, largely military in character, and caused by climatic changes and political and economic tensions. They have also emphasized the internal weakness and disintegration of the Byzantine and Persian empires, thus minimizing the Arab achievement.

All these and similar interpretations, justifiable though they may be within their own limits, cannot explain away the evident spiritual basis of the Arab revival, nor destroy the fact that Arab rule, conduct, learning, and morals were inextricably tied up with the religion of Islam, and were progressive and creative to the extent to which they—and Islam itself— remained true to the rise of the Arab spirit to a new and nobler conception of life. In the first two or three centuries following the Prophet Muḥammad, the original vision and ideals were potent, and with them the vitality and creativity of the Arab empire and civilization. When the vision was dimmed, and the ideals gradually lost sight of, political life became a mere contest for power between rival dynasties, parties, sects, and races, and the process of disintegration set in.

The same was true of Islam as a religion, which was closely interwoven with Arab life and culture. So long as it preserved its original urge and spontaneity, it acted as a leaven vitalizing the political system, opening before the people ever new and wider horizons in the realms of action and of contemplation. When, however, it became reduced to a set of doctrines to be taken on credence, and a code of laws and morals to be applied rigidly and blindly it turned out to be, as other religions in the same state, a burden rather than an inspiration, a paralysing shackle instead of a liberating force, the letter that killeth all real endeavor and progress.

The driving force, the creative element, in Arab civilization was not only the spiritual but also the universal in outlook and practice. It would be more correct to say that it was universal by virtue of its spirituality. In the realm of belief it started with the conception of the unity of God, the creator and the sustainer of this universe, the judge of the actions of men, and the ultimate guide of human destiny. All things are derived from Him and dependent upon Him. He is the principle of order, of stability, of growth in the universe and in human life. Men may be divided in race or country; their ultimate loyalty remains that which ties them to God and makes them brethren within Islam. There is therefore an essential unity in humanity, derived from the unity of God.

Now it is true that this unity was limited to those who were within Islam itself. The same may also be said of the other great bloc in medieval times: the Christian world. Each of these two systems was complete in itself, each looked upon the other as being outside the fold, material for conversion or for conquest, so that humanity as a whole was not united in practice or, strictly speaking, even in belief. In other words there was, if one could say so, more than one universalism dominant in the medieval world. But I should like to venture the suggestion that the two universalistic systems, the Christian and the Moslem, were essentially alike, or at least closer to each other than either of them is to the modern naturalistic view of the universe. They proceeded from similar basic claims and used essentially the same kind of reasoning. Despite their frequent controversies and violent disputations, they understood each other far better than any of us who has embraced the modern this-worldly outlook would understand them.

So long as the universalistic outlook was dominant in Arab civilization, and so long as those who belonged to this civilization felt that they were bound by a common loyalty which was grounded on the unity of God and the resultant unity of the universe and the unity of man, the empire which the Arabs built maintained its internal strength and steady progress, and Arab civilization remained growing and creative. But as has happened in the case of other civilizations both before and after, this fundamental universalistic belief gradually lost its effect in practice. Within the Arabic empire, Arabs, Persians, Turks, Berbers and others turned one against another, each seeking to gain political predominance and rule; individuals and dynasties began to struggle for power; partisan and sectarian rivalries asserted themselves and shook the foundation of the state. The universal loyalty was broken up by lesser and narrower loyalties, with the result that the motivation became the gain of power rather than the realization of a transcendent ideal.

It should be stated, however, that this weakening and final break-up of the universal outlook in practice affected the political realm more than it did the cultural. Even after the various races, parties and sects became divided against themselves in a contest for power, their representatives continued to collaborate in the realm of culture. What politics divided, culture kept co-operative and united. The traveler who wandered in the Arab world passed through many states and political entities, often at war with one another, but wherever he went, from Central Asia to Spain, he found one common culture, with a common language, Arabic, and a basically unified world-view.

Underlying this fundamentally universal outlook of Arab civilization was a faith not only in the unity of God and the unity of the believing community, but also in the unity of truth. Truth was to Arab thinkers not subjective and relative, but objective and absolute, and the duty of man was to learn it and abide by it.

Arab thinkers received truth through two ways: the one, the way of revelation, the word of God as revealed to the Prophet Muḥammad and embodied in the Koran; and the other, the way of wisdom or philosophy, as worked out by the ancients, particularly Plato and Aristotle. To them these two truths were but two facets of the one and only truth. Thus their duty was to learn them adequately and fully (hence the great activity of commentation which they embarked upon) and then to try to reconcile them. There were, no doubt, extremists on both sides who did not follow this path: certain philosophers, on the one hand, who explained religious texts away by allegorical interpretation; and the religious traditionalists and reactionaries, on the other, who damned all philosophy as essentially pagan and sinful. But the main tradition of Arabic philosophic and theological thought rested on the belief in the fundamental unity of the two truths, and set itself the task of bringing out this underlying unity. Thus

Arabic thought, like that of the Latins, is one of reconciliation and synthesis. Arab philosophers and theologians bent themselves to the duty of seeking the common ultimate truth through its different manifestations. Since Reality is one, truth should be one.

In addition to the philosophers and the theologians, there were the mystics, who stressed even more fully and nobly the essential unity of God, of humanity, and of truth. They were those soaring spirits, the climax of the achievement of creative religion, who rise above the letter of the doctrine or the law, who look upon the human personality as a whole, who value love above belief, who are truly universal in their yearning for the good life. Below the divergences of nature they see the One Reality: God. "O God," one of them declares, "I never listen to the cry of animals or to the quivering of trees or to the murmuring of water or to the warbling of birds or to the rustling wind or to the crashing thunder without feeling them to be an evidence of Thy unity and a proof that there is nothing like unto Thee." Stressing spiritual experience rather than codes and doctrines, they become open to truth, from wheresoever it comes, and in this way they assert its unity and the unity of humanity, across the various boundaries which divide peoples and religions.

> My heart has become capable of every form; it is a pasture for gazelles
>   and a convent for Christian monks,
> And a temple for idols, and the pilgrims Ka'ba, and the tables of the
>   Tora and the book of the Koran.
> I follow the religion of Love, whichever way his camels take. Love is
>   my religion and my faith.

In this mystic urge we have one of the best fruits of Arab, as well as of the more general Islamic civilizations; indeed of every creative civilization. And it provides the indisputable proof that such abundant and life-giving fruits can grow only in a soil saturated with a true universalism, a deep conviction of the unity of God, of humanity, and of truth.

These attitudes of Arab civilization—the spiritual urge, the universal outlook, the deep-seated belief in the unity of truth—had far-reaching effects in practice. One of the most remarkable and distinctive of these was the co-operative nature of Arab culture. When the Arabs came out of the Arabian Peninsula into lands that had been saturated with the achievements of successive civilizations going back to the dawn of history, they did not—as did other conquerors, ancient and modern—destroy or eradicate the marks of those civilizations. On the contrary, animated by an open mind and a tolerant spirit, they encouraged the continued growth of the cultures of the various peoples that participated in the empire, and provided the conditions for the unification of those cultures into one whole.

Thus Arab civilization is not the achievement of one people; it is rather a co-operative enterprise undertaken by many peoples of various racial origins, cultural backgrounds, and religious affiliations. Moslems, Christians, and Jews; Arabs, Arameans, Persians, Turks, Berbers, and others—all shared together in this common effort. Each provided its own distinctive contribution. The Arabs brought in the original spiritual urge represented in Islam, the remarkable genius of the Arabic language, and their sharp literary sensitiveness. Persia provided its administrative tradition, its belles-lettres, and its art; India its wisdom literature, its astronomy, and mathematics; and, above all, the Hellenized Syriac and Coptic speaking Christians of Syria, Mesopotamia, and Egypt contributed their philosophical, theological, and scientific traditions. Berbers, Jews, and Arabicized Spaniards collaborated with the Arabs, and under their patronage built up the glorious civilization of Moorish Spain. And the same is true of Sicily and Southern Italy, of Central Asia, of all the other regions that came within the compass of Arab life. Thus exclusiveness and complacent self-satisfaction are not in the true Arab tradition. If they had been, Arab civilization would not have been possible.

To the concrete achievements which each of these peoples provided, we must add the more evasive but no less effective elements in their social life, their mental attitudes, their moral conceptions, their varied natures and temperaments. Their collaboration in everyday life and cultural activity, even when torn apart politically, is evident in the synthetic nature of Arab science, philosophy, theology, architecture, the minor arts—indeed in almost every aspect of Arab culture and civilization.

Arab civilization has been criticized as a hodgepodge of many heterogeneous elements, thrown side by side without organization or order. Had this been the case, Arab civilization would not have been creative. Its contributions in science, philosophy and art, which are being increasingly recognized by Western scholars, could not have been possible except on the basis of a unity of outlook, of endeavor, and of final accomplishment. Arab culture is a finished tissue in which threads of various makes and colors are woven. It is not a mixture, but a compound. It has unity; and this unity—as in every other individual or social phenomenon—is the basis of its strength and creativity.

A second criticism is directed at the Arabs themselves. What, it is asked, did the Arabs contribute to this process? Leaving aside the distinctive contributions of the Arabs—the original spiritual revival, the genius of the language, the faculty of expressing condensed experience in sharp clear-cut verse or prose, the individual achievements of Arabs in the various disciplines—leaving aside all this, I wish to venture the suggestion that even if the Arabs had themselves offered no single element to this whole, it is sufficient to their undying credit that they provided the original spirit and the necessary conditions for the bringing together and the co-operation of all these various peoples in one common effort. It was they who started the empire on a policy of tolerance, who opened their gates in Damascus, Baghdad, Cordova, and elsewhere to scholars of all races and sects, who sought scholars and books from the ends of the earth, who gloried in the patronage of the arts and the sciences. This alone is a most distinct contribution, more important than any single achievement in science or philosophy or art, and entitles the Arabs to a marked place in the history of civilization.

THE NATION-STATE SYSTEM IN MODERN AFRICA AND ASIA*

Robert Montagne

[T]erritorial and maritime conquests were recorded and celebrated by the people who undertook them. They also gave rise among the conquered —conquerors of yesterday—to resentments which still smoulder. Today, when the world has become smaller, when men and ideas travel with increasing ease, when all tongues are mingled and rival political ideas confront each other, the memories of these great expansions are still alive in international assemblies. It is indeed easy to understand that the imperial powers should try to save what remains of their achievements. The inhabitants of the colonies of yesterday, now set up as "modern states"—a bold Western innovation—relentlessly demand their place in the sun. The representatives of the old nations are confronted by those of the new, whether in U.N.O. or in its Committees, and are concerned to found a new international law of *a static character* which would forever erase the memory, as yet all too near, of these great historic expansions. Conquerors and conquered are to be seen there, wearing the same clothes, obeying the same diplomatic conventions, appealing to the authority of the same modern constitutions. Watching and listening to them, one could easily

* Robert Montagne, "The 'Modern State' in Africa and Asia," *The Cambridge Journal*, V, No. 10 (July 1952), 583–600). Reprinted by permission. Robert Montagne is former Directeur d'Études Sociologie Nord-Africaine, and author of *La Civilisation du Disert-Nomades d'Orient et d'Afrique* (1947), *Naissance du Proletariat Marocain* (1951), and *Revolution au Maroc* (1955).

come to the conclusion that a modern world, stable and united, is already in existence and that colonization had been merely an unfortunate and passing phase. But what is the reality like? What are these modern states which rise up on the ruins of the old empires? Is the world, which is now changing so fast, giving birth to entirely new societies? Or is it that what we see are only ephemeral structures, mere juristic phantoms, which only hide from us the obstinate survival of ancient ways of life able to resist indefinitely the influence of the West? This can be found out only by studying the structure of these new nations and states. . . .

Events and institutions can . . . according to a comparative method which is no longer strictly historical, be classified in a series. Without having to admit that humanity always passes through the same stages in its history, we can see in certain regions the existence, at different epochs, of identical social structures and of similar developments. . . . In this manner we accustom ourselves to move in thought not only through time but also through the "time-space," which is an often reversible complex, inside which past and present, East and West, no longer stand in opposition.

In order to measure this time-space, and at the risk of shocking the historians, I propose to take in thought a fast aeroplane. This is the only practical way which will allow us to survey in a bird's-eye view the far-reaching frontiers of our subject. In this way, also, we shall feel that beneficent shock produced on the mind by the impressions afforded by a variety of stopping-places, impressions which will sharpen by their contrast our analytic abilities. . . .

[T]he plane indifferently cuts through the frontiers of the various states which we see on the multicoloured sheet.

If we are travelling in America, Africa or the Near East, the invisible frontiers over which we are flying will have, nearly all of them, a common feature which is of great importance. A great many of these frontiers are geometrical lines: parallels, meridians or obliques. These are abstract and theoretical divisions which contrast with the supple lines—mountain ranges or valleys—within which most of the states of Europe and Asia have developed throughout their long history. These straight lines are the marks that the white man's hand has left while forming, *ab nihilo,* these "modern states" which we are soon to inspect. These lines are those with which an arrogant pen, at a meeting of experts, has imperiously fixed the lives of the coloured peoples, by drawing on the map on a diplomat's table the contours of a new society. . . .

But let us confine ourselves to Africa and the Near East, regions where the expansion of the West is still going on in various ways. All over these regions the existence of frontiers in straight lines serves to remind us that the era of zones of influence apportioned among rival nations and of the scientific division of continents is hardly ended. Let us examine these frontiers carefully.

Sometimes, the straight lines start at a given point from which a number of frontiers diverge fanwise. If this abstract network covers inhabited areas, then there will be convenient nests for smugglers who, passing successively from one compartment into the other, will make their profits out of the impotence of the customs and the financial controls. The corner of eastern Morocco squeezed in between Algeria and the Spanish Rif is such a region, another is the *bec de canard* in Syria, between Turkey and Iraq ... Often also, when the theoretical dividing line is drawn through densely populated regions, it breaks so many ties among men that, in practice, it proves necessary for Frontier Delimitation Commissions to make concessions to topography. We then get those saw-like frontiers, purely theoretical straight lines to start with, later made a little more human; such frontiers are those which separate the Cameroons from Togoland, under French and British trusteeship. Yet, in spite of these re-arrangements, the cries of the victims are still heard. The Ewes of Togo-land, for instance, last year denounced through U.N.O., the arbitary division imposed on them, a division which they described as a kind of vivi-section. It is true that their protest may not have been altogether spontaneous, and that it was meant to provoke the intervention of the Trusteeship Committee in the question of the division of Africa between the European nations.

There are also still more ingenious frontiers which have resulted in even more complicated geometrical figures. I am thinking of those curious poly-gons drawn by British political officers to form the neutral zones in the desert claimed by Saudi Arabia on the one hand, Iraq and Kuweit on the other. Even though here also it is a question of linear frontiers, we see a touching effort on the part of Westerners to recognize the rightness of the native conception of political geography, which is so different from ours. Before our arrival in Asia and Africa, a frontier was never actually a line but a no-man's-land, where one ventured only at one's own risk. In Black Africa today, wise administrators, by making use of this concept, have established in small neutral zones, without injury to the interests of any party, schools, missions, experimental farms and nurseries. For this, they chose these no-man's-lands which have always existed between the vari-ous hitherto hostile chieftainships. There is no end to the curious fancies of "scientific frontiers," drawn by the geographers and the diplomats of the West. One has only to think of the Spanish Sahara cut up into three zones separated by parallel lines, each of which has a separate status. But the nomadic camel breeders, heedless of the Europeans, are always cross-ing these zones, in search of the fickle pastures conjured up by the rain.

Or better still, there is the last-born of these partitions, the Palestinian checkerboard, cut up into six squares, each three joined together at their extremities, in order to separate Jew from Arab.

And yet, what powerful reality those lines drawn on the map possess, lines which neither nature nor the inhabitants, left to themselves, would have brought into being. The West is there, in these invisible frames which it has drawn on its own maps, come to undertake its gigantic task. To be made aware of this, it is enough for us to examine our surroundings during the first stop of the plane on one of the landing grounds near a large African town—Kano, for example. What strikes us near the rest house where the passengers are received is the variety of the races around us. In this vast continent (yesterday a sea of peoples on the move, throwing up disparate invasions following one on the other) the Western peace, at the end of the nineteenth century, suddenly came to freeze these human waves. The positions of the conquering races, and of innumerable small surviving islands of conquered peoples which have taken refuge in the mountains and become shut in on themselves, are everywhere to be seen. Hundreds of different tongues, thousands of dialects have kept these human groupings apart from one another; the different physical characteristics of those whom we see around us are enough to testify to the far-reaching antiquity and of the isolation of these small communities so jealously guarded for many centuries. And suddenly, on those advancing waves, on those scattered islands, a Western power has thrown its net to catch these heterogeneous societies, like fish which, caught in the trap, cease at last to devour each other. But in spite of the diversity of ethnic types, we will hear only one language spoken, a language imposed on all by the conquering colonial power, which has also imposed its currency and its exchange controls. Its customs authorities too are here to levy (after a long and suspicious inspection that no smile can pacify) various duties on the goods brought in, no matter how insignificant. And here also are the police, and the native army. Even though we are in the heart of Africa, we are left in no doubt that here is a modern state set in the midst of other modern states, run and administered in the same way. The elected representatives of the neighbouring countries, the *conseilleurs généraux*, the M.P.s, the Councillors of the Republic and of the French Union all sit at the table in this rest house. In the English-language newspapers on the table, we read that the local parliament, the House of Assembly, has just held its annual session and begun its work with a prayer modelled on that read at Westminister...

These things which we observe now in Africa, no matter how curious they may be, are not new. The introduction by conquerors of Western institutions is quite the rule. When Portugal was imposing its authority on the delta of the Congo, in the sixteenth century, the African kings used to receive coats of arms from Lisbon and codes of laws compiled by Christian lawyers, and their vassals used to become marquesses and counts... And this went on until some revolt would re-establish the African order and expel the missionaries.

Let us not think, however, that this is a question of mere appearances. The extremely powerful machinery of the modern state (which establishes itself with its numerous adjuncts, financial, economic, judicial and cultural) will somehow exercise from the outside, on the innumerable native societies, imprisoned henceforth within their "scientific" frontiers, a pressure of such power and efficiency, that it breaks them up and scatters them like the shell of a cracked nut....

Within the limits laid down by conquest or the mutual rivalries of the Powers, the West has established the modern state. This State is immediately supplied with all the techniques essential to it: those of finance, economics, justice, education, and defence. It is moreover given, in fact or in law, a constitution which regulates the relations of the state authorities with the local populations.

Often, especially at the beginning, paradoxical as it is, a kind of systematic and temporary consolidation of the previous political institutions takes place. This is really because the conqueror is under the necessity of husbanding his available forces, unavoidably limited, in order to direct and control the life of the people. Sometimes the new masters, hesitating to demolish at one stroke an often ancient civilization, manifest a desire to keep intact the respectable elements of social life which sustain it. The treaties of Great Britain with the Indian princes, the Demischel treaty with Emir Abd el Kader, the protectorate conventions in Morocco and Tunisia, the treaties signed with the Foulbé Emirs in the middle Niger, the recognition of the Negro chiefs from the time of the Congo kings of the sixteenth century down to the chieftains of the Rwanda-Urundi in the twentieth century—such are the different manifestations of this state of mind. But, however resolved the new masters may be to observe these treaties scrupulously, the stabilization of these native sovereignties soon confronts them with problems difficult to solve. The arbitrariness of the rulers was tempered in the past by the fear of war and rebellion; the support of the notables was therefore essential to enable the rulers to govern the people. But from now onwards, in this modern state rigorously pacified, their domination runs no more risks. They are naturally tempted to exercise it without any check. The old abuses speedily reappear, multiplied at all the steps of the hierarchy, with nothing to stand in their way. The tyranny of the great, the degradation of the masses go on increasing, unless a vigilant supervision succeeds in re-establishing justice for a short while, as it does, but alas, only too infrequently. Absolutism sets itself up in the shape of democratic doctrine. This is to be noticed in Africa and in Asia wherever the power of the native ruler exceeds the influence of the Western Adviser whose duty it is to check the evil. The reaction will then be swift. The will of the conqueror suppresses such extensive sovereignties as those of the big chiefs in the Algerian South, of the Emirs of Mauritania, of the King of Abeokuta in Nigeria and of so many others. . . .

At the same time, notables from the civil service or the merchant class will reap fortunes for themselves by making use of modern economic methods in a society where the weak can no longer have recourse to rebellion. They increase their landed properties and often use improved techniques on them. This is what happens in Iraq, in Egypt, in Morocco, under conditions which sometimes endanger the social equilibrium of the rural populations and paralyse the settlement of the nomads.

But what we see most of all is a rapid decline of the basic institutions and social units, which takes place in the course of only two or three generations. Tribes, chieftainships, theocratic fiefs, ethnic and religious minorities, and at last that fundamental cell, the patriarchal family, all are destroyed: a destruction which the modern state brings about blindly and inadvertently.

Let us consider some aspects of this decline. In the first place, the tribes cannot survive in a pacified state where men can move freely. Each of these tribes, one of the thousands who have parcelled out among themselves, in tiny territories, the area between the Persian Gulf, the Atlantic, the Mediterranean and the Tropics, used to be a kind of large exclusive family, shut in on itself, ensuring its own defence and regulating its life in the midst of warring populations. In the peace which reigns today, the tribe languishes, and the moral ties between its members are loosened. Men get away, sell their lands and marry outside the tribe. The tribe itself becomes a mere territorial command until the day, not so far off, when even its chiefs, through a too rapid decline, will relinquish their position to the benefit of officials from the town.

In Muslim countries, the theocratic fiefs used to be places of refuge and protection. And they were also little spiritual fatherlands. But the territorial unity of command does away with them. On the other hand, as the pretext of the Holy War (which used to justify their existence) has disappeared, in a social and political environment which aspires to other things, their masters too fall into a decadence rendered more rapid by idleness.

The same is also true, and sometimes even more so, of the innumerable Negro chieftainships which gather into a community thousands of inhabitants around a kind of priest-king, spokesman of a highly hierarchical community, conceived in the image of a complicated and mysterious spiritual world. Men and women, lured by the charms of a life freer and more full of amusements, begin to leave the small territory for workshops and public works, for military service and for commerce; they reject the oppressive traditional customs of the elders and lose faith in the efficacy of the rites which once determined their behaviour. They free themselves from this powerful tyranny which, for the common good, often made them go so far as to sacrifice themselves to the divine powers.

Even the numerous religious, ethnic and linguistic communities in the East, and here and there in North Africa, who have remained in the midst of the Muslim and arabized masses, wilt and die. Their members who, in the past, were dangerously dispersed among hostile populations are now (thanks to the improved communications and the attractions of town life) concentrated in one place. And there, modern education serves to approximate these hitherto isolated and fearful minorities to the majorities which persecuted them. In the greater freedom their exclusiveness disappears.

While this rather mechanical levelling of complex societies goes on, and while the work of assimilation, unachieved through long centuries, is completed in a couple of generations, the patriarchal family, last fortress of the past, begins to crumble and fall. Schooling gives the children the advantage over their ignorant parents and upsets the authority of age. Moreover, the modern state will, in matters of rationing, allowances to soldiers' families, and widows' pensions, recognize only the limited household . . . The architects will build only small houses for these reduced families. In the proletarian tenement where a single room must do, there is no place for a bigger grouping.

Finally, the inhabitants of the new state cease to belong to these traditional, coherent and ordered societies, every one of which had its part to play in the collective life. They become grains of dust driven in the wind of circumstance. Their mass, ever growing but discrete, congregates around the modern towns created by the West. The proletariat appears in the towns of Egypt, on the coasts of Africa, wherever modern economic effort creates new possibilities of work outside the customary bounds. In these overcrowded neighbourhoods, where patriarchal discipline disappears so rapidly, Africa and the East are in decomposition; they are dying of a gigantic moral disorder, before the West has succeeded in building the order which it has designed.

It would be quite unfair to emphasize only the destructive effect of the "modern state." Out of the ruin it brings, a new society is slowly, perhaps too slowly, emerging, but emerging everywhere at the same time.

Here is an innovation for which these peoples were not at all prepared.

The individual is called upon to become a free person by the training he receives at school and by the responsibilities he is given in his various positions in the State. We force him to think for himself, to become an independent centre of will and power. It is enough to read the newspapers and periodicals published in Black Africa, to realize from the articles written by native teachers how much will power and sometimes heroism this attitude requires, and how seriously these men take their task. I know no more touching formula of this new state of mind than that which R. Delavignette heard last year from the mouth of a man from the West Coast of Africa: "Now every Black must be his own White."

The education of girls aims at an even more complete liberation. In the Berber districts of North Africa it saves them from the narrow and oppressive supervision by the agnates. In Negro territories it raises them from the depths of the polygamous family to the rank of human persons enjoying all their natural rights as we understand them. To realize the revolutionary character of such a liberation, we must appreciate the importance of economic specialization for the Negro woman—among the Bantus for instance, she is strictly imprisoned within the framework of an amazingly primitive agriculture, and tied down to the production and sale of certain kinds of produce.

Few of these changes would be permanent if these men, deeply imbued as they are with a religious attitude, went on conforming to the old local beliefs which, only yesterday, regulated the cycle of rural and human life. But for these ancestral practices new faiths are being substituted, faiths more suited to the needs of the members of these bigger communities henceforth subjected to the mighty currents of modern ideas. We may observe, in fact, that as an indirect result of the advance of the modern state, a rapid diffusion of Islam and Christianity is taking place.

The Islam, which goes on with its conquests under our surprised eyes, is no longer that of the *marabouts*, with a merely local or provincial significance; and even less is it that of the unassuming devotion still fervently given by country women to saints represented by stones, by trees or by magic enclosures. It is a purified and reformed religion, sometimes strict and fanatical, but one which unifies everywhere belief and practice. This religion may at times become, as we shall see, the spiritual manifestation of the political ambitions of a vast community spread over half a continent. Even without organized Muslim proselytism, the faith in the One God, expressed in the Arabic language, advances gradually, thanks to the greater facility of communications and the free movement of peoples. It takes hold (this time for good) of those regions conquered superficially, often centuries ago, where rural and nature cults, modest but tenacious plants, survived, humbly hidden within stone enclosures. We

may expect, therefore, a deepening of the influence of Islam in the domain
it had already conquered, and a further diffusion of it along the principal
commercial routes and in the ports. Islam, in becoming modern, completes
its historical expansion. Henceforth it will be master of the Northern third
of the African continent. And converts are everywhere being gained on
the East Coast of Black Africa and on the principal commercial routes of
the interior. Taking advantage of the same favourable circumstances, the
decline of the tribes and chieftainships, the liberation of the individual,
the free circulation and unmolested activities of missionaries, Christianity
also takes up its work again, work which from the third to the eighteenth
century has often been discontinuous and hazardous. Helped by powerful
organizations, Catholics and Protestants erect their churches and found
compact communities. Indeed we may sometimes wonder whether these
communities (owing to the spiritual and temporal forms which they take)
will not become in the minds of the Negroes a substitute for the "chieftainships" which have disappeared. Another generation of effort, and two-
thirds of Black Africa will be transformed into a region in which the
Christian populations will preponderate. This is a historical event from
which innumerable practical consequences will flow, making possible, in
such unexpected circumstances, the development of these "modern states"
in the midst of which the new churches spring up.

The peace which reigns inside the frontiers, the freedom of communications, the development of an economy henceforth linked with that of other
parts of the world, have still another unforeseen and unreckoned result,
the importance of which will appear in the building of the new states and
which may often modify their structure: certain remarkably endowed
races, so far still in the background of the political scene, are playing a
role which is becoming steadily more important. Everywhere some ethnic
groups reveal today unsuspected aptitudes for commerce, industry, for the
liberal professions, and for medicine. Often, by a remarkable paradox,
these newcomers (who will easily get rich and win the highest positions)
are the pariahs of the past who will, by their success, reduce to poverty
and impotence the warrior peoples of yesterday. That is how the Kabyles
and the Mozabites of Algeria, formerly looked down upon by the nomads
of the table-lands, the Chleuhs of Sous in Morocco, despised by the urban
population, the Djerbians and Sfaxians from Tunisia, find their way into
the higher social ranks. In Mauritania, the Zenaga, Berber merchants with
Negro blood, enrich themselves in the commerce of the Sudan, while the
noble Hassan shepherds, their former masters, become paupers. The Ibos
of Nigeria, once primitive and anarchic, have become in the space of
twenty years business men and artful politicians who aspire to control the
destinies of their former conquerors, the Muslims of the north. In the

Sahel which runs along the south of the Sahara, the Peuhl conquerors fall
into decadence, while the Bamaleke, only yesterday despised, but organized now in strong commercial communities (modernized versions
of their animistic fraternities), gain control of the coastal trade. The importance of this new characteristic, revealed in the course of the liberation
of these peoples by the West, can be hardly exaggerated. Indeed, the soul
of the future nations may undergo a change through the intervention of
these newcomers whose constructive genius has not up to now, in the warlike existence of the peoples, found an opportunity to express itself.

The reconstruction of the human communities of Africa and of Asia on
entirely new bases assumes the destruction of ancient structures and the
adoption of modern plans originally designed for territories a hundred
times larger and for populations infinitely more numerous. This reconstruction obviously cannot take place without causing serious moral and
social crises. How can these men and women, prompted so quickly by the
West to the dignity of membership of a modern state, be able to forget a
past which formerly enslaved them so narrowly and left no room for the
free play of personality? What spiritual resources have these transitional
generations, so poor and so isolated, to enable them to find the means to
reconcile the ancient laws with the discipline of the new life? We can
recognize the psychological drama which takes place in the consciousness
of all those who suddenly find themselves in contact with the West. Their
first, spontaneous reactions should be studied with care.

Nothing, indeed, is more touching than the ardour of these young Negro
neophytes when confronted with the diverse forms of our civilization,
their naïve and trusting admiration of our techniques, their enthusiasm for
our intellectual principles.... This confidence that they have in us, a confidence that demands a breakaway from the past, implies also a violent
opposition to their traditional beliefs. It is not without danger. A young
teacher from a small township in the Gaboon, transferred to a school in
the bush, will feel around him the suspicion of the witch-doctors and the
power of those who cast spells, whose vengeance is ready to overwhelm
the deserter. When he is afraid that owing to the decay of Europe the
tyranny of the idols will be restored, he will say to the white inspector:
"Look, Sir, the bush is gaining on us. May France remain strong!"

Others will cast an invincibly suspicious eye on these innovations destructive of the ancient way of life, and will remain convinced that the old
order of things is still incomparably superior to that of the West. I myself
will never forget the way with which an old Arab Beduin from the plains
of the Gharb in Morocco dismissed with condescending contempt the
merely relative value of the most modern machines which we were com-
placently exhibiting. This was in 1919, on the occasion of a *moussem,* a

big summer fair, on the confines of the Spanish Zone. The French authorities, in order to put an end to the false rumours spread by our neighbours that German planes (said to be invincible) were coming back, had arranged for a French seaplane to demonstrate over the heads of the assembled peasantry. When the seaplane, after a long and noisy flight, came to anchor silently in a lagoon in front of the simple farmers ready to go into ecstasies, the old Beduin, pious Muslim that he was, let fall these words which I heard from his lips: "There is nothing astonishing in all this: the Christians have got hold of the secret of Sidna Daoud—the Prophet David—on him be peace. They have thus been able to make the motor. This motor they put in boats which become steamers; in locomotives, and it makes trains; in cages, and they fly in the air . . . There is neither might nor strength except in God."

This was, of course, only the popular version of a more profound system of thought, that of Djamal ed Din El Afghani who initiated the awakening of Islam; for him, the civilization of the West was nothing but a material force which it would be easy to vanquish by studying in Europe and wresting the secrets of its technical weapons. This material force, once mastered, would be put at the disposal of a purified religion which, confident in itself and in its destiny, would once more take up its providential mission to rule the world. I sometimes wonder if a small number of Oriental students in our universities, do not, even today, share this easy belief. May they realize however that there is not, at the source of our power, a secret like that of Sidna Daoud. . . .

Sometimes a complaint is heard, deeper and more poignant, which reveals the confusion of a soul close to nature when we imprison it within the abstract bounds of our laws. The Africans have not, perhaps, in spite of the talent of those of them who write in French, formulated it in terms as eloquent as those of Rabindranath Tagore, the Bengali poet, who has expressed his dismay when faced with our complicated machines, which seem to him so terrible and so tyrannical. I quote these words of his from his little book, *Nationalism*, now thirty years old, so deep and concentrated, and so tragically to the point in the India of today:

A nation, in the sense of the political and economic union of a people, is that aspect which a whole population assumes when organized for a mechanical purpose. Society as such has no ulterior purpose. It is an end in itself. It is a spontaneous self-expression of man as a social being. It is a natural regulation of human relationships, so that men can develop ideals of life in co-operation with one another. It has also a political side, but this is only for a special purpose. It is for self-preservation. It is merely the side of power, not of human ideals. And in the early days it had its separate place in society restricted to professionals. But when with the help of science and the perfecting of organization this power begins to grow and brings in harvests of wealth, then it crosses its boundaries with amazing rapidity. For then it goads all its neighbouring societies with greed of material prosperity and consequent mutual jealousy, and by the fear of each other's growth into powerfulness. The time comes when it can stop no longer, for the competition grows keener, organization grows vaster, and selfishness attains supremacy trading upon the greed and fear of man, it occupies more and more space in society and at last becomes its ruling force.

And he also says, even more clearly:

In the West the national machinery of commerce and politics turns out neatly compressed bales of humanity which have their use and a high market value; but they are bound in iron hoops, labelled and separated off with scientific care and precision. Obviously God made man to be human; but this modern product has such marvellous square-cut finish, savouring of gigantic manufacture, that the Creator will find it difficult to recognize it as a thing of spirit and creature made in His own divine image.

Alas! Tagore was only too right, and today we see India broken up into different and hostile nations under the influence of the concept of the modern state. The imperious call of the West continues to be heard, though the Westerners have departed. Its voice reaches further than that of a Gandhi who gave his life in vain trying to save his dream. Like Asia, the whole of Africa, black and white, and even Central and South America, teem with nations in which men, troubled and divided against themselves, mourn, without knowing it sometimes, their lost gods. The poetic voices, welling from among the peoples, which used to extol the free life, have now in the present glorious misery become, for a time, silent. . . .

Let us once again move through the "time-space" constituted by Black Africa and the Arab countries in the last two centuries. By introducing there under various forms the concept of the modern state, the nations of Western Europe, perhaps without intending it, and in spite of the crises their action has brought about, have made a constructive contribution. Already the American continent is organized into living nations which, whether separate or federated, have acquired prodigious wealth. And now the misfortunes of Europe are giving them a leading role in the destinies of the world of which none of us would have dreamt forty years ago. The empires founded by Europe in Asia are also breaking up into nations; nations as yet fragile and indeterminate, but which instinctively model themselves on their Western prototypes. What will happen to the Near East and to Africa? Is the African continent destined to become, as its position in relation to Europe would indicate, a kind of political extension of our continent supplied with similar political institutions, as South America became an extension of North America? And if this transformation, now only beginning, is accelerated, what will its rhythm be?

History, Geography, Sociology, combining their insight and resources, try to throw light on a future still obscure. We can distinguish three tendencies. The first and oldest is a little out of date perhaps in the eyes of some, but it cannot yet be taken as condemned by the progress of the world; it lies in the direction of extensive assimilation into European culture. The results of this tendency, within the space of a century, are considerable. One can see them in the changes which have taken place in Angola and the Senegal, linked as they are to European "parent-states," also in America, in the West Indies and the Guianas, which have remained European enclaves. One can also see the results in the growth of such vigorous and sympathetic personalities . . .

A second tendency, purely national, can also be traced. Nations have been constituted in the whole Arab East, in Ethiopia and in Liberia. Other nations are being formed on the Gold Coast, in the Anglo-Egyptian Sudan, through the persevering endeavours of British administrators who try to endow the skeleton of the modern state with a powerful collective soul. . . . To what extent have the old forms of social life, so incompatible with the establishment of a true national solidarity, weakened in their resistance, to allow the birth, as the West would like, of a new feeling of fraternal equality? Would not the artificial and forced development of a nation out of such a disparate collection of peoples such as Nigeria, produce, as in India, violent dislocations? In Nigeria, the Northern Muslim Provinces form a virtual Pakistan, while on the Coast, formerly animistic and now partly Christianized, enterprising and adaptable intellectuals are stirring, already accustomed to Western ways of thinking, but seemingly devoid as yet of that political wisdom necessary to weld a society still divided and attached to its ancient traditions.

A third kind of development, totally different, can also be observed: the establishment, in the Arabian Peninsula, in North Africa, and in Black Africa, of extensive unions, almost continental in size, based on race or religion, making use of the fragile frames of nations still too young. The weakened state of Europe allows Islamic or pan-Arab Leagues, United States of the Negro World, to be organized or planned under our very eyes. Today nations, formed some twenty years ago, are so impatient and ambitious as to tear the breast which has nourished them; and in their midst the forces of the past, defeated at one point, rise up unexpectedly at another, no longer merely conservative and static but nevertheless opposed to progress. These forces then take on the aspect of a new racial or religious imperialism which for these nations is infinitely seductive. We see these hardly formed nations amalgamate themselves by alliances and confederations into vast unions, which with a little imagination and bold-ness, could be represented (after the latest Western political fashion) in the international organizations, as the "regional organizations" of the world. Such is the case of the Arab League which claims, in advance, the growing nations of Tunisia and Morocco, and which tomorrow, advancing towards the Anglo-Egyptian Sudan and the Negro states of Tropical Africa, would reconstitute, stronger than ever, the Arab empires of the Umayyads and the Abbassids ...

It is, then, in this world of manifold appearances and ill-defined possibilities, that we must try to trace the slow and difficult formation of the African and Oriental nations.

PART TWO

THE QUEST FOR POWER IN MULTI-STATE SOCIETIES

CHAPTER TWO

Gauging the Power of a State

In the course of history, men have devised lists of the component elements of political power in order to determine whether their own states or coalitions were more or less powerful than those that threatened them. We call the development and use of these political yardsticks "gauging the power of a state." Not only have Western scholars and statesmen worked on such schemes, but non-Western leaders of premodern times were also intrigued by such programming.

Stephen B. Jones's essay "Gauging Power in the Western State System" discusses the power inventories of a number of leading European and American commentators. Some compilers have striven for conciseness; others have been concerned with detailed elaboration. For reasons explained in the article, either of these two indices must be used with considerable care and prudence. Familiarity with the task of the analyst of national power is an important first step in understanding state behavior. National strategy, or "the art of using power for the attainment of goals in competition," is an interrelated aspect of the problem. "What one can do," Professor Jones points out, "is influenced by what one has, but what one has is influenced by what one does, in world politics at least." How the various components of power and the requirements of national strategy interrelate—requiring the student of international relations to develop "political binocular vision"—makes up the second major theme of the article.

Professor Jones believes that "so long as there is politics among sovereign states there will be estimation of power." The ancient political literature of the non-Western world supports his statement. Interest in establishing a reliable power index, as well as its fruitful incorporation into the decision-making machinery of government, has not been restricted to our era or civilization. As early as the fourth century B.C., Hindu political theorists devoted considerable attention to a discussion of the various

75

factors of state power and their importance in the formulation of policy goals. From Kautilya's writings we learn that a state had seven constituent elements of sovereignty: (1) the king or sovereign; (2) the ministers serving the state; (3) the rural areas, including the people residing there; (4) the fortresses, or fortified urban areas; (5) the treasury, or the financial resources of the state; (6) the standing army; and (7) the allies or friends of the state. How these factors were used to construct a seven-item schedule for programming power is explained in the next selection.

U. N. Ghoshal's article makes clear that the application of power (*śakti*) to foreign policy (*guṇas*) was a well-understood lesson in the Mauryan period of Indian history. His essay summarizes what is, to our knowledge, the earliest attempt of any civilization to design a formula to measure the relative strengths of independent political communities. It also introduces to students of world politics the level of refinement attained by premodern theorists.

GAUGING POWER IN THE
WESTERN STATE SYSTEM*

Stephen B. Jones

A familiar sight in the newspapers and weekly magazines is a world map (often, I regret to say, on the Mercator projection) on which population, oil production, or similar information is shown by rows of small men, barrels, or other appropriate symbols. These maps are often interpreted in caption or accompanying text as indices of national power. No one denies that such information is relevant to power, but no reader of this journal needs to be cautioned that such information is only a first step toward an evaluation. The present paper spells out that caution and tries to take another step or two. Its thesis is: An estimate of national power has two aspects which are related, in a figurative way, like the two rays of a triangulation. Either ray gives direction, but it takes the two to give distance. A better analogy, perhaps, is that of two searchlight beams groping through the dark until they intersect on the target. One ray or

* Stephen B. Jones, "The Power Inventory and National Strategy," *World Politics*, VI, No. 4 (July 1954), 421–452. Reprinted by permission. Mr. Jones is Professor of Geography, Yale University, author of *Boundary Making* (1945), and coauthor of *Geography and World Affairs* (1950).

beam is the conventional inventory of the elements or factors of power. It gives the power resources of a nation, using "resource" in a broad sense. The other ray is here called "national strategy."

This thesis is not fundamentally original, except perhaps in presentation. Clausewitz (thinking only of military strategy, of course) wrote of superiority as a function of absolute strength and of the skillful use of that strength. [Others] differentiate between the tools and techniques of statecraft, and the distinction is implicit in other books.

Definition of Terms

"Power" is here defined as "that which permits participation in the making of decisions," . . . This is perhaps not truly a definition; it tells not what power is, but what it makes possible. It has the virtues of including constructive uses and of saying that power is not solely material or possessed only by those who have a lot of it. Power, like radiant energy, can move in many directions at once. . . .

"Strategy" is used with some misgivings, since the word has many meanings, from the strictly military one of the conduct of campaigns to such figurative usages as "the strategy of raw materials." It is defined here as "the art of using power for the attainment of goals in competition." (The subordinate clause is perhaps implied by the main one.) The extension to other forms of power and other types of competition than military seems justified in this age of cold war and total effort. "Strategy" is preferred to "policy" for present purposes. Policy is more concerned with setting goals than with the art of attaining them . . .

"National strategy" has been adopted in preference to "grand strategy" or "global strategy," for a nation's strategy may be neither grand nor global. To speak of national strategy does not imply a genre of strategy peculiar to a state, though, to be sure, no two states can have identical national strategies, if for no other reason than that they are geographically distinct. The national strategy is not necessarily wrought with logic. It may contain as much prejudice as plan. If a plan exists, rarely will it be consistently followed.

We use the term "resources" in a very broad sense, somewhat like the familiar reference to a man "calling up all his resources." In discussions of power, there may be some confusion among the terms "resources," "natural resources," "sources," "reserves," and "raw materials." "Resources" is the broadest of these terms. We use it to mean anything a nation has, can obtain, or can conjure up to support its strategy. The items of an inventory of power resources are commonly called either "elements" or "factors." There is, we believe, a shade of difference between these two terms.

The distinction may not be important and probably will not be adopted by others, but in making it we may clarify a concept that will be useful later. An element is a basic, separable part, commonly thought of in terms of its own properties. A factor, in the words of the dictionary, is "one of the elements that contribute to produce a result." A factor is commonly thought of in terms of the specific whole of which it is a part, of what it does rather than what it is. One might say loosely that there are elements of potential power, factors of actual power, but both "potential" and "actual" need to be subdivided and clarified, as we attempt to do on a later page.

The concept we are endeavoring to establish is simply that inventories of power resources may contain items at several levels of organization. [Hans] Morgenthau, for example, lists natural resources, industrial capacity, and military preparedness among his eight elements of national power. This is no sin, of course. A manufacturing firm would include in its inventory raw materials, semi-finished goods, and finished merchandise. The important point is that estimates of national power are made for comparative purposes and that valid comparisons are possible only if levels of organization are taken into account.

An inventory of power resources, or, briefly, a power inventory, could be a few lines or many pages in length. Taxonomists divide themselves into "lumpers" and "splitters" and the terms are appropriate here. An extreme lumper could compress the whole inventory into the familiar three factors of production of economics: land, labor, and capital. This is not to say that all power is economic. Even the older term, "political economy," is not broad enough to cover all the items of power, such as military competence and morale. But these items, though outside the conventional bounds of economics, may be considered either attributes of labor (using that term for all useful population) or mental capital.

The splitter will immediately go to work on this basic group. Land includes two categories of resources. One might be called "area resources," including the size and the shape of the country and immobile resources like landforms, soils, and climates. The other is the mobile mineral and biological resources. Location, sometimes considered an attribute of land by economists, will be treated later in another manner.

The factor of labor is perhaps better called "human resources." There are likewise two parts. First is population, considered as to number, age structure, and so forth. Second is what might be called "mental resources," the social, political, economic, and military systems of a country and the stock of skills, leadership, and patriotism.

Capital is better called "equipment resources," since it includes not only economic capital goods but also military equipment and the material apparatus of government. An additional item is supplies or stockpiles of consumable materials and goods—foods, metals, merchandise, munitions, etc.—and the financial stockpile of precious metals and credit.

There is of course a high degree of relationship among the items mentioned. Equipment is produced by organized skill operating on mobile natural resources. In turn, it may be used to extract further natural resources. Whether an ore deposit of marginal tenor is usable or not depends on skill, organization, and equipment. Leadership and patriotism are like enzymes in metabolism. In the final analysis, without them there is no power.

The foregoing paragraphs list resources as tangible as soil, as intangible as leadership, as measurable as population, as difficult to measure as patriotism. There is no common unit and no statistical summation is possible. Cost has been suggested as a measure of tangible items. Because of the importance of the budget in national housekeeping, there is a tendency to express many problems in terms of cost, but even as a measure of armaments it has its limitations. That a carrier might cost twenty times as much as a destroyer does not mean that twenty destroyers equal one carrier, in the operational sense. "Power value" rather than cost would be the significant figure if it could be measured, as sales value rather than cost is the real criterion for the inventory of a store. The Maginot line was costly, but its power value turned out to be nil. Cost is therefore not an adequate index of power. It does have its use as a "modifier" of inventory items, as will be discussed on a later page.

Even though one must give up the seductive hope that the power inventory can be summed up in dollars, kilowatt hours, or some other common unit, there remains the possibility that some key items may be used as rough indices of the probable total. The hope, of course, is to find measurable items that will so serve. Manpower of military age or the output of fuels, steel, or all heavy industry are some of the possibilities. Such data unquestionably are basic and under some conditions give a correct estimate of relative power. The longer a war lasts, the more likely are such data to be significant. They are particularly applicable when a country has limited access to external supplies. One could write a history of World War II in terms of supplies, with a measure of truth. But with far less than the whole truth: equally important is what was done with the supplies. Poverty of resources correlates with the weakness of Italy but does not explain the military failures against Greece or, for that matter, against the British at sea and in North Africa. Too little oil and too much intuition were long-run handicaps for Hitler, and it would be difficult to say which was the greater. Had his long-range strategy been sounder, he might have created a sufficient synthetic oil industry. Even in estimating potentials one must consider the strategic ray. To be sure, our analogy does not imply that the strategic ray is the more important, but only that *both* rays are important.

National income and its close relative, gross national product, have been considered possible indices of national power. They are operational in nature, rather than being inventory items, but this would be no disadvantage if they measure what can be done with a given inventory. For one thing, they give an idea of the dislocations to be expected from the diversion of resources from civil to military purposes. Their chief value is as tools, not as indices, however. Sherman Kent has commented adversely upon the search for indices of national power, and upon this use of national income data in particular. He stresses the importance of fat, slack, and flexibility in the national economy.

That quantifiable items like manpower or the output of heavy industry or economic aggregates like national income cannot serve as indices of national power does not, of course, mean that quantification is useless. Much of science consists of efforts to narrow the range of guessing. Since there is, inevitably, a large element of guesswork in an estimate of national power, quantitative information is highly desirable for all items for which it is obtainable. But, for the same reason, there is no use refining quantitative data to a high degree.

Modifiers of the Power Inventory

If the power inventory is thus essentially a check-list, with some quantifiable items, it becomes desirable to run through the concepts that must be kept in mind when the check-list is used. If we take any item of the list of power resources, we find that a chapter or a book or possibly a shelf of books can be written about it. It can be qualified almost without limit. We might start with population, for example, and find ourselves many pages later discussing the rate of training of civil defense workers in the use of Geiger counters. Such thoroughness may be necessary and desirable for some purposes—for a detailed mobilization program, for example. For general thinking about power, more generic concepts are desirable. These generic concepts we shall call "modifiers" of the power inventory. Not all the modifiers are applicable to every item of the power inventory, though with some imagination most of them can be applied. . . .

One of the most obvious modifiers of the power inventory is quantity. In some commentaries on national power, quantity is the only modifier considered. That the United States produces three times as much steel as the Soviet Union closes the argument for some people. But quantity is a whole family of modifiers. Its principal genera are availability and change.

Availability has two subdivisions, the space and time aspects. Spatial availability is summed up in the term "location." The effect of location on steel supplies is shown by the fact that the United States during World War II needed a third more steel for shipbuilding than for ordnance and other direct military uses. Location has two subspecies, accessibility and mobility. To illustrate, Mackenzie River oil is highly inaccessible but highly mobile. The Canol pipeline (another non-combatant use of steel) did not improve the accessibility until after the need had passed. "Tonnage" ores like iron are less mobile than ores that can usefully be measured in pounds. Labrador iron ore probably could not have been made accessible during World War II even had the need arisen. Manpower is relatively mobile and with a man move his skills, but the mobility of manpower varies with culture. Aboriginal natives need fewer supplies than do more civilized troops and workers, but at the same time they may be more essential to the economy of their villages, which have no labor-replacing machinery.

The time aspect of availability appears in the familiar phrase "lead-time," which stands for the period required to convert plans into production. Lead-time is a phase of the problem of potential power. That there is a difference between actual and potential power is obvious, but these two terms are too vague to be of much service. A geographer is likely to think of ore and fuel reserves when he hears the word "potential." An economist is likely to think of factories convertible to war production. A military man may think of the reserve corps or of mothballed ships. A fivefold classification of states of availability is here proposed: (1) power resources available immediately; (2) power resources available after activation; (3) power resources available after conversion; (4) power resources available after development; and (5) power resources available hypothetically.

Immediately available resources include such things as armed forces in being, munitions in depots, money or credit at hand. (There is of course a locational immediacy as well. A division in Germany and one in Texas are not equally immediate in availability for a given emergency.) Resources available after activation include such things as reserve troops and officers, mothballed ships, money and credit requiring legislation before use. Resources available after conversion include such things as factories suited for war production, and manpower untrained but adaptable to military or industrial service. This category is one that the United States has banked on heavily in the past, thanks to Britain, France, and the Atlantic Ocean. Resources available after development form another group that has given much comfort to Americans in the past but which is less comforting now. Such things as minerals known to exist but not in production and products known to be practical but not available in quantity, like synthetic rubber in 1942, are included. Hypothetical power resources remind one of the story of the diplomat who spoke most feelingly of his country's claims to some tropical territory. "It is full of rich resources," he exclaimed, "all undiscovered!" But hypothetical power should not be laughed at. The atomic bomb was hypothetical until 1945.

These availability states are of course not rigidly separated pigeonholes, but they do differ in kind as well as in degree. They should permit sharper thinking than do "actual" and "potential." A given power resource is not confined to one category. Many exist in all five states. Oil, for instance, may be immediately available in storage tanks. Idle wells and refineries may be activated. Non-essential use can be curtailed—this would be conversion. New wells may be drilled in proven fields—this is development—and favorable structures may be wildcatted on the hypothesis that oil exists in them. Intangibles like leadership can exist in all five states. How power resources are distributed through the availability series reflects the national strategy. The United States traditionally has left as much of its power as possible in the convertible and developable states. The trend is to push many items into higher states and to step up the pace of conversion and development. Not even the most spartan of nations could keep all its resources in a condition of immediate availability, but simple trust in "the power and potential of American mass production" goes the way of the faith that a million Americans would spring to arms overnight if their country were attacked.

The term "potential" has another connotation than that of availability. It also implies the maximum sustainable rate of production, or, more precisely, of expenditure, of a given item of power. Maximum sustainable rates follow different rules, depending upon the nature of the resource, the time element, and national strategy. Where natural resources are ample and the rate of production depends largely upon capital and labor, long-continued increases are possible, though perhaps at the cost of diverting capital and labor from other items. American steel production, for example, is capable of much further growth, if low-grade and foreign ores are utilized. In other cases, the maximum sustainable rate may vary with the period of time involved. The expenditure of manpower, if in excess of natural replacement, is an obvious example. To estimate the maximum sustainable rates of power expenditure therefore requires knowledge of both resources and their probable strategic use.

The availability states discussed above are closely related to three aspects of the national economy discussed by Sherman Kent: fat, slack, and flexibility. Kent defines these terms as follows:

By *fat*, I mean such things as some of the things Britain had at the start of World War II: extensive external assets, a large merchant marine, access to necessary raw materials and the credits to buy them without going into current production, a large and up-to-date supply of capital equipment, a large inventory of finished goods, a national diet of three to four thousand calories per day, etc. Important elements of German fat may be said to have existed in the excess capacity of machine tools, a large amount of brand new plant and new housing. The Italians had practically no fat, indeed little enough lean.

By *slack*, I mean such things as the 40-hour week, twelve to sixteen years of education for youth, small proportion of women in the labor force, unemployment of both labor and capital, only partial utilization of equipment, etc.

By *flexibility*, I mean the capacity of the economy to beat plowshares and pruning hooks into swords, and that in jig time. I mean the ability of technicians to make typewriter factories over into machine gun factories, and put the manufacturers of dry breakfast food into the shell-fuse business. I mean the ability to make synthetics from scratch where the natural sources have dried up.

"Fat" and "slack" correspond to "resources available after activation." Steel production, for example, is expansible in several ways. Plants may be operating below capacity. To activate this unused capacity would be taking up slack. Or they may be operated temporarily above capacity by postponing repairs. This would be using up fat. "Flexibility" covers the two concepts of "conversion" and "development." The quotation from Kent illustrates both. Making war goods in typewriter and cereal factories is conversion. Making synthetics from scratch (if the basic processes are known and not hypothetical) is development. The difference is significant because the lead-time of change is likely to be greater for development than for conversion and the investment of money, manpower, and materials larger. The expansion of steel production by building new mills is development, and involves the temporary diversion of steel from other uses.

These terms can be applied to persons as well as to commodities or plants. The conversion of clerks into soldiers, of housewives into welders, is familiar. The longer process of producing physicians, physicists, or general officers is more appropriately called development. The population factor as a whole can be developed, as by the importation of labor, alliances, and public health measures. The long-term effect of pro-natalist policies on the birth rate is still somewhat hypothetical.

The importance of change in relation to quantity needs no emphasis. Change has two aspects, rate and range. Rates of production, mobilization, conversion, expansion, etc., need no discussion. Changes of rates, or accelerations and decelerations, are also important, and one may need to consider changes in the changes of rates. The higher derivatives of change are significant in demography, where one wishes to know not only the death rate, for instance, but whether it is rising or falling and how the rate of rise or fall is changing. Rates of resource accumulation or wastage are important. Secular changes of vast consequence may be taking place almost unperceived by untrained observers, such as soil erosion, climatic alteration, or the aging of the population. The range of change obviously applies to fluctuating quantities like temperatures or harvests. Better knowledge of the range of Russian winter temperatures would have aided Hitler in 1941–1942. Range may also apply to rates. There is an upper limit to the rate of oil production from a given field, for instance, beyond which recovery declines and salt water may intrude.

Rates and ranges of expansion are major considerations in estimating power. The expansion of American production during World War II surprised even optimists, though whether time will be available in a future conflict for similar expansion is debatable. Soviet recovery after World War II was also surprisingly rapid. Expansion has its converse, contraction. The ability to do without may be important in war. Many contractions are effected for the purpose of expanding or maintaining supply or effort in other lines or places. Rationing of gasoline to civilians permitted expanded military consumption. But expansion without concomitant contraction is of course possible, as in the activation of unused plants. Use of the electrolytic process of tin-plating instead of the dipping process gave more plate from less tin, so that a reduced supply of a raw material was not reflected in an equivalent contraction of the product.

Substitution is another modifier of quantity. Substitution can be looked at from two sides. One can ask if an item in short supply can be replaced by a more abundant or a synthetic product, or one can ask if some item which is abundant may have other uses. We usually think of the former—glass for tinplate, synthetic for natural rubber—but the latter may be significant when weighing the power resources of other countries. An American thinks of potatoes as food, primarily, but they are an important source of industrial alcohol in the Soviet Union. Substitution of machines for men is a favorite American occupation. The high degree of automation possible in peace may be deceptive as to the possibilities in war, when destruction and disruption may make muscle-power indispensable. The reverse substitution of men for machines has its limitations also.

The doctrine of limiting factors in biology means, for example, that a plant needing nitrogen is not helped by an excess of phosphate. Man's ingenuity in finding substitutes makes this doctrine only loosely applicable to human affairs. Nevertheless, limiting factors do appear, particularly in war and under conditions of blockade and attrition. Substitution very often requires time and imports, which may not be available. The limiting factors may be rates. For instance, there was no doubt that the United

States could create a synthetic rubber industry adequate for its needs. The question was whether it could be created in time.

The Quality Modifiers

Quality is a second family of modifiers. The two main branches of the quality family are the quality of materials and goods on the one hand, and of operation on the other. These terms are meant to apply very broadly. American schoolboys or African natives are materials in the present sense, having certain qualities in that condition. Trained as workers, soldiers, professional men, etc., they might be called goods, their qualities in that state depending not only on inherent vigor and intelligence and childhood environment but upon specific training. Operation is also used broadly, to include business management, military organization, and government.

Quality of course connotes the question, "How good?" For our study, the question really is, how well does something serve its strategic purpose? An example of the distinction is the use by the Communists in Korea of obsolete wooden-frame airplanes for night bombing, because these old planes give poor radar echoes.

Quality is often placed in opposition to quantity, the ideal of "the mostest of the bestest" being difficult to attain. It is not necessarily unattainable, however, and quality often has been improved while quantity was being increased. The *a priori* opposition of quality and quantity possibly dates from handicraft days. The Battle of Britain is often cited as a triumph of quality over quantity, British planes, pilots, and operations being considered superior to the German. Because of these qualitative superiorities and the fact that fighting took place over British soil, the Royal Air Force sometimes obtained local quantitative superiority. A different relationship of quality and quantity can be illustrated by a famine-struck area. The difference between high- and low-grade wheat would mean little. Quality would be negligible in comparison with quantity and availability.

Change of quality must also be considered. This has three aspects, durability, obsolescence, and variation. Durability and obsolescence might be lumped as life expectancy of materials or goods. The significance of durability needs little elaboration. The United States was able to get through four years of war with its initial stock of private automobiles, in part because the cars proved durable beyond customary expectation. (Gasoline and tire rationing of course lengthened car life by reducing use.) The durability of railroad equipment, machine tools, and the like was important. Materials and labor needed for maintenance and replacement of non-combatant equipment of course must be drawn from the supply available for military use. Durability can be obtained at excessive cost and can be offset by obsolescence. Military equipment, however, is subject to very hard usage, and expenditures to increase its durability usually are justified. Breakdowns are likely to occur at the worst possible time and place when the equipment is overworked during an emergency.

High durability and low rate of obsolescence are major criteria of materials and goods that are to be stockpiled or mothballed. To judge when obsolescence has so reduced power value that goods should be scrapped requires something like clairvoyance. [Bernard] Brodie argues cogently against prematurely scrapping obsolescent naval ships, on the grounds that quantity may offset a modern qualitative inferiority. The destroyer-for-bases deal of 1940 is a supporting illustration. Whether the great stock of slow Liberty ships is a real or an illusory asset in event of war is a question currently debated. Rommel repeatedly refers to the gradual obsolescence of his tanks relative to those of the British. Rommel's victories actually increased his problems, for the Germans came to think him a miracle worker who could win with any weapons, while the British were compelled to replace their equipment and had fewer competing demands for their best tanks. There is perhaps more danger that obsolescent items will be rated too highly in terms of power than that they will be scrapped prematurely, but pruning the power tree of its fading branches does not strengthen it unless there is concomitant new growth. In the inorganic world of ships, tanks, and the like, new growth does not come spontaneously.

Variation in quality may involve the familiar phenomenon of "the weakest link." Ships in line of battle can steam no faster than the slowest vessel. One defective shell can jam a gun. All troops in combat may have to fall back if one unit gives way. In the first battle of El Alamein, Auchinleck directed major counterattacks at Italian divisions, forcing the Germans to limit their own drives. On the other hand, the phenomenon of "the strongest link" sometimes is encountered. Rommel's crack Afrika Korps saved many critical situations and kept the Italian army in battle long after it would otherwise have collapsed.

Variations in the quality of leadership—economic, political, military—are important modifiers of the power inventory and of course are difficult to assess. A change of leaders may change the power value of a military unit almost overnight. Even push-button warfare will require not only a man to push the button but, more important, a man to say when to push the button. This ineluctable individual factor may be overlooked in the power inventory because it cannot be treated statistically. It is apt to be neglected in the economist's or the geographer's approach to the study of power. Uncritical historians, on the other hand, may give too much attention to individuals. "The Gauls were not conquered by the Roman legions but by Caesar," said Napoleon, whose own history showed the potency of genius, but also that manpower, weather, and nationalism were not to be ignored.

Operation: Focus of Inventory and Strategy

When we speak of operation and of the quality of operation, we are at or near the common focus of the inventory and strategic beams of our opening analogy. We use "operation" in the broad sense of "the way things work." How well things work is a major modifier of the power inventory. We can apply this concept of working quality to items in wide variety—a squad of soldiers, a mine, a factory, an army, the whole of an economic or political system. This aspect of quality may be illustrated by Russian experience in the first five-year plan, when modern factories were built but sometimes nothing came off the assembly lines.

Operation has two main parts, motivation and organization. Motivation—involving reward, punishment, loyalty, leadership—is essential even for the most prosaic effort. To return to the example of petroleum as a factor of power, the motivation of the seamen on tankers may be a critical matter. Motivation for the long-haul usually demands pecuniary or other material rewards. But material motivation is not enough; it has proved insufficient for high quality of work even in purely economic activities. In this respect, however, states may go to the other extreme. As has been said, without patriotism there is no power, but one cannot expect patriotism to replace pay checks year after year. Americans seem particularly reluctant to admit that political and military operation really works from the top down, though checked and criticized (in both senses of criticism) from below. Patriotism, luck, or *le bon Dieu* may not provide administrators of high quality if pay is inadequate.

Organization may be divided into control and integration. Control is essential in government, industry, or battle. Loss of control is a nightmare of the military commander and all sorts of communication devices are used to provide a mechanical guard against it. Control involves motivation. A General Patton might control where a weaker man might lose control. Control is necessary for a rationing system and for maintaining secrecy in government and the armed forces. Integration means how the parts of an organization mesh together. One aspect is illustrated by the integration of Negro troops into white units in the United States Army.

This step multiplied many-fold the power value of the Negro soldiers and removed from them the stigma of "the weakest link." The operations of alliances are generally hampered by imperfect integration. The faulty integration of American railroads early in World War I led to intolerable congestion. The converse of congestion—shortages—may also arise from faulty integration, even when ample materials or goods are available.

The pace of operations is an important aspect of their quality. Equipment of high quality is necessary but not sufficient for fast pace. [Derwent] Whittlesey has pointed out that the time-dimension of human activities has three derivatives, velocity, pace, and timing. A jet airplane may have a velocity near the speed of sound. The pace of air operations depends on many other velocities than those of airplanes. It depends, among other things, on the rate at which intelligence reaches the commander, on the rapidity with which plans are formulated and orders issued, upon the speed of servicing and repair. Pace—"the average tempo of trajectories in a specified area"—may thus be more significant than velocity. The sluggishness of bureaucratic pace is notorious. Fortunately, it is also world-wide, though this does not permit us to be complacent about it. One purpose of war games is to step up the pace of operations that may some day be performed in the face of the enemy. Perhaps all branches of administration should hold war games.

Operational quality is roughly synonymous with some meanings of "efficiency" but not necessarily with that which relates output to input, if we measure output and input in conventional ways. Diplomatic operations of high quality are not necessarily economical of time or money. It is debatable whether the decision of 1953 to concentrate war production in the most efficient factories was wise or unwise as a long-run policy, since dispersal among more plants not only might decrease vulnerability but might permit faster acceleration of production in event of war.

Vulnerability and Cost

Vulnerability is a modifier of the power inventory that of course now affects the innermost parts of the home front. The power value of two factories may depend, after war begins, more on their vulnerability than on their efficiency. The vulnerability of Britain to air attack weakened Chamberlain's hand at Munich. Theoretically, the states with atomic weapons have the power virtually to blow each other to bits. Whether they will do so is debatable. Atomic warfare might resemble the strategy of the fleet-in-being, the threat of atomic weapons being used to tie up the resources of the opponent. Vulnerability will nevertheless be a factor, for the side that has attained the best defense against atomic weapons can make the most aggressive threats. Distressingly little attention has been paid to the reduction of vulnerability during the period of rapid construction since World War II. Some records have been stored in underground vaults, but little has been done to safeguard the really essential resources of labor and equipment, without which records have little meaning.

Simplicity is one of the classical principles of war. A major reason is the vulnerability of complicated operations, especially in the face of an active enemy. Simplicity is difficult to attain in industrialized war, in spite of modern methods of communication and control. Simplicity in plan may be obtainable only through complexity of control, as in assembly-line manufacturing. In industry, simplicity is not sought for itself but only if costs can be reduced or sales increased. In fact, the search for cheaper supplies or more extensive markets often results in complicated cross-hauling of materials and goods and in duplication of delivery and marketing systems. Much of this complexity, efficient though it may be in a capitalistic economy in peace, would have to be eliminated in time of war, especially if the home front were heavily bombarded.

Cost as an index of power or a measure of power value has been discussed on an earlier page. In spite of its limitations in these respects, it remains a significant modifier. In part, this is because of the subjective importance given to the cost of national defense by taxpayers and their Congressional representatives. There is a persistent clamor for social security and insurance sells steadily, but that national power is the most basic form of social security and insurance, without which the others are illusory, is commonly forgotten in time of peace. The subjective importance of cost is of course greatest in the democracies where public opinion is most effective in government.

Cost has objective as well as subjective importance. Cost, in relation to national power, implies the question, "How much of our resources are required to increase our supply of a given item, or its readiness for use?" Japan, for example, could build warships with cheaper labor than could the United States, but the cost in terms of available steel was proportionately greater to Japan. Japan could man a warship for a small part of the payroll of its American counterpart, but the oil for fuel came from a much more limited resource. World War II showed that most nations can sacrifice living standards for war to a degree hardly thought possible and that national bankruptcy can be staved off for years. Nevertheless, drain on resources is a reality, if replacement does not keep up with use. The attrition on manpower is perhaps the most obvious form, but drain on equipment, if there is insufficient reinvestment to maintain or replace it, may be serious.

The Strategic Beam

The power inventory has now been provided with a set of modifiers—a check-list for a check-list, so to speak. A question may arise: Are the modifiers so numerous and so indeterminate that they reduce the inventory to a pulp? This thought can be dismissed with little comment. So long as there is politics among sovereign states, there will be estimation of power. Even though the best estimates are only rough, they are better than reliance on intuition or emotion. It is true that the modifiers are warning signs rather than guideposts, that they point out traps rather than show where the path lies. Nevertheless, insofar as they conform to realities they should be useful. . . .

One of the most serious of the problems that beset the student of national power is how to avoid encyclopedism. The modifiers of the power inventory are no protection against this. In fact, the mechanical application of a check-list to a check-list would yield compound encyclopedism. Encyclopedism is likewise a problem in basic intelligence research. What facts to collect, in how much detail to present them, how far to go in evaluation without treading on the sacred ground of policy-making? These and similar questions plague the intelligence research worker. Roger Hilsman has challenged the encyclopedic method in intelligence and calls for workers to be "manipulative, instrumental, action-conscious, policy-oriented." In terms of our analogy, what Hilsman appears to desire is that the intelligence worker get more light from the strategic beam and not work only by the inventory beam, where he is forever stepping into shadows. The aptness of this analogy will be attested by many who have worked in intelligence, though they may not be optimistic about the practical solution of the problem.

If one looks at power along the inventory beam, one is asking, "What have I?" If one looks along the strategic beam, one is asking, "What do I need?" Each question of course connotes the other, but most will agree that, as in personal finances needs run ahead of funds, among nations it is strategic needs rather than love of statistics that sets us counting our power resources. This analogy can easily be strained, however. In the first place, neither the power inventory nor strategic needs can be expressed completely in monetary or even statistical terms. Second, the public purse is much more elastic than the personal one. A nation does not live on a fixed income, and it is production rather than the budget that really counts. Third, it is not so much a case of shifting one's line of sight from the inventory to the strategic beam as of looking along both. It takes binocular vision, so to speak, to see national power in full relief. What one can do is influenced by what one has, but what one has is influenced by what one does, in world politics at least.

This paradox, if it is one, will be discussed under four heads: (1) the harmony of resources and national strategy; (2) the augmentation, or reduction, of resources by national strategy; (3) the allocation of resources in relation to national strategy; and (4) the relativity of power in the light of national strategies.

Harmony of Inventory and Strategy

That national strategy must be in harmony with national resources may seem like a truism, but the statement is true only in a very general sense. It can be a very misleading doctrine if resources are considered to be a fixed sum and if national strategy is conceived in strictly military terms and only in isolation. The doctrine has been used by some isolationists, who argue not that the United States *can* isolate itself (by means of some wonder-weapon, perhaps), but that it *must* isolate itself because it cannot afford a broader strategy. One possible answer, of course, is to say that the broader strategy may be the cheaper in the long run. Walter Lippmann took a different tack: he held that a state must balance its commitments and its power, but he goes on to say of the "true statesman": "Having determined the foreign commitments which are vitally necessary to his people, he will never rest until he has mustered the force to cover them." In other words, if two strategies appear equally good, we may choose the cheaper, but if it is penicillin we need, aspirin will not do.

Harmony of resources and needs may be all very well, but what if a state cannot muster the force to cover its vitally necessary commitments? One answer, too popular with Americans, is to recalculate the risks and cut the commitments. Another answer, popular with Americans and justifiably so if the limitations are realized, is to turn to science. The development of wonderful new weapons is much in mind, but should the brunt of war remain on the shoulders of the ground forces, even more important may be the use of science to augment natural resources. A kinder deity might have given this country limitless high-grade iron ore and never-failing oil wells, but we know of other ways to meet our needs, such as beneficiation of lean ores and the distillation of oil shales. But such expansion of resources does not come about automatically or with the ease of comic-strip art. It requires research, capital, labor, and time, all of which must be comprehended in the long-term national strategy.

Import and stockpiling programs are of course another way of augmenting a state's resources or of conserving domestic supplies. Since the

United States has traditionally discouraged imports and since large stock-piles are uneconomic, in a business sense, such programs require a con-sciously strategic viewpoint.

A state may augment its resources through the acquisition of colonies or the formation of alliances. An alliance may be the only resort of a small state, short of outright annexation to a great power, by which it can "muster the force to cover its vitally necessary commitments." In estimat-ing the power of an alliance, due consideration must be given to strategic aspects. The power of an alliance is never the simple sum of the power inventories of its members. The total may be much less than the sum if organization is weak or if the members cannot easily support each other. On the other hand, the joint power of the United States and Canada is potentially more than the sum of their separate resources, because to-gether they form a coherent block of North America reaching into the Arctic instead of splitting the continent along a long, weak boundary.

A state may augment its power by building up the power of its allies or, without an alliance, of its presumptive friends. This of course is an objec-tive of American foreign aid programs. The motivation of foreign aid programs ranges from pure humanitarianism through the belief that sound independent nations are "safe" to the strictly military desire to build up foreign facilities and sources of supply. This last is sometimes called "geologistics" and augments resources by cutting down "transmission losses" and taking advantage of lower wages and prices.

Power resources can be reduced instead of augmented if the national strategy is unsound or obsolete. Clumsy diplomacy or a speech or act that is stupid in relation to foreign policy may cut national power or, looked at another way, may require an increased use of resources to achieve a given end. Wishful thinking plays a role in national strategy. A state's resources may be as effectively reduced by it as by the drainage of an oil field or a drop in the birth rate. Two ingrained American habits of mind are faith in machinery and a desire to pull back from overseas commit-ments. Any strategic theory that embodies or seems to embody these ideas is sure to find advocates. The popular enthusiasm for wonder-weapons finds support in these mental habits. Wishful thinking is by no means con-fined to the man-in-the-street and the professor-in-the-tower. The fateful conferences of Munich and Yalta show that statesmen are not immune.

The Problem of Allocation

One of the knottiest problems of national strategy is the allocation of resources, between private and governmental demands and among the various branches of the government. In a democratic country, such allocations are strongly influenced by habits, moods, and political pressures held or generated by the public. Certain clichés crop up. For instance, it becomes said that the civilian economy can bear only so much military or foreign aid expense. At bottom, this is a rationalization of American hedonism. Pushed to the test, a state must pay the price of victory or lose. If there is sufficient solidarity, spontaneous or enforced, civilian consumption can be pared to the bone.

The division of resources among the armed forces may bring up the cliché of "balance," which usually means that increases and cuts in the budget shall be equally shared. Certain criticisms of "balance" are, however, not without clichés themselves. The argument is heard that air power has the greatest inherent capabilities of any arm, because of the velocity of its vehicles and their global, three-dimensional medium of operation; the air arm should therefore receive the lion's share of appropriations. The conclusion may be true, but it does not follow from the premise as stated in general terms. Capability, like balance and allocation, is a vague word unless we are told, capability for *what*. Even within an armed service we find arguments about allocation of resources. Hitler's navy was torn between the submariners and the advocates of a balanced fleet, with each side claiming that the war would be lost if its counsels were disregarded.

Allocation of resources therefore can be discussed rationally only in the light of given national strategies. National strategy is to the power inventory as management is to the materials inventory of a factory. What is produced, and when, depends on the judgment of the management. The decisions of course are not free or unlimited. They depend not only on the resources of the factory but upon the milieu—the cultural and natural environments offering possibilities and imposing limitations. It hardly needs to be said that national strategy usually is less logical and consistent than industrial management. The play of interests makes the national strategy a sort of vector sum of ideas that are often divergent and sometimes diametrically opposed. The struggle between isolationists and interventionists in the United States in the interwar period is an obvious example. The single vote in the House of Representatives that renewed the selective service act might be called the vector sum in that case.

The strategy of industrial management is tested promptly. The statement of profit and loss gives the answer. There is no such easy test for national strategy. That a state has survived thus far may be all that we can claim, and we may not know for sure whether this is because of, or in spite of, its national strategy. Even the lessons of war are not conclusive. Witness the different conclusions that have been drawn from strategic bombardment in World War II.

Generally speaking, there are two philosophies of resource allocation. One holds that a country should cleave to the strategy that seems best in terms of its own resources. The other holds that the "best" strategy is always relative to opposing strategies and calls for more flexibility, or for less complete commitment to one program. Strategic air power provides an illustration. Advocates of concentration on this arm have a number of arguments. There is the "inherent capabilities" doctrine: the long range and great pay-load of a strategic bomber. There is the argument from American strengths and weaknesses: the United States has a lively technology but not unlimited manpower; Americans like machinery and speed; they detest infantry service but will take any risk if they can do it sitting down. The Soviet Union is the most important enemy, and the doctrine of hitting the core rather than the extremities of enemy power has much to recommend it. But there are three terms of the equation of power that weigh against the foregoing: first, the unexpectedly rapid Soviet development of atomic bombs, making it unlikely that the United States will initiate their strategic use again; second, the Soviet strategy of limited risks and aggression by satellite; and third, American reluctance and unreadiness to turn a limited war into a general one. The evaluation of all these terms necessarily changes with time, technology, and national mood. Flexibility currently is dominant, and strategic thought seems to be seeking in tactical atomic missiles a means of combining flexibility, relatively conventional three-arm warfare, and American predilections for small armies and mechanization.

Neither the "one-basket" nor the "flexibility" philosophy of resource allocation can guard against obsolescence. As cavalrymen loved horses, so sailors love ships and airmen love airplanes. Whether anybody but a scientist can love an intercontinental rocket is a question, yet conceivably it might make other military implements obsolete. Steel and oil are sinews of war, as everyone knows, but one can imagine a titanium-hulled, uranium-powered missile that would make no great demand for steel or oil even in the manufacturing stage. This is of course dream-stuff today, but it shows that the projection of the inventory ray into the future must be checked against possible projections of the strategic ray.

National power must constantly be re-evaluated in terms of the methods and instruments available to national strategy. If Lower Slobbovia plans war on Upper Denturia, relative power is not determined solely by the fact that the former has bigger piles of rocks and more men to throw them. Can it bring its power to bear? If a wide, swift river separates these two countries, does Lower Slobbovia have the needed vehicles for crossing? Is its organization good enough to land its rock-throwers en masse, not in driblets? Are its emissaries loud braggarts who infuriate the Denturians or shrewd operators who may settle the dispute without fighting? All this bears on such questions of allocation as whether the Slobbovian *Führer* should put some of his rock-gatherers to canoe-building and send some of his rock-throwers to a school of diplomacy.

Allocation in Space and Time

Power resources exist in space and time. This may seem an obvious statement, yet it is an aspect that may be neglected. In the language of physics, there are space and time dimensions of the field of power. Strategy is the art of movement in such a field.

In a sense, space and time are resources. The nation that has them can adopt strategies that would be suicidal without them. Space consumes more than time: it consumes fuel, supplies, and manpower. Yet trading space for all of these is generally a sign of unpreparedness rather than of wisdom. But space and time are more than resources. They are conditions of resource allocation and use. Here, again, the strategic ray of the power triangle is valuable. Space and time aspects may be left out of an inventory. They are integral parts of national strategy.

[Harold and Margaret] Sprout made use of space as a strategic condition when they compared British sea power, based on an island close to the continent where the main rivals lay, with American sea power, facing two broad oceans. Whittlesey, we have said, lists three derivatives of time: velocity, pace, and timing. Velocity and pace have been touched on above, under operational quality. Timing was implicit in the discussion of the five availability states. Availability is strategically meaningful only in terms of how long it takes to bring a given item to the state of "immediately available." Locational availability also can be translated into terms of time and timing. Thomas' discussion of the "railway revolution" in war shows that even a century ago mobilization was not something that just happened. In the Battle of Britain, radar helped the British get their planes to the right place at the right moment. One might say that radar gave the RAF a complete picture of the space-time field which helped offset the fact that the Luftwaffe was the larger force and held the strategic initiative.

The Problem of Relative Power

That national power is always relative is almost axiomatic. In the eyes of Lichtenstein, Switzerland is a great power. A superficial approach to the relativity of power has been to compare the power inventories of the states or alliances under discussion, with emphasis upon actual or potential power according to the purpose or leanings of the writer. Such a simple method has of course long been rejected by those more deeply concerned with the problem. No substitute formula, simple or complex, will come from the present paper. The emphasis upon the interplay of the inventory and strategic beams leads only to greater uncertainties, when two or more states are considered.

Emphasis upon the strategic aspect of relative power does not render the power inventory useless. Basic data on such fundamentals as man-power, steel production, and the like are indispensable, and it is generally true in world politics as in pugilism that a good big man is better than a good little man. What the strategic approach does is to ask how good the man is, as well as how big. If strategic considerations make the estimation of relative power more complex, they may compensate by making it less fatalistic. It is less necessary to kneel before statistical superiority, unless the margin be great. The free world has had no reason to fear the Soviet Union—statistically. But generally the Soviet Union has held the initiative in world affairs. If the statistically weaker country has often called the tune for the statistically stronger, a reversal of roles is at least theoretically possible.

The simplest statement about relative power is that the margin of power between A and B is more significant than the absolute power of A or B. Unfortunately, we cannot express a margin of power statistically any more accurately than we can measure absolute power. We must make the best informed guess possible.

Relative power is sometimes discussed as if a state had only its own resources. But tight blockade is rare. Alliances, trade with neutrals, con-quests of territory, scientific substitution, all may increase relative power. On the other hand, we cannot assume that a state necessarily commands all its own resources. Some may be highly vulnerable (like the French coal fields in both world wars); some may be withheld by public unwillingness to sacrifice; administrative clumsiness may prevent full employment of resources. In short, the modifiers we have discussed apply to the calculus of relative power.

Power relations are never simply between A and B. They take place in the configuration of international politics. Even in the so-called bipolar world of today, many states are involved. The shift of China from the non-Soviet to the Soviet camp profoundly affected the relative power of the United States and the Soviet Union, without changing the absolute power of either of these countries by itself. The relative power of the United States and Communist China in Korea was profoundly affected by the mere existence of the Soviet Union in the background. Even weak states affect relative power if they influence when or where competitive crises arise. The weakness of the states of the Eurasian rimland is the despair of the American strategist.

If it is the margin of power that really counts, one must ask for how long a period the margin must be maintained and what sort of competition is taking place. In a short war, margins of skill and readiness may count for more than relative potentials. There are some who hold that a little more skill (especially in handling Soviet minority peoples) and a little more readiness (for Russian winters) might have given Germany military victory over the Soviet Union. In long wars, relative potentials obviously become more significant, if the disparity in skills is not too great. In short crises not leading to war, relative diplomatic skill may be decisive. The long-term competition called the Cold War has demanded skills and other resources in combinations of unusual nature. The Cold War is a competition for entire peoples. Diplomacy is no longer merely the communing of diplomat with diplomat but a problem of mass communication of many kinds. Skill in communicating ideas and methods on a wide range of topics —government, subversion, farming, birth control, etc.—may tip a country like China or India to an extent that military power is almost incapable of offsetting.

Relative power, considered item by item, must be evaluated differently if the given item is scarce or abundant. If some element is scarce, the margin between just enough and not enough may be very significant. If both parties to a competition have some item in plenty, some derivative factor may be significant. Both the United States and the Soviet Union have large coal reserves, for instance. Whether they will last four hundred or four thousand years makes no immediate difference; they suffice for the present. Much more important are such derivatives as the rate of production, how much it could be increased, the man-power requirements of coal-mining in the two countries, and the speed with which a hydrogenation industry might be developed if liquid fuels run short.

Our opening analogy stated that the power inventory must be triangulated by national strategy. To extend the analogy to relative power, not only a state's own inventory and strategy must be considered but also the inventories and strategies of the other state or states involved in the political configuration. Theoretically, in this age of global competition, this would mean sixty or more strategic beams sweeping the international skies—with an effect more dazzling than illuminating. And, actually, it is in such a spider-web of beams that we are caught, when Germany and China, Iran and Guatemala, Indochina and British Guiana may hit the headlines the same day. The speed of communication and reaction in world politics, as well as the global scope, calls for more background in strategic thought than has been the American custom. Otherwise we are repeatedly surprised, "for, to the blind, all things are sudden."

The complicated interrelationships of national strategies and relative power may be somewhat simplified if we consider national strategy to have two aspects, one of which we may call "autonomous," the other "responsive." There is not a dichotomy between these but, rather, a gradation. For example, England was not forced to adopt sea power as its principal weapon. In fact, there was little attempt to employ sea power independently until the reign of Henry III. Insularity permitted the British to rely on sea power but did not command it. Similarly, the decision of Britain to maintain a fleet equal to the two closest rivals was an autonomous decision, for Britain was free to adopt a smaller or greater ratio, limited only by the willingness to risk and the willingness to sacrifice. The location of the principal British naval bases was less autonomous; it depended on the probable enemy of the period and that enemy's resources and possible strategy. The distribution of British ships among the fleets and bases was also not fully autonomous; it was responsive to the political changes and the moves of the opponents.

A state faced with rising unemployment might make autonomous decisions on combating it. It might widen military training, thus tightening the labor market by removing young men and increasing economic activity by orders for military equipment and supplies. Or it might pay men for raking leaves or expand unemployment insurance. One policy enhances available power, the other doesn't, though the theoretical potentials remain unchanged. If, having failed to train its men, the second state is attacked, it is forced to make a convulsive responsive effort. Enemy power must be matched if possible, when and where and however it is used.

The autonomous aspects of national strategy are extremely important. They are the main aspects about which decisions are made in advance of conflict. These decisions are likely to be swayed by factors extraneous to the true problem. These decisions may weigh heavily in the scales when one comes face to face with an opponent and must respond to his moves. The decision of the Truman administration to take a stand on immigration to Palestine was autonomous. Extraneous factors of domestic politics played an important part. The effect of this and subsequent decisions on American power in the Middle East was and continues significant.

The last aspect of relative power that we shall discuss might inelegantly be called "historical peristalsis." In both politics and technology, change is endless but not continuous. Nor is the phase always the same from one country to another. The peristaltic changes in naval technology, the political responses to such changes, and the relative power relations resulting from both are so well brought out in Bernard Brodie's *Sea Power in the Machine Age* that no discussion here is needed. Similar processes take place in diplomacy, propaganda, and all the other implements and methods of national strategy. To use a more refined but less apt analogy, the light of the strategic beam fluctuates. Hence the evaluation of the power inventory must change.

Thought is subject to many kinds of distortions, many of them quite unintentional. One common distortion is polarization. One polarization that is germane here is the tendency to place in opposition the long and the short views. The phenomenon of "historical peristalsis" indicates that both long and short views are necessary and complementary. A statement about national power really should carry a date.

Another form of polarization also is germane: The "and/or/versus" distortion. If one mentions, for example, "the spirit and the sword," it takes the merest twist of the tongue to change it to "the spirit or the sword" and but an intonation to give "or" the meaning of "versus." When we have spoken of power inventory and national strategy, *and* means *and*, not *or* or *versus*. Especially is it not intended to polarize material and imponderable aspects of power. There are non-material as well as material items in the power inventory and national strategy requires the availability of both. Even a national strategy of complete pacifism requires for inventory a stock of Grade A martyrs, as complete militarism requires a stock of Grade A brutes. Though a sound national strategy should reduce the wastage of resources, strategy is not a substitute for resources but is the art of using them.

GAUGING POWER OF THE HINDU STATE*

U. N. Ghoshal

Besides introducing into Hindu public life the concept of an elaborate State-system, the early *Arthaśāstra* gives us the first classified list of forms

* U. N. Ghoshal, "The System of Inter-State Relations and of Foreign Policy in the Early Arthaśāstra State," in *India Antiqua* (Leiden: E. J. Brill Ltd., Publishers, 1947), pp. 136–145. Reprinted by permission. U. N. Ghoshal is former Professor of History, Presidency College, Calcutta, and author of *The Agrarian System in Ancient India* (1930), *A History of Hindu Public Life* (1945), *Studies in Indian History and Culture* (1957), and *A History of Indian Political Ideas* (1959).

of foreign policy (*gunas*), together with the principles of their application. These rules, it is needless to say, systematise the branches of foreign policy known at that time. The number of six *gunas*, as mentioned by the Teacher,[1] comprises the classes *sandhi, vigraha, yāna, āsana, samśraya* and *dvaidhībhāva*. We can understand the significance of these terms in the light of their definitions by Kautilya and Kāmandaka. From this it appears that *sandhi* means dependant alliance sought by a weak Prince *in extremis* and accompanied with agreement of surrender. *Vigraha, yāna, āsana* and *samśraya* means respectively war, marching, neutrality and seeking protection by a weak Prince from his powerful neighbour. *Dvaidhībhāva* means verbal surrender (evidently with treachery at heart) by a weak Prince to two powerful enemies. A careful consideration of the above shows that some types are more fundamental than the rest. . . .

[I]t appears that the application of the six-fold policy in the context of certain specific conditions of States was not unknown to the early masters of the science. In the passage there quoted, the Teacher says that the Prince shall adopt *sandhi* when the condition of stagnation is expected to produce equal results within the same time. The full import of this extract is to be understood in the light of Kautilya's fuller treatment of the subject. Starting with the category of three conditions of States, Kautilya says that increase stands for the *guna* in which the Prince finds himself competent to undertake his own works and prevent those of the enemy, the "works" being defined as relating to forts, irrigation-works, trade-routes, colonisation of waste-lands, as well as the working of mines and forests. [D]ecline, according to the same authority, means the *guna* causing hindrance of the Prince's own work, but not that of the enemy. Lastly, stagnation is that *guna* which causes neither increase nor diminution of the Prince's own work. In the background of these definitions, Kautilya recommends the Prince to follow the *guna* leading to increase, but not that causing decline. What is more, Kautilya shows how the Prince should adopt the policies of *sandhi*, or indifference, according as the results of these conditions manifest themselves in the future. It is permissible to think that while the passage from the Teacher quoted above refers to stagnation and its future consequences alone, the two other conditions of increase and decline along with their tendency to produce prospective results were also known to that early authority.

If the above arguments can be accepted as correct, they would indicate the early Arthaśāstra State as marking an important stage in the development of Hindu public life. For in the first place foreign policy is here regarded as a means of acquiring relative strength, or at least of avoiding

[1] Kautilya frequently quotes an unnamed "Teacher" in his writings—Ed.

relative weakness. In the second place, Kauṭilya's specific references would point to one of the main objectives of international diplomacy in the Arthaśāstra State. This is nothing short of carrying through, and at the same time denying to the enemy, a comprehensive programme of economic and military self-sufficiency, which involves the construction of forts and irrigation-works, colonisation of waste lands and the exploitation of mines and forests.

From another reference in Kauṭilya we learn that the early Arthaśāstra State also knew the application of foreign policy in relation to what is called the "Power" (śakti) of the Prince. In the passage referred to, the Teacher is quoted as declaring will-power to be more important than material power, and the latter again to be more important than power of deliberation. We can realise the full significance of this text in the light of Kauṭilya's fuller account of the subject. Kauṭilya ... mentions a category of three śaktis. This consists of strength of knowledge, strength of finance and army, and strength of valour. Kauṭilya winds up by recommending the Prince to secure for himself śakti (power) as well as siddhi (fruition). In the context from which we have quoted above, Kauṭilya asks the "conquest-seeking Prince" (vijigīṣu) to march after making himself sure of his own and the enemy's śakti as well as the proper place and time and so forth. We may conclude from the above discussion that the early Arthaśāstra masters knew the category of three "powers" of the Prince in relation to foreign policy in general and the policy of marching in particular. This introduces us to a new factor in the evolution of Hindu public life, namely, the conception of the State as Power and the application of Power-politics to the sphere of international relations. From the above, it also follows that the Arthaśāstra State, having the sources of its strength in the Prince's qualities of intellect and will and in his possession of army and finance, was fundamentally a secular institution.

The Teacher's comparison of the three Powers of the Prince, together with Kauṭilya's criticism of the same, is of high interest as exhibiting different estimates of their relative importance from the pen of two Arthaśāstra authorities. Justifying his preference for will-power to material power, the Teacher argues that the Prince who is heroic, strong, healthy, and well-armed, can by himself and with the help of his army subdue another Prince possessing merely material power, while the Prince with material power but without will-power is sure to perish. Again, in support of his preference of material power to the power of deliberation, the Teacher says that the Prince with the power of deliberation but without material power becomes barren in intellect, while his want of material power destroys his well-thought-out plans, "just as drought destroys the sprouts of seeds." This view, by putting a premium upon will-power,

is at the opposite pole of the philosophy of Kauṭilya who ranks deliberation as the foremost power and the power of will as the least important. . . .

As regards the policy of marching, the Teacher is quoted in one place
as comparing the relative advantage of marching against a vulnerable
Prince in great trouble and an enemy in slight trouble, and giving his
decision in favour of the former. In the same context, the Teacher is
quoted as declaring that the Prince with impoverished and greedy subjects
should be marched against instead of one whose subjects are neglected.
For the impoverished and greedy subjects can be easily won over or suppressed, but the subjects who are neglected can only be reduced by controlling the leaders. Kauṭilya quotes both views only to refute them with
his counter-arguments. The importance of his quotation, however, lies in
showing the dominant part played by the attitude of the subjects in shap-
ing international policy in the Arthaśāstra State.

It is characteristic of the minuteness of inter-state relations in the
Arthaśāstra that it describes under appropriate technical terms the subdivisions of the forms of foreign policy above-mentioned. We can safely
trace back such analysis from references in Kauṭilya and Kāmandaka to
the early Arthaśāstra times. Kauṭilya quotes the Teacher as comparing
successive pairs of allies from the point of view of the advantage obtainable from them. From this standpoint the Teacher prefers the ally who is
long-standing but not submissive to his opposite, and the allies being
equally submissive, the one who is of great help but temporary to his
reverse. The Teacher also prefers the ally who is powerful but difficult
to rouse to the one who is the reverse, the ally with scattered troops to the
one with unsubmissive troops, the ally supplying troops to the one supplying money and the ally supplying money to the one supplying land.
Kauṭilya, as usual, quotes the above views only to refute them. Apart
from the question of these specific gains, the early Arthaśāstra also compared different types of gains in general. [T]he Teacher describes his
preference of small but quick gain to large but distant gain,—a view which
Kauṭilya himself contradicts.

[T]he Teacher declares his preference for land that is rich but constantly menaced by the enemy on its borders to its opposite. This view, as
usual, is contradicted by Kauṭilya with counter-arguments. . . . Kauṭilya
quotes the Teacher as preferring the creation of forests yielding economic
products to those sheltering elephants. In the latter chapter Kauṭilya cites
the same authority as preferring elephant forests with few but spirited
elephants to those with numerous but tame elephants, mines with costly
but scanty yields to those yielding inexpensive but ample products, water-

routes to land-routes for commercial traffic and the Himalayan route to the Southern route.

The above extracts suggest a number of reflections. In the first place they indicate some of the broad objectives of international diplomacy in the Arthaśāstra. These comprise the acquisition of concrete gains in the shape of allies, money and land as well as the accomplishment of definite objects in the form of construction of civil and military public works, colonisation of waste lands, exploitation of mines and forests and so forth. In the second place, we find in the arguments of the authors an attempt to assess the military and economic advantages of different classes of allies and different kinds of lands, mines, forests, trade-routes and the like. Let us illustrate this point by a few examples. An ally with troops, says the Teacher in preferring the ally who supplies troops to the money-supplying ally, commands great authority and can, when roused, accomplish all works. Again, he says, in preferring the (money-supplying ally) to the (land-supplying) ally, that money because of its mobility can stand expenditure. Kauṭilya, on the other hand, in refuting the above views, says that unlike troops money is always at hand, while troops as well as all other desired objects can be won by money. Again, he says that both the ally and the money can be acquired by means of land. Evidently the Teacher realises that money (unlike land) was ready for use at any time and that troops (unlike money) could be effectively used for carrying out all works. On the other hand, Kauṭilya understood that money could procure troops and that land could be used for acquiring both money and troops. Again, the Teacher justifying his preference for forests yielding economic products to those sheltering elephants says that the former is the root of all works and yields a rich store, while the latter is just the reverse. Kauṭilya says *per contra* that unlike the forests yielding economic products the elephants cannot be created on many varieties of lands and that elephants bring about the destruction of troops. In preferring the water-route to the land-route, the Teacher says that the former is inexpensive and brings great profit through the huge volume of merchandise carried along it. In justifying the contrary view Kauṭilya says that the water-route is liable to obstruction, it is not open at all seasons, it is attended with great dangers and it is incapable of defence.

CHAPTER THREE

Balancing Power with Power

The balance-of-power concept has long disturbed many Americans. Some observers deplore its usage; others deny that it has application to United States foreign policy. In 1916, one scholar advised the public to consider balance of power "a vicious and disastrous principle," a "pernicious doctrine," and an "*ignis fatuus*" that should be abandoned.[1] Some forty years later, another professor stated that "the mere acceptance of the idea of a balance of power would undermine the basis of voluntary association among free partners and convert [the United States] into an empire with satellites to be ordered about. It would convert the United States from a federal Republic to an empire and ultimately destroy the Republic."[2]

Many men have refused to accept these dramatic conclusions, but few have answered the detractors of balance of power more succinctly than James Reston of *The New York Times:* "For years we have been complaining about 'power politics' and 'the balance of power,' but there are no other kinds of politics in the world today, and when the chips are down the balance of power is usually decisive."[3]

The adaptability of balance of power to the vicissitudes of inter-state and international relations is the subject matter of this chapter. Two selections review the balance-of-power politics of the Western nation-states before the United States and Russia assumed their current dominant roles in world affairs. Edward V. Gulick surveys the ways in which European leaders since 1500 have adjusted the fundamental idea of balancing power

[1] Philip M. Brown, *International Realities* (New York: Charles Scribner's Sons, 1917); quoted in Frederick H. Gareau, *The Balance of Power and Nuclear Deterrence* (Boston: Houghton Mifflin Co., 1962), pp. 97–99.
[2] Frank Tannenbaum, *The American Tradition in Foreign Policy* (Norman: University of Oklahoma Press, 1955), p. 167.
[3] *The New York Times*, May 7, 1961, p. 14E.

with power to meet the changing needs of the continental states for a measure of stability in external affairs. He suggests some inherent limitations of balance of power, and tries to explain why the concept has provoked both bitter tirades and vigorous defense. Martin Wight's essay cogently characterizes the various phases of development of European balance of power and discusses its principal operational features. Careful consideration of these articles should give the student some basis for determining the validity of Professor Wight's assertion that "the balance of power is as nearly a fundamental law of politics as it is possible to find." Subthemes in both readings are the disparate meanings that the concept can denote; such as, a law of international politics, a policy of a particular power, and an equilibrium or a preponderance of power. Those who wish to become proficient in this area of international politics must learn to decipher the meaning(s) the author intended to convey—often not an easy assignment.

Professor Gulick believes that "odds and ends of balance of power practice may have been used in many state-systems" in the premodern, non-Western world, but that "there was an unusually high, systematic and complex development of the system in Europe without parallel elsewhere." The next two articles—describing the theory and operation of the *maṇḍala*—offer evidence that this assertion is incorrect.[4] Political commentators of the Mauryan period of Indian history were considerably more than superficial, elementary practitioners in the intricacies of balancing power with power. The early Hindus felt that a state's geographical location determined its foreign policies. Wherever remoteness existed between two kingdoms, there would be an absence of enmity, hatred, and rivalry. Alliances were possible between those "natural" friends that did not share a common boundary. On the other hand, contiguous states were destined to be enemies. From this model of inter-state relations, the Hindu version of the balance of power, built around the doctrine of *maṇḍala*, emerged.

---

[4] Confucian statesmen of China also understood the value of balancing power, although they were considerably less elaborate than the Hindus in working out plans for its use. One document that describes the Chinese version of balance of power deals with the military strategy that might be used against the British in 1842. China was quite unprepared to meet successfully the Western military tactics and weapons that the British employed. In the resulting crisis, Chinese leaders advocated a typically Confucian idea, namely, the use of barbarians to control barbarians. Some modern Sinologists maintain that this doctrine is the Chinese counterpart of the Western balance-of-power concept. See Ssu-yü Têng and John K. Fairbank, *China's Response to the West* (Cambridge, Mass.: Harvard University Press, 1954), pp. 28–35. But see also Mark Mancall, "The Persistence of Tradition in Chinese Foreign Policy," *The Annals of the American Academy of Political and Social Science*, CCCXLIX (September 1963), 18–19.

U. N. Ghoshal's short selection lists the twelve component members of a *maṇḍala* and designates their geographical positions. The next article, by Benoy Kumar Sarkar, develops the theory underlying the Hindu king's struggle for power in his inter-state relations and shows how Kautilya and a later Hindu author, Kamandaka, fashioned a mathematical design for establishing alliances. Does this fourth-century description of methods of balancing power have any relevance to modern European international relations? One Hindist has noted:

When applied to the map of Europe the ancient Indian *maṇḍala* supplies a perfect pattern for the issues and vicissitudes, understandings and seeming mis-understandings, that have underlain our almost incessant wars. At the opening of the modern period, in the sixteenth century, France found herself threatened with encirclement when Spain and the German Empire became united under the dynasty of the Hapsburgs. The subsequent struggle for hegemony between the French kings and the emperors in Vienna—from the time of Francis I (1515–1547) and Charles V (1519–1556)—continued until the dismemberment of the Austro-Hungarian Empire in the Treaty of Versailles in 1919. Louis XIV (1643–1715) . . . secured the support of the Mohammedan Turks in the rear of the Hapsburg dominions in Eastern Europe, and these then invaded the enemy territories from what is now Yugoslavia, and through Hungary, while the armies of France fought the German Imperial forces in Flanders and along the Rhine.

The neighbor to the rear, or at the flank, of one's own neighbor and rival is the born ally: that is the supreme principle. Moral and religious considerations, matters of ideology, and common spiritual traditions do not have the force of this simple geometrical fact. The Christian king did not hesitate to betray and endanger the Christian civilization of Europe by inspiring and supporting an invasion by the very power that had been the primary common foe of Christendom for the past thousand years . . . Anxious to preserve the political independence of the territory of the Holy See, Alexander VI, supreme shepherd of the Christian flock, vicar of Christ on earth, and the very tongue of the Holy Ghost, joined hands, in 1494, with the sultan Bayazid II, to defeat the imperial ambitions of Charles VIII of France. Half a century later, Suleiman the Magnificent became allied with the French king, Francis I, against the Holy Roman Emperor, Charles V; and the subsequent Moslem advance into Eastern Europe . . . even enjoyed the tacit approval of Pope Paul III.

In the French *maṇḍala* of alliances, when the power of Turkey began to decline, that of rising Russia took its place, as the natural ally at the back of the immediate neighbor to the east. Napoleon in 1805 and 1810 accordingly made friends with the emperor of Russia, in order to check Prussia and Austria . . . Napoleon also resurrected Poland, as a second ally for himself at the back of Germany, by restoring those portions that had fallen to the share of Austria and Prussia in the partitions of Poland between those powers and Russia at the close of the eighteenth century. And following the same absolutely dependable logic of the *maṇḍala*, France again won the cooperation of Russia in her policy of encirclement just before the First World War—a classic pincer movement on the chessboard of the powers that would compel her immediate neighbor to fight a war on two fronts. France at the same time supported Serbia against Austria, as the ally at Austria's rear, and then Romania, as a dagger in the back, at the crucial hour when Germany had failed in the Battle of Verdun and was suffering defeat along the Somme sector of the Western Front. With the Treaty of Versailles a comprehensive maṇḍala policy was inaugurated by France to hold the crushed enemy in check. A ring of Slavic powers, from Poland and Czechoslovakia to Romania and Yugoslavia, was brought into being, threatening the rear of Germany and what was left of Austria. The new allies were provided with loans for armament and development. To which the reply of Germany was the Rapallo Treaty, in 1922, with Russia—a natural ally now, to the rear of Poland and Czechoslovakia . . .[5]

In the final article of this chapter, "The Balance of Power in the Missile Age," Glenn H. Snyder depicts the reasons why political scientists and military strategists alike, since 1945, have had to discard many of the balance-of-power shibboleths of the past. As essays earlier in this book have indicated, the development of nuclear and thermonuclear weapons, along with their fantastic means of delivery to any place in the world, has resulted in a bipolarity of power. Classical balance-of-power politics has undergone a drastic revision, and it is often easy for students to become lost in a welter of military terminology when considering the contemporary scene. Dr. Snyder's selection discusses the current politico-military situation in a way that a non-West Point graduate can understand. "International relations theory," he says, "must come to terms with the weapons revolution and the logical place to start is with the balance of power concept." His article is a significant contribution toward this end.

[5] Heinrich Zimmer, *Philosophies of India*, ed. Joseph Campbell (New York: Meridian Books, Inc., 1956), pp. 115–118. Reprinted by permission of Bollingen Foundation, New York, the original publishers.

THE WESTERN CONCEPT OF BALANCE OF POWER IN HISTORICAL PERSPECTIVE*

Edward V. Gulick

It is instructive to examine the implications . . . of the balance of power, . . . because that has been one of the dominant frames of refer-

* Edward V. Gulick, "Our Balance of Power System in Perspective," *Journal of International Affairs*, XIV, No. 1 (1960), 9–14. Reprinted by permission. Mr. Gulick is Professor of History, Wellesley College, and author of *The Balance of Power* (1943) and *Europe's Classical Balance of Power* (1955).

ence for international competition...One finds, first of all, that serious literature on the balance of power system is scanty, and the study of the balance of power, in spite of its interest and importance, is rather torpid. There is no systematic use of the term in our period, and the phrase possesses a disconcerting number of meanings, being commonly used in the sense of an aim, a policy, a diplomatic way of life, or a state of affairs. It may appear as a principle or as a systematic lack of principle, depending on whether one reads Metternich or Cobden; it may be synonymous with power politics and replete with unpleasant connotations, or presented as the most rational means for buttressing a state-system; it is forever being held, pursued, overthrown, upset, reconstituted or redressed.

Basically, it is applied to a state-system whose members, animated by a desire to remain independent, aim primarily at preventing domination of the system by any one state. On this basis the balance of power system may evolve into a relatively elaborate diplomatic way of life in which institutions, policies, and devices are geared to the central task of maintaining the system itself; and in which typical means emerge, such as holding the balance and reciprocal compensation. Although odds and ends of balance of power practice may have been used in many state-systems such as in the Chou period in China, in the early and middle feudal periods in Japan, in the era of the break-up of the Alexandrine empire, among the tribes of the Congo or North America or in dozens of other places, there was an unusually high, systematic and complex development of the system in Europe without parallel elsewhere.

In modern history, the concept of this type of system was one of our many great gifts from the Italian peninsula, where it was "invented" in the fifteenth century, and tested in the laboratory of the local state-system. Here a multiple balance prevailed among Florence, Rome, Venice, Milan, and Naples, each determined to prevent domination of the system by its neighbors. The system was soon wrecked by the French invasion of Italy in 1494, but within a few years the concept had moved out into the larger European arena where its history from 1500 to 1945 may be broadly seen in three phases, each of some 150 years' duration. The first (to 1648) witnessed its adoption by the decisive political figures in the Europe of that day, the new national monarchs; and ended with the achievement in the treaties of Westphalia of sovereign independence for Europe's states and their firm establishment in a state-system as the basic, continuing condition of European international affairs. Thus 1648, by installing, securing, and rendering apparently permanent the historically bizarre norm of a state-system, became one of the decisive years in world history and is strikingly relevant to our affairs today.

The second phase (1648–1815) took this base and built upon it the intricate, baroque structure of Europe's classical balance of power system. In a narrative sense the period saw the evolution of a dominating dualism between Hapsburg and Bourbon during the age of Louis XIV, and its supercession in the 18th century by a return to a multiple balance, this time dominated by a Big Five of England, France, Prussia, Austria, and finally Russia. These powers presided over and made viable a complicated, interrelated group of hundreds of sovereign units. This second phase, although bewilderingly full of diplomatic shifts, maneuvers, alliances, coalitions, and wars, was also the most respectable period of the evolving balance of power system. A host of contemporary documents testified to this by stating or assuming its virtues as a systematic approach to statecraft.

It was in this Golden Age of the European equilibrium that the system was most highly developed. There was considerable group-consciousness among the member states, and a rough consensus on the appropriate use of intervention, alliances, reciprocal compensation, holding the balance and warfare. It was a system of tidy calculations wholly appropriate to the Age of Reason. There was widespread concern over preserving the key components of the system, and a surprising amount of moderation. Statesmen of the period were greatly helped in their work by the rather well-defined framework (*i.e.*, the understood membership of the system), and the relative homogeneity within it—all sharing certain common features of the historic European culture. The system was nearly demolished by Napoleon, but in 1814–15 his conquerors restored it at the Congress of Vienna and reintroduced a multiple balance. As events turned out, the ensuing years saw the end of the widespread popularity of the balance of power system, and the Vienna arrangements proved to be the last major peace settlement which could be based unanimously and consistently on an avowed balance of power policy.

It is interesting to note that the system remained even at this late date almost wholly a *European* system. Among its leading states neither Austria nor Prussia had overseas commitments; France's were minimal; Russian policy was still concerned more with its western interests than with central or eastern Asia; and even Britain with ranging trade connections, a growing Indian empire, and recent acquisitions of the Cape Colony and Ceylon, construed the 1814–15 settlement as primarily European.

The third major phase began with the post-Napoleonic years and lasted to 1945. As it unfolded, deep changes overtook the system itself—industry and transport were revolutionized, trade with non-European areas burgeoned, large accumulations of capital sought overseas investments, and mission activity flourished. Coincident with those developments, the great powers, caught in the usual, tense European relationship, and having harnessed the industrial revolution to their militarism, were now more nearly capable of destroying each other. At this juncture, with mutual danger thus greatly enhanced, they found a temporary outlet for their dynamism by turning to the weaker, non-European areas of the globe which had by now been brought effectively within the European ken. Between 1880 and the Anglo-Russian agreement of 1907, Europeans burst into these regions like a host of carpetbaggers, and staked out an astonishing assortment of African and Asiatic spheres, protectorates, bases, coaling stations, and colonies. Although world war may have been postponed by this unusual expansionist outlet, the period ended, as each period had before, with a holocaust, in this case the double holocaust of World Wars.

Reflecting on the 1815–1945 period, we see that it contained two of the most brilliant manipulators in balance of power history, both German, Metternich and Bismarck; it saw an astonishing increase in size of the separate units through the freakish imperial expansion; it witnessed the spread to the rest of the world of what was primarily a Europe-based and Europe-centered technique of analysis and policy-making. It also embraced the most creative institutional advance in the evolution of the balance of power, since the period both began and ended with the Concert: opening with its 1815–22 phase and ending with its elaborated counterpart, the League-UN. The latter, usually misconstrued as unrelated to the balance of power system, should be viewed rather as its culmination. The component states retained their sovereign independence and continued their basic relationship as members of a state-system, each desirous of maintaining its independence, each relying on preserving the system and preventing its domination by any one member state. They had simply evolved a more elaborate, and sensible method for achieving the same aim. Balance of power writers had long urged this type of improvement.

Looking over the total history of the system to 1945, one finds that the balance of power has a record of much wreckage, but many successes. Among the latter we may number the preservation of the separate components of the state-system between 1648 and 1792—nearly one and one-half centuries, the checking of Louis XIV, the subsequent reduction of the Napoleonic over-balance, the maintenance of peace among the great powers during Bismarck's Imperial Chancellorship, and the creation of conditions suitable for the fulfillment of a rich national development for many European peoples.

The year 1945, like 1494, 1648 or 1815, marked a decisive shift. With it we entered a new phase in which we have been confronted with a new pattern. For one thing, the major components of the system have grown. This shift to larger and larger units has occurred in each major phase in the past, the perspective on our own period being particularly striking when one considers that Milan and Venice were "Great Powers" in the original system. Each successive phase has also altered and expanded the framework from the Italian state-system of the *quattrocento* through numerous changes up to the late 19th century empires, and on to the present global limits. In size, our post-1945 system represents an increase of several times over its 19th century grandparent, and hundreds of times over its original Italian ancestor.

The present system is characterized, moreover, by a dramatic exodus of power from western and central Europe for the first time in five centuries (disregarding the powerful Manchu Empire of the 17th and 18th centuries, since the latter lay outside the framework under discussion). Decisive power has flowed to two, new, Europeanized superpowers, both accompanied by a cluster of allies and associates, and both rushing down opposite slopes toward mutual annihilation. What might appear as a hopelessly unmanageable number of bulky states for a state-system . . . is given structure and apparent viability by the self-appointed "executive" of The Two and their semi-permanent coalitions.

On the one hand we have in the USSR a superpower which is more the disrupter, the aggressor and the subverter, stirred by a largely unrestrained ideological and power evangelism, and more in the tradition of Napoleon than Metternich. In simplest terms, it is a throwback to an anti-balance of power type. The United States, on the other hand, evangelical in its own way, has been thrust into a more conventional balancing policy, showing more restraint, more inhibitions, more lethargy, more negativism, and more sense of conserving the system—in short, a posture more Metternichian than Napoleonic.

There remain today remnants of regional balances. We have them in varying stages of development in the Arab areas, the Caribbean, Southeast Asia, Turkey and the Balkans, and Europe itself (most flabbergasting of all). One finds earlier illustrations of these "inferior balances" in the Balkans before World War I, in warlord China during the 1920's, Scandinavia in the 18th century, and elsewhere. But, where there could once have been an independent existence for such sub-systems (the Baltic powers in the early 18th century, for example), today each would be hard-put to pretend its policies were unrelated to the over-riding competition of the superpowers. Regional frameworks have ceased to have a separate identity or any real meaning by themselves. One cannot reasonably consider the balance between North and South Korea as unrelated to the central struggle of the US and the USSR.

Then, too, techniques of competition, of thrust-and-parry in the balance of power system, have broadened. In place of the exalted ambassador.

the dynastic marriage, the analysis of court diplomacy, the fraternization of international aristocrats, the bilateral alliance and occasional wartime coalition, all based on the essential acceptance of the balancing system itself, there is now a more systematic resort to subversion by highly organized propaganda, new in the 20th century, and the use of "Trojan Horse" local parties, not new, since Napoleon used this device (although more amateurishly). There is more eagerness to supplant the government instead of dealing with it, a profound change from the homogeneous state-system run by cosmopolitan snobs in 1750 or 1815, but again, resembling Napoleonic policy.

We see in our own period the steady resort to *peacetime* coalitions, not new but unusual when one considers that the coalition has chiefly been used in wartime and held together only with extravagant difficulty and mutual exacerbation. Churchill found that "there is only one thing worse than fighting with allies, and that is fighting without them." An outstanding feature of the present competition between the two sides is the extensive use of economic weapons now being widely and sometimes very skillfully used—for commitment, subversion, and ultimate control by one; for profit, stable economies and defense against Communism by the other —not new, but again, vastly increased in scale.

One of the marked differences between our present system and the classical balance of power appears in the prevalence of "neutralism." Although not a novel phenomenon in diplomatic history it is, like so many other features of the present balance of power, on a larger scale and involving greater and more powerful units. This group, despite the addiction of some of its members to double standards of neutralism, has served as a cushion in the competitive balance, giving a good deal of play to the Russo-American dualism. Future gains by either side are more apt to be from the group of neutralist or uncommitted nations than from the committed ones. Although neither side is yet at the desperate stage for affiliates, gains from now on will have great importance, for example, in Indonesia with its 90 million people. This is particularly true for the West, since Communist gains are much more apt to be consolidated ones with scant chance of their being undone, whereas a power can always leave the West as the Bandung states did, withdrawing at least as far as neutralism. Yugoslavia's departure from the Cominform illustrates the extreme difficulty and instability of such severance on the Communist side.

THE MECHANICS OF BALANCE OF POWER AMONG WESTERN STATES*

Martin Wight

The central principle in what we might call the "mechanics" of power politics is that of the Balance of Power, which describes the way Powers group themselves in a state of international anarchy. The Balance of Power is a phrase with two distinct meanings. It can be used either objectively or subjectively—to describe either a "law" or principle of international politics (a general statement of how Powers in fact behave), or a policy which may be adopted by a particular Power.

In the first sense, as a principle of international relations, the Balance of Power is an application of the fundamental law of self-preservation. If there are three Powers, of which the first attacks the second, the third cannot afford to see the second so decisively crushed that it becomes threatened itself; therefore if it is far-sighted enough it supports the second. When one Power grows dangerously strong, other Powers combine against it. The Balance of Power thus comes into play each time that a Dominant Power has tried to gain mastery of the world. The Dominant Power usually has a small entourage of vassal-states which are more frightened of defending their independence than of collaborating, and of jackal-states which have private local interests to pursue; but arrayed against them there arises a grand coalition of superior strength which finally wins. This is the extreme illustration of the Balance of Power.

The Balance of Power develops through various phases. First there can be a *multiple* balance, i.e., a balance similar to a chandelier. This was the normal state of Europe in the eighteenth century. In Western Europe and overseas there was the balance between Britain, France and Spain; in Central and Eastern Europe there was the balance between Austria and

* Martin Wight, *Power Politics*, published by the Oxford University Press under the auspices of the Royal Institute of International Affairs (Looking Forward Pamphlet No. 8), 1946, pp. 42–54. Reprinted by permission. Mr. Wight is Dean of School of European Studies and Professor of European History, University of Sussex; author of *Power Politics* (1946), *The Development of the Legislative Council, 1606–1945* (1946), *The Gold Coast Legislative Council* (1947); and editor of *British Colonial Constitutions* (1947).

Prussia, Russia and Turkey. The balances interacted, and were completed by the smaller Powers. The Great Powers changed partners when their interests shifted as in a quadrille: in 1740 Britain and Austria were allied against France and Prussia, in 1756 Britain and Prussia were allied against France and Austria. The multiple balance broke down, first with the War of American Independence, and then decisively with the Revolutionary and Napoleonic War. The Vienna Settlement tried to restore it: Britain had unchallengeable supremacy outside Europe, Russia took Poland, Austria was predominant in Italy, Prussia was given the Rhineland, and all together in the Quadruple Alliance formed a counterpoise against the recovery of France. But the multiple balance can only last so long as there is international tranquillity and no vital issues arise to split the Great Powers. When this sooner or later occurs, the Great Powers divide into opposite camps, and the multiple balance is replaced by a *simple* balance: it is no longer a chandelier but a pair of scales. This was what happened in Europe with the creation of the Franco-Russian Alliance in 1893 against the Triple Alliance of Germany, Austria-Hungary and Italy; and again with the creation of the Berlin-Rome Axis in 1936 against the League Powers. The period of the simple balance is marked by heightened tension, a race between the two groups in armaments, and uneasy oscillations which we know as *crises*. Mr. Churchill has brilliantly described a crisis, writing of the pre-1914 Balance of Power:

The great Powers marshalled on either side, preceded and protected by an elaborate cushion of diplomatic courtesies and formalities, would display to each other their respective arrays. In the forefront would be the two principal disputants, Germany and France, and echeloned back on either side at varying distances and under veils of reserves and qualifications of different density, would be drawn up the other parties to the Triple Alliance and to what was already now beginning to be called the Triple Entente. At the proper moment these seconds or supporters would utter certain cryptic words indicative of their state of mind, as a consequence of which France or Germany would step back or forward a very small distance or perhaps move slightly to the right or to the left. When these delicate rectifications in the great balance of Europe, and indeed of the world, had been made, the formidable assembly would withdraw to their own apartments with ceremony and salutations and congratulate or condole with each other in whispers on the result.

It was the same with the crises of the 1930's, except that the courtesies had worn thinner and the power was more naked ... And in due course the manoeuverings for position cannot be prolonged, and the Balance of Power overbalances into war.

But there is not only the distinction between a multiple and a simple balance. We must also consider the confusion arising from the fact that the word balance itself has two meanings: it can mean *equilibrium,* and it can also mean *preponderance,* as when we say we have a balance in the bank—i.e., a plus, not an equality between assets and debits. This is the distinction between the objective and the subjective view of the Balance of Power. The historian will say that there is a balance when the opposing groups seem to him to be equal in power. The statesman will say that there is a balance when he thinks that his side is stronger than the other. And he will say that his country *holds* the balance, when it has freedom to join one side or the other according to its own interests. To hold the balance is a policy specially suited to a Sea Power that is partly detached from Europe: it has been the classic policy of Britain . . .

Politics, as Bismarck said, is not an exact science, and there are no "laws" of politics without any exceptions. The Balance of Power is as nearly a fundamental law of politics as it is possible to find: it is easy to see from history that it is the way most Powers have pursued self-preservation in most cases. But rulers often make mistakes in their forecasts of power, and sometimes have other motives besides the interests of the state they rule . . . For we may notice that the law of the Balance of Power is the more true of states according to their strength, confidence and internal cohesion. Weak and corrupt states, and especially those ruled by an unrepresentative despotism or clique, tend to gravitate *towards* the Dominant Power; it is popular states without deep social cleavages (whether their governments be parliamentary democracy or a mass-party dictatorship) that tend to *gravitate away from* the Dominant Power.

There are three chief ways in which the Balance of Power operates: by compensation, by intervention, and by the establishment of buffer states . . .

In the simplest form compensation means giving a state the equivalent of something of which you deprive it . . . This applies, of course, only to victorious Powers and their satellites; defeated Powers are usually deprived of territory without compensation. But in its more developed form, compensation means that one state cannot afford to see another increase its power without obtaining a proportionate increase, i.e., equality of aggrandizement . . .

By the principle of compensation, a Power can be forced to take part in an international transaction against its will . . . It is the principle of compensation that made Russia join in the Second World War against Japan after the defeat of Germany; whatever the Russian desire for rest and recuperation, Stalin could not afford to see his allies settle the Pacific without an equal say himself.

Intervention means interference by a Power in the internal affairs of another Power. We may classify it as either defensive or offensive, according to whether it aims at preserving or at altering the Balance of Power. The principle of defensive intervention might be stated thus: no Power can allow the Balance of Power to be decisively altered in its disfavour by a change of regime or policy in another state . . . Offensive intervention is a technique of penetration and expansion, aimed at provoking a change of regime in another state or even at destroying its independence altogether . . .

There is also non-intervention. Non-intervention, like neutrality, requires unassailable confidence and strength to be an effective policy, and a non-intervening Power is liable to have its hand forced if it cannot make other Powers follow non-intervention as well . . . Thus non-intervention is itself usually a positive, not a negative policy: a holding of the ring with a subtle bias in favour of one of the combatants . . . Hence the truth of Talleyrand's sardonic remark, that "non-intervention is a political term meaning virtually the same thing as intervention." . . .

Intervention is frequent in the relations between a Great Power and its satellites. The classic example is the relations between the United States and Latin America. The United States proclaimed the Monroe Doctrine in 1823 to prevent intervention by the European Powers in Latin America; but as it grew in strength it turned the Doctrine inside out to justify intervention in Latin America on its own part . . .

A buffer zone is an area occupied by a weaker Power or Powers between two or more stronger Powers. It will be the vital interest of each stronger Power to prevent the other from controlling the buffer zone, and each will pursue this interest in one of two ways, according to its strength: either by seeking to establish its own control over the buffer zone, transforming it into a protectorate or a frontier province, or by maintaining its neutrality and independence. Buffer states can therefore be roughly divided into neutral states and protectorates. Neutral states are states without an active foreign policy at all; protectorates are states whose foreign policy is controlled by another power. . . .

It is broadly true that politics, like nature, abhors a vacuum; and buffer states cannot achieve stability and security on their own. This was the great weakness of the belt of East European Powers between Germany and Russia under the Versailles Settlement—the Middle Zone. It came into existence while Germany and Russia had temporarily ceased to be Great Powers, but it could not be maintained without relation to them; least of all could it be, as the Allies seem to have hoped, a wall to hem them both in. As soon as the two had resumed their strength they moved into this vacuum again, as the prelude to conflict between themselves. But the Second World War, by destroying Germany, France and Italy as Great

Powers has turned the whole of Europe into the buffer zone between Russia and Anglo-America. In Eastern Europe Russia is building up a frontier belt of friendly and satellite states, a glacis against invasion; the West European seaboard, with Britain as the great outpost, is equally vital to America. In between lies the vacuum of defeated Germany; and it is in its partition into spheres of influence, its neutralization, or its movement into the orbit of one or other of the victorious Great Powers, that we shall trace the shifting or stabilization of the Balance of Power in the next twenty or thirty years.

THE HINDU CONCEPT OF BALANCE OF POWER: CONSTITUENTS OF THE MANDALA*

U. N. Ghoshal

The basis of the Arthaśāstra view is a State-system (*mandala*) which consists of an aggregate of Princes radiating from the most ambitious of them all, technically called the *vijigīṣu* ("conquest-seeker"). According to the standard definition of *mandala*, it comprises besides the *vijigīṣu*, (a) a set of five Princes in front functioning alternately as his foes and his friends but with receding degrees of this relationship according to their distance from the Central Prince, (b) another set of four Princes in the rear similarly functioning alternately as his foes and his friends in the fashion just described, and (c) two neutral Princes.... The list of Princes belonging to the *mandala* of the standard type is as follows:

1. *Vijigīṣu* ("conquest-seeker"), in the centre
2. *Ari* ("enemy"), in front of No. 1
3. *Mitra* ("ally"), in front of No. 2
4. *Arimitra* (ally of No. 2), in front of No. 3
5. *Mitramitra* (ally of No. 3) in front of No. 4
6. *Arimitramitra* (ally of No. 4), in front of No. 5
7. *Pārsnigrāha* ("rearward enemy"), in the rear of No. 1

* U. N. Ghoshal, "The System of Inter-State Relations and of Foreign Policy in the Early Arthaśātra State," in *India Antiqua* (Leiden: E. J. Brill Ltd., Publishers, 1947), pp. 136–145. Reprinted by permission. U. N. Ghoshal is former Professor of History, Presidency College, Calcutta, and Author of *The Agrarian System in Ancient India* (1930), *A History of Hindu Public Life* (1945), *Studies in Indian History and Culture* (1957), and *A History of Indian Political Ideas* (1959).

8. *Akranda* (enemy of No. 7), in the rear of No. 7
9. *Pārsnigrahāsāra* (ally of No. 7), in the rear of No. 8
10. *Akrandāsāra* (ally of No. 8), in the rear of No. 9
11. *Madhyama* ("intermediate Prince"), adjoining No. 1
12. *Udāsīna* ("neutral Prince"), adjoining No. 11

Such, then, is the famous category of *mandala* which is beyond doubt one of the most notable contributions of the Arthaśāstra to the development of Hindu public life. The severely literary character of this concept is apparent on the surface. We can read it in the conventional numbers of the constituent States and above all in their schematic arrangement on the basis of their geographical situation. In practice, it is evident that not only would the number of the members vary with changing circumstances, but their relations instead of being permanently fixed by geography would be shaped by the harmony (or conflict) of vital interests. Nevertheless, the *mandala* concept embodies a great advance. It marks the stable (and even stereotyped) grouping of a number of allied and hostile as well as neutral States around the central figure of an ambitious potentate—an Indian Louis XIV or Napoleon. It thus lifts foreign relations to a plane in which they can truly be called inter-national.

THE HINDU CONCEPT OF BALANCE OF POWER: THEORY OF THE MANDALA*

Benoy Kumar Sarkar

The conception of "external" sovereignty was well established in the Hindu philosophy of the state. The Hindu thinkers not only analyzed sovereignty with regard to the constituent elements in a single state. They realized also that sovereignty is not complete unless it is external as well as internal, that is, unless the state can exercise its internal authority unobstructed by, and independently of, other states. . . .

* Benoy Kumar Sarkar, "Hindu Theory of International Relations," *The American Political Science Review*, XIII, No. 3 (August 1919), pp. 400–414. Reprinted by permission. Benoy Kumar Sarkar is former Professor of History, National Council of Education, Bengal, and author of *The Science of History* (1912), *Chinese Religion through Hindu Eyes* (1916), *The Political Institutions of the Hindus* (1922), and *The Politics of Boundaries and Tendencies in International Relations* (1926).

The doctrine of independence implied in this conception of external sovereignty was obviously the foundation of the theory of the state in relation with other states. And it gave rise to certain categories of *droit des gens* or *jus gentium* which normally influenced Hindu political thinking from at least the fourth century B.C. These concepts can more or less be grouped under the doctrine of *mandala,* that is, sphere or circle (of influence, interests, ambitions, enterprise, and what not).

This doctrine of *mandala,* underlying as it does the Hindu idea of the "balance of power," pervades the entire speculation on the subject of international relations. . . .

In the first place the doctrine of *mandala* is essentially the doctrine of *vijigeesoo* (aspirant to conquest) or *Siegfried.* It is the cult of expansion. . . . The doctrine becomes necessarily a spur to the struggle for existence, self-assertion and world domination among the *Siegfrieds.* The conception is thus altogether a dynamic factor calculated to disturb the equilibrium and *status quo* of international politics.

First, then, in regard to the doctrine of *vijigeesoo.* According to Kautilya, it is the ambition of each state to acquire "strength and happiness" for the people. The *elan vital* of a ruler in Kamandaka's conception also lies in the "aspiration to conquer." The king, says he, should establish in himself the *nabhi* (or center of gravity) of a system. He should become the lord of a *mandala.* It is part of his duty to try to have "a full sphere around him" just as the "moon is encircled by a complete orb." The "full sphere" is, of course, the circle of states related to the *Siegfried* as allies, enemies and neutrals. Perpetual "preparedness" must therefore be the first postulate of *Realpolitik* in Hindu theory. "One should be ever ready with *danda*" (the "mailed fist"), declares Manu naively, "should always have one's might in evidence and policies well-guarded, as well as be ever on the look out for the enemy's holes." Further, one should "bring to subjection all those elements that are obstacles to the career of triumph."

The *rationale* of this preparedness is very simple indeed. It is as elemental as human blood itself. It goes without question in *Shookra-neeti* that "all rulers are unfriendly," nay, they are "secret enemies to those who are rising, vigorous, virtuous and powerful." "What wonder in this?" asks Shookra and his solution is given in another query which carries its own answer: viz., "Are not the rulers all covetous of territory?" Such being the data of international psychology, Kamandaka frankly suggests that "in order to do away with one's enemies their kith and kin should be employed" whenever possible. For, is not poison outdone by poison, diamond cut by diamond, and the elephant subdued by the elephant? "Fishes, again, swallow fishes, similarly relatives relatives." . . .

The *vijigeesoo,* then, cannot by any means afford to indulge in pious wishes or have faith in the Utopian statecraft of idealistic dreamers. What under these conditions are likely to be the relations between the hypothetical Siegfrieds ... These firebrands are normally endowed with a war-mentality and a bellicose attitude. The world in their eyes is a theater of warfare and equipment for warfare, and they proceed on the assumption that nothing can be unfair in war. . . .

Let us now examine the other aspect of the doctrine of *mandala,* that of the struggle for existence and "place in the sun" among the states. To a *vijigeesoo* . . . "right is that which a strong man understands to be right"; and the international *mores* of the *Mahabharata* is summed up in the dictum that "victory is the root of right," just as its creed of life for the individual appraises "death as better than lack of fame." How, then, is this quest of fame, victory or world domination to be regulated by each state in competition with the others? Are there any rules or methods by which the competing states may guide themselves in this conflict of aspirations? . . .

The "proper study" of the *vijigeesoo* . . . is . . . his own and his enemy's spheres. And how are these spheres located in his imagination? . . . We are told that the enemies diminish in importance according as they are remote from the "centre of the sphere." First to be dreaded by the *vijigeesoo* are those who are situated around or very near his own state, then those who live farther away, and so on. With the remoteness of location, enmity, hatred or rivalry naturally declines. Whether a state is to be treated as inimical, indifferent or friendly depends *per se* on its propinquity or distance. The geographical distribution of states influences their psychology in regard to their neighbors as a matter of course in such an order that the positive antipathy of the nearest dwindles into tolerable apathy of the next and gives way to active sympathy and even friendliness of the farthest distant. This, however, is not the only possible grouping of powers in a *vijigeesoo's* estimation. The *Shookra-neeti* gives another order in which the states may be distributed. According to this computation, first are situated the enemies, then come the friends, next the neutrals, and the most remote on all sides are the enemies again.

These are the elementary principles of international dealings of which elaborate accounts are given in the writings of Kautilya and Kamandaka. The theory holds that there is a hypothetical tug-of-war always being fought between the *vijigeesoo* and his *ari* (the enemy). These two are the combatants or belligerents. Along with these are to be counted another two states in order to furnish a logical completeness to the hypothesis. The *quadrivium* consists of the following members:

1. The *vijigeesoo:* the aspirant, e.g., an Alexander "mewing his might," bent on "conquering and to conquer";

2. The *ari* (the enemy): the one that is situated anywhere immediately on the circumference of the aspirant's territory;

3. The *madhyama* (the mediatory): the one (located close to the aspirant and his enemy) capable of helping both the belligerents, whether united or disunited, or of resisting either of them individually;

4. The *udaseena* (the indifferent or the neutral): the one (situated beyond 1, 2, and 3) very powerful and capable of helping the aspirant, the enemy and the mediatory, together or individually, or resisting any of them individually.

These four states, then, constitute the smallest unit of international grouping. From the standpoint of the *vijigeesoo* all other states are either his own allies or the allies of his enemy. Such states are held to be eight in number according to the hypothesis. How, now, is the "aspirant" to pick up his own allies from the crowd? He need only study the geographical position of these states with reference to the belligerents, i.e., to himself and to his enemy.

The *madhyama* (the mediatory) and the *udaseena* (the neutral) may be neglected by the Siegfried, for the time being, in his calculation of the possible array of forces directly allied or inimical to his career of conquest. The two belligerents, with the eight others (divided in equal proportion as their allies *in potentia*), are then located in the following order of *entente cordiale* by Kamandaka and Kautilya:

The "aspirant" occupies, of course, the hypothetical center. Next to his front is the "enemy." Now we have to calculate frontwards and rearwards. Frontwards: next to the "enemy" is situated (1) the aspirant's ally, next to that is (2) the enemy's ally, next (3) the ally of the aspirant's ally, and last (4) the ally of the enemy's ally. Rearwards from the aspirant: First is situated (1) the rearward enemy, next is (2) the rearward ally, then comes (3) the ally of the rearward enemy, and last (4) the ally of the rearward ally.

There is nothing queer, archaic or unworkable in this conception of international relations. A simple illustration would show how humanly the political theorists of India approached the foreign policy of nations. Thus, for instance, according to the Kautilyan doctrine of *mandala,* the "natural enemies" of France engaged in studying the *modus operandi* for "the next war" would be Spain, England and Germany, and her "natural allies" Portugal, Scotland, Ireland and Russia. A French *vijigeesoo,* e.g., a Napoleon, embarking on a war with Germany, should begin by taking steps to keep his "rear safe." With this object he should have Spain attacked by Portugal, and manage to play off the anti-English forces in Ireland and Scotland in such a manner that England may be preoccupied at home and unable to attack France in support of Germany. As Germany, on the other hand, is likely to have China as her natural ally (supposing there is no other state between Russia and the Far East), the French *vijigeesoo* should set Russia against China, and so on. It is obvious that the diplomatic feats conceived by the Hindu political philosophers could be verified almost to the letter by numerous instances in European and Asian history, especially in ancient and medieval times when Eur-Asia was divided into numberless nationalities.

... the group of ten states or a *decennium* constitutes one complete *mandala*. The *vijigeesoo* is the center of gravity of this sphere. Now each state can have the same legitimate aspiration, that is, each can be fired by the same ambition to form and figure out a sphere of its own. The inevitable result is a conflict of interests, a pandemonium of Siegfrieds united in discord. The problem of statesmen in each state is to find out the methods of neutralizing the policies of others by exploiting the enemies of its rivals in its own interest. The doctrine of *mandala* thus makes of *neeti-shastra* or political science essentially a science of enmity, hatred, espionage and intrigue, and an art of thousand and one methods of preparedness for "the next war."

We need not go into the details of the *Machtpolitik* conceived in Kautilya's *Artha-shastra* or in the sections on warfare in the *Shookra-neeti*. But it is already clear that the doctrine of *mandala* has launched us at last into *mâtsya-nyâya*, the logic of the fish, the Hobbesian law of beasts, anarchy. The doctrine assumes and is prepared for a world of eternally warring states. While "internal" sovereignty dawns as the "logic of the fish" sets, "external" sovereignty postulates the existence of the same logic as a fact in international relations. In one instance *danda* or punishment, that is, "sanction" of the state, is exercised to crush anarchy, but it is apparently in order to maintain a world-wide anarchy that *danda* or *Faustrecht* is employed by one state against another. The theory of the state is thus reared on two diametrically opposite conceptions:

1. The doctrine of *danda*, which puts an end to *mâtsya-nyâya* among the *praja* or members of a single state;

2. The doctrine of *mandala*, which maintains an international *mâtsya-nyâya* or the civil war of races in the human family.

From one anarchy, then, the state emerges only to plunge headlong into another. This is the dilemma that pervades the political philosophy of the Hindus.

BALANCE OF POWER IN THE MISSILE AGE*

Glenn H. Snyder

The idea of "balance of power" is still the central theoretical concept in international relations. However, its meaning is now undergoing fundamental change because of the development of nuclear weapons and long-range ballistic missiles. This article attempts to explore the impact of these developments and to suggest some changes in the traditional concept to take account of them.

The "power" that was balanced in the pre-nuclear balancing process was essentially the military power to take or hold territory. Moreover, territory, and the human and material resources on it, was the predominant source of power. The motive for engaging in the balancing process was to prevent any single state or bloc from becoming so powerful that it could make territorial conquests with impunity and eventually achieve a hegemony over the other states in the system. The objectives were, first, to *deter* the potential disturber from initiating war by forming alliances and building up armaments sufficient to defeat him, and secondly, if deterrence failed, to *defend* or restore the balance by engaging in war.

Nuclear weapons, long-range aircraft and missiles have superimposed a new balancing process over the old. The new balance, which we might call the "balance of terror" (to borrow Churchill's striking phrase), centers on a different form of power—not the power to contest control of territory but the power to inflict severe punishment and to deter by the threat of such punishment. One might say that the new technology has tended to split apart the twin objectives of deterrence and defense by making it possible to deter simply by the threat to inflict terrible costs, quite regardless of the relative balance of capabilities to take or hold territory. Moreover, the capabilities to punish may have little value for defense in the traditional sense, and their actual use may generate costs for both sides which are far beyond the value of most conceivable objectives. Calcula-

* Glenn H. Snyder, "Balance of Power in the Missile Age," *Journal of International Affairs*, XIV, No. 1 (1960), 21–34. Reprinted by permission. Mr. Snyder is Associate Professor of International Relations, University of Denver, and author of *Deterrence by Denial and Punishment* (1959) and *Deterrence and Defense* (1961).

tions of probable cost have become at least as important as calculations of the probability of winning.

Thus nuclear weapons and long-range delivery systems have done much more than simply add higher levels of potential destructiveness to the balance of power. They have changed the very nature and meaning of "balance." Two balancing systems—the strategic balance of terror and a truncated tactical balance of power—now operate simultaneously, each according to somewhat different criteria.

The Balance of Terror

In its "pure" form, the balance of terror would have to do only with the deterrence of, and defense against, all-out nuclear attack. However, the threat of nuclear retaliation may also deter lesser contingencies. To simplify, we may assume that each nuclear power is interested in deterring two types of attack against itself—all-out strategic nuclear attack and a major conventional attack. We may postulate a "minimum" and a "maximum" deterrent for each of these contingencies. Thus we have four salient levels of "balance" in the balance of terror, although these do not exhaust the possibilities.

SECOND-STRIKE DETERRENCE OF NUCLEAR ATTACK. A country has a *minimum second-strike deterrent* when it has just enough nuclear striking power—*after* subtracting the forces which the potential aggressor would be able to eliminate in a surprise attack and by his air defenses—to cause damage to the opponent's economy and population, thereby more than offsetting the value which the opponent places on his objective.

If both sides have at least this capability, they are in the familiar condition of "nuclear parity" or "stalemate"—neither side can prevent unacceptable damage to itself by striking first at the other side's nuclear forces. To consider this condition an automatic corollary of nuclear armament, as we have been somewhat prone to do in the recent past, seems ill-advised in the light of recent thinking. Whether, even now, the United States and the Soviet Union are in nuclear stalemate is a matter of conjecture. The balance may shift against the United States in the years immediately ahead if the Soviets develop the substantial lead in ICBM production which is officially conceded as possible. If such a "missile gap" develops, a minimum second-strike capability for the United States may have to depend, for a time at least, on keeping a certain portion of the SAC long-range bomber force in the air at all times—a difficult and costly measure.

One hesitates to make even qualified predictions in the face of the technological revolution now taking place, but it seems likely that achievement of "balance" in this sense will become progressively easier as long-range missiles begin to make up a considerable portion of the striking forces on both sides ... If appropriate protective measures are taken, such as "hardening," concealment, mobility and deployment of missiles on submarines, the balance of terror should become quite stable, at least as compared to the present and the three or four years immediately ahead when the fear of a surprise counter-force attack will still be an important factor in strategic calculations. Of course, we should not forget that an unexpected technological breakthrough—such as the development of a near-perfect defense against missiles or a method of accurate peace-time tracking and near-simultaneous destruction of a nation's fleet of missile-firing submarines—would give one side a temporarily decisive advantage, but there is no evidence that such a development is likely.

A minimum second-strike deterrent should provide high confidence of deterring a deliberate nuclear attack. It might be irrational, after the attack, for the deterrer actually to use such a force as threatened—i.e., "all-out" against the enemy's cities. He would not be able to defeat the aggressor, he probably would insure that more of his own cities would be destroyed than otherwise, and he would be throwing away whatever bargaining power remained to him. But for the aggressor to expect his victim to act rationally in the wake of a massive nuclear attack would itself be a form of irrationality. However, there is always the possibility of accidents, lunacy in the aggressor's leadership and miscalculation—for example, miscalculation by the aggressor in estimating his counter-force capability, or by the deterrer in estimating the level of potential retaliatory damage necessary to deter. Considering these possibilities, the deterrer may be bothered by the fact that, should deterrence fail, he could not hope to "win" with a minimum second-strike force. He might wish to have the nuclear wherewithal to defeat the attacker—i.e., to force the latter to capitulate, or to destroy his economy and war-making capacity, including his unused strategic nuclear forces—or (more reasonably, perhaps) to persuade the attacker to terminate the war on the basis of the territorial *status quo*, after a series of limited retaliatory strikes. He might want, in other words, a *maximum second-strike deterrent*. Such an objective would require a much larger number of bombs and delivery vehicles than a minimum deterrent designed to produce just barely unacceptable costs for the enemy.

FIRST-STRIKE DETERRENCE OF GROUND ATTACK. For the deterrence of conventional ground attack, unaccompanied by a surprise nuclear strike, the relevant nuclear capability is of course the "first-strike" variety. Conceivably, deterrence of ground invasion might be effective with a *minimum first-strike* force—just enough to cause sufficient damage to the attacker to offset the value he places on conquest of the country attacked.

For a small country such as Holland, an ability to wipe out perhaps only one or two Russian cities would probably meet this criterion. For a larger country such as West Germany, the requirement might be a little higher. But to retaliate with such a minimum force would be irrational, it seems, since conquest could not be prevented and severe nuclear counter-retaliation would very likely follow. If a country wished to vindicate its honor (a "rational" aim perhaps) there are less costly ways. But the prospective aggressor—e.g., the Soviet Union—cannot be sure how rational the prospective victim is, and it must consider that under the stress of war, reason can easily become unhinged, or the victim may retaliate more or less by reflex action because of a previous commitment to retaliation for deterrent purposes. It seems clear that a major Soviet surface attack on a West Germany able to "take out" five or six large Russian cities would pose a grave risk for the Soviet Union, even without considering West Germany's possible alliance connections with other nuclear powers such as the United States. The more the victim's damage-producing capacity exceeds the minimum the aggressor can accept, the more reluctant will he be to undertake the risk of attack.

But for a completely credible nuclear deterrent against ground attack, a *maximum first-strike* force is necessary. This is a strategic nuclear force able not only to inflict unacceptable costs on the aggressor after he has launched a ground attack, but also to defeat him (or at least force him to accept the *status quo ante*) *and* in the process—by attrition of the enemy's nuclear forces and by passive and active defense measures—to limit one's own costs to a level which makes all-out nuclear war preferable to subjugation.

It seems quite obvious that such a force is beyond the reach of any small country against a superpower opponent, and it may become unattainable even for the latter *vis-à-vis* each other. Not only is the quantitative requirement very high, but the qualitative requirements are more stringent than for a minimum force. A good part of the maximum force must be composed of very accurate and very powerful weapons—such as piloted aircraft carrying high-yield bombs, and missiles based relatively close to the enemy—weapons suitable for destroying small and highly-protected military installations such as missile sites, bomb stockpiles, deep-sheltered aircraft, and communications centers. A minimum capability—either the first or the second-strike variety—requires only enough accuracy to hit cities. The maximum first-strike force and the minimum second-strike force are, in a sense, reciprocal; if one side has the former, its opponent, by definition, cannot have the latter.

If a nuclear power wishes to deter either conventional or nuclear attack on other countries, its maximum first-strike requirement is considerably higher than for deterrence of attack on itself. Since all countries naturally value their neighbors' independence somewhat less than their own, they will defend others by strategic nuclear means only at the prospect of less costs to themselves.

These categories are intended as benchmarks for discussion rather than as an exhaustive listing of the various levels of capability which a country might wish to have for deterrence. A small country might want to have somewhat more than the bare minimum for a first strike, even though it did not attempt to achieve a minimum second-strike force. The extra forces would not increase the credibility of its deterrent threat, but they would insure against underestimation of the aggressor's civil and air defenses and his level of unacceptable damage. The threat of greater costs to the enemy might also offset the latter's doubts about the deterrer's willingness to use his forces. Of course, if the deterrer's forces are highly invulnerable, the quantitative requirement for a second-strike minimum might not be much beyond that for a first-strike minimum.

A country with a minimum second-strike capability might want to have some additional forces for the reasons just mentioned, and also to hedge against underestimation of the aggressor's first-strike force. If the extra forces were of a counter-force nature (even though the total did not approach the maximum first-strike requirement) they might increase to some extent the country's ability to deter tactical ground attack or a strategic attack on its allies. Or they might provide the means to make a credible threat of limited retaliation in these contingencies.

In none of the categories mentioned above does "balance" mean *matching* the enemy in offensive striking forces or having a slight margin of superiority over the enemy in such forces, as in the traditional concept of balance of power. Both of the minimums probably require less than the enemy's forces and both of the maximums require more. In the balance of terror, the striking forces do not exist primarily to fight each other for the control of territorial objects, but rather to pose for the opponent the prospect of unacceptable costs. "Balancing" means introducing into the enemy's risk calculus a prospect of cost which will be sufficient to offset his prospect of gain, *after* discounting the costs by some factor representing the enemy's doubts about one's willingness to inflict them.

An important characteristic of any balancing system is its degree of stability—i.e., the strength of tendencies for the system to remain in balance once an equilibrium has been reached. The most dangerous form of instability is that which tends to move the system in the direction of war. In general, the stability of the balance of terror at any particular time depends on three prime factors: the vulnerability of striking forces, the accuracy of striking forces, and the number of such forces on each side.

Instability is greatest when the forces on both sides are both highly vulnerable and highly accurate, so that with roughly equal numbers of forces on each side, one side could practically eliminate the forces of the other in a single blow. Even if both sides wished fervently to avoid war, each would be forced to consider that the opponent had both the capability and the incentive for a knock-out blow, the incentive arising from the opponent's desire to forestall such a strike against himself. From such considerations, the "first" side would develop an incentive for a first strike, and the second side, knowing this, would have his own incentives reinforced. Clearly, this is an explosive situation.

Maximum stability would be obtained when both sides, by virtue of the invulnerability of their forces, have something approaching maximum second-strike capabilities—i.e., a capacity virtually to destroy the opponent's economy and society even after the opponent has had the advantage of the first strike. Stability would be fairly great even if one side had only a little more than a *minimum* invulnerable second-strike force, because the other side would then not have to fear being the recipient of a surprise attack. Only a small increase in the capability of the latter side, however (possibly because of some secret scientific development), might give it a maximum first-strike force—i.e., deprive the opponent of its minimum second-strike capability—and thereby make a deliberate attack rational.

Differences and Interaction between
Balance of Terror and Balance of Power

The traditional "tactical" balance of power continues to operate in conflict situations in which strategic nuclear retaliation cannot be credibly threatened or rationally employed. In modern strategic theory it survives chiefly in the concept of "limited war." Before considering the interaction between the balance of terror and the tactical balance of power, it may be useful to note certain important differences between the two systems in their "pure" form.

One difference has already been noted: the irrelevance of quantitatively matching the opponent's military capabilities in the balance of terror. Another concerns the strategic value of territory and of territorial boundaries. In the tactical balance, the strategic value of territory, and the human and material assets associated with territory, continues to be high. The traditional "elements of national power," such as manpower, natural resources, industrial strength, space, geographic separation, command of the seas and so on, continue to be the primary sources of power and they are important criteria for determining the existence or non-existence of a tactical "balance."

These territorially-based elements are also a source of power in the balance of terror, but their significance is less and considerably different than in the tactical balance. Strategic nuclear weapons have reduced the importance of geographical separation between opponents in the balance of terror, since ICBM's can reach from continent to continent.

However, distance still retains some significance in the strategic balance of terror. An aggressor can reduce the required range and hence increase the accuracy and possible payload of his missiles by obtaining control of territory between himself and his prospective nuclear opponent. He may also increase the points of the compass from which he can attack, thus complicating the opponent's warning and air defense problem. He may increase the space available for dispersal of his striking forces, and he may obtain useful staging bases and post-attack landing points for his long-range aircraft.

The acquisition of industrial and resource assets by conquest may increase a nuclear power's capability to produce additional strategic weapons. While "raw" manpower is not a significant source of power in the balance of terror, an aggressor may turn to his own uses the scientific brainpower of a conquered nation. On balance, however, the strategic value of territory and its associated assets is probably smaller in the balance of terror than in the tactical balance.

"War potential" is a source of power in the tactical balance not only prior to war but also after the war has begun. Stockpiles of raw materials, standby war production plants and the like can be translated into actual military power during the progress of the war, provided of course that the forces ready in advance of the attack can hold off the enemy until the additional power is mobilized. But in the balance of terror, industrial potential provides only pre-attack power, not post-attack power. Once the war has started, if it is not destroyed, its usefulness probably would be limited to survival and reconstruction.

In the tactical balance, alliances are useful for both deterrence and defense, in roughly equal proportion; if deterrence fails, the costs of war are low enough and the incentives to prevent the conquest of an ally are high enough that allies are likely to see a balance of advantage in coming to each other's aid. Nuclear powers may also find it advantageous to ally themselves for deterrent purposes in the balance of terror, but the alliance's value for defense is likely to be low. For example, two countries which cannot separately muster a minimum second-strike force against the prospective aggressor may be able to do so by combining. But it would be irrational for either to retaliate when the other is attacked unless its own forces plus the undamaged forces of the attacked ally were sufficient to reduce the residual forces of the aggressor to a level which was tolerable for the supporting ally.

However, even if this condition did not hold (in which case the allies would not intend to carry out their obligation) the alliance would still have deterrent value because of the aggressor's uncertainties, and because deterrence does not depend on absolute credibility. A nuclear attack on a single country would be a very momentous act which might stimulate enough emotional reaction and irrationality among the victims' allies to trigger their retaliation. The aggressor would have to realize that the *possible* damage he might suffer at the hands of the whole alliance would be very much higher than the value he placed on conquest of the single victim. The magnitude of the possible retaliatory damage might very well offset in his mind the low credibility of an alliance response. If so, he would have to consider striking simultaneously at all the alliance members; presumably he would be deterred from this move if the alliance could muster a minimum second-strike force with respect to such a simultaneous attack.

A country with a minimum second-strike force might have little interest in alliances even for deterrent purposes if it was confident of being able to maintain such a capability at bearable cost in the face of an aggressor's expansion. But if it lacked such confidence, it might wish to make a deterrent pledge to aid friendly nuclear powers, even though it did not intend to carry out the pledge for lack of an adequate first-strike, counter-force capability.

The Choice between Strategic Deterrence and Tactical Defense

The great dilemma which faces nuclear powers and alliances concerns the degree to which deterrence by threats of nuclear punishment can substitute for a capacity to defend territory with conventional or tactical forces. Or, to put it another way, to what extent can the scope of the balance of terror be enlarged to reduce the burden of maintaining a position in the tactical balance of power?

Since the end of World War II, the United States has used its dominant position in the balance of terror to deter a considerably wider range of contingencies than direct nuclear attack on itself. The *means* of the balance of terror, in other words, have been applied to the furtherance of certain *ends* in the tactical balance of power, notably the deterrence of a large-scale Soviet ground attack in Western Europe. Consequently, in US and Western policy, the scope of the tactical balancing process has shrunk to the deterrence and defense of "limited" aggression, primarily outside Western Europe. The validity of this concept became increasingly questionable after 1953 and 1954, when the Russians exploded a hydrogen bomb and then demonstrated that they had a modern, long-range delivery capability. Disclosures since 1957 have underlined the fact that the Soviets have achieved or are near to achieving a substantial second-strike capability. The logical consequence of these disclosures is to reduce the plausibility of the strategic nuclear threat, for contingencies other than direct nuclear attack on the United States, and to reinstate the tactical balancing process in something approaching its pre-nuclear dimensions.

However, it is a commonplace that world politics do not turn entirely on logic. The balance of terror may not be narrowed to its "pure" form—the deterrence of strategic nuclear war between nuclear powers—when both sides lack a maximum first-strike force. This would be the case only if both sides were omniscient with respect to each other's risk calculations and degree of rationality, and if both actually *were* rational. Since the aggressor can never be sure how the deterrer estimates and costs the consequences of war, or how prone he is to emotionalism and lapses of reason, there may still be some range of major tactical aggressions which can be deterred with fairly high confidence by strategic nuclear threats, even though the deterrer's nuclear forces fall short of a maximum first-strike capability. But what is the limit of this range? Major ground invasion of a country possessing strategic nuclear forces of at least minimum first-strike dimensions probably falls within the range, especially if this country is allied with other nuclear powers. Perhaps security against conventional ground attack against an area, such as Western Europe, which one or more nuclear powers considers "vital," could safely be left to the strategic deterrent. This would mean that tactical forces must be provided for the defense of all countries considered important but not "vital" by the nuclear powers.

The range of enemy moves on the ground which can be left to nuclear deterrence depends on how *effective* the nuclear threat is judged to be, and *how costly* the consequences of the failure of deterrence would be, with respect to each move. The cost would be counted in terms of the expected cost of war if the nuclear forces can defend successfully at acceptable cost; if they cannot (i.e., if the threat is a bluff) the cost would be in the currency of territorial and other values lost in not carrying out the threat. More precisely, the balancing power or alliance must, in some sense, calculate a *product* of the probability of war and the cost of war (appropriately modified to take account of uncertainties and the disutility of gambling at high stakes) and compare this product with a similar product for the alternative of ground defense, after adding to each product the peacetime cost of providing the forces for each alternative. Nuclear deterrence rather than ground defense would be relied on for those contingencies for which the nuclear alternative promised the lesser aggregate of peace-time preparedness cost and "expected cost" in war. The factors involved in such a calculation are highly intangible and immeasurable but some sort of intuitive judgment along these lines is basic.

Interaction between the Strategic and Tactical Balances

If we assume that the strategic nuclear threat may still deter certain major tactical moves by the enemy, certain interactions between the balance of terror and the tactical balancing process within this "intermediate" area are worth noting.

A prominent idea in current NATO strategic doctrine is that although the ground force "shield" in West Germany is insufficient to block a determined Soviet push, it may be considered adequate to make any Soviet gains dependent on a decision to initiate war at a level of violence high enough to implicate the Big Deterrent with significant credibility. The validity of this concept is greater, the larger the strategic counter-force capability available to the West. When strategic forces are large enough, and of such a kind, that they *might* be used in a first strike, the aggressor will be aware of some critical level of violence in the lower-case balance of power which will either signal an objective large enough, or stimulate a sufficient degree of emotion or irrationality in the leadership of the West, to produce an intolerable probability of all-out war.

It would seem that there is an upper limit to the size of ground forces necessary to produce this "trip-wire" or "triggering" effect—a limit which is considerably below the level of tactical forces necessary to hold or defeat the Red Army. Once the shield is at the level at which it produces maximum support for the retaliatory threat (it may be there now) and the West does not have and cannot muster sufficient strategic first-strike capability to make its retaliatory threat plausible, there is little point in further *small* increases in the shield; it must become large enough, at least when supplemented by well-trained ready reserves, to block a full-scale Soviet ground attack. Under these conditions, the utility of tactical means for complementing the strategic threat drops to zero. The security of Western Europe then can no longer be left to the balance of terror, and becomes dependent on the achievement of a tactical balance of power in Europe.

It should be noted that there may be other means, within the context of the balance of terror, which may be substituted in part for a US all-out retaliatory threat which has lost its credibility—notably the creation of nuclear deterrents controlled by the European countries themselves, either independently or on a group basis, and the development of a strategy of limited retaliation by the United States. These alternatives may turn out to be useful or necessary to counter Soviet attempts at nuclear blackmail, even if the Soviets are balanced tactically.

Within this intermediate range of contingencies, where both types of balancing are operative, the balance of terror may also complement the tactical balance. Thus, the US threat to respond with nuclear weapons outside the immediate battle theater in case of new outbreaks of war in Korea and Indochina may operate in Asia to discourage aggressions so blatant that they would raise an uncomfortable probability of the threat being carried out. They might contribute to holding the enemy's force commitment to a level which could be dealt with effectively with the limited conventional forces available.

There is an important interaction to be noted between the *stability* of the strategic balance and the stability of the tactical balance. When the strategic balance is unstable—i.e., when both sides have a substantial first-strike counter-force capability—the tactical balance tends toward stability. Limited aggression will be undertaken with reluctance, and once started, will be carried out and defended against with caution because of the danger that at some point one side or the other will be provoked into striking first at the strategic level. But when the strategic balance is stable —when both sides have the capacity to strike back powerfully after absorbing a first strike—the tactical balance tends to become unstable because limited attacks can be undertaken and limited wars can be carried to fairly high levels of intensity without serious danger that either side will decide to initiate all-out strategic warfare.

I have rather simplified the "real world" in assuming only two balancing systems. It would be more realistic to speak of several systems, each centering on a rather well-defined type of conflict. Ranging from low to high cost, the categories might be non-military "cold war," violent revolutionary conflict within a state in which outside powers participated only with material aid, civil war participated in by "volunteers" from the outside, limited inter-state conventional conflict between organized military forces, "tactical" nuclear warfare in a limited geographical area, limited strategic warfare involving the territories of the superpowers, and finally all-out war or the ultimate balance of terror. Each major contending power would then have in mind several "critical points," each representing the intensity of action at each level which would pose an unacceptable probability that the opponent would cross the boundary into the next or higher levels. The incipient aggressor would then be "balanced" if he could not win his objective at any level without crossing the critical threshold into another balancing system in which he would either lose or suffer unbearable costs. He would not be balanced if there were one or more weak links—i.e., levels of conflict at which he could achieve his goal at acceptable cost without crossing the point of critical risk.

Speaking very generally, the defender can balance at each level in either of two ways: by providing a capacity for effective defense, or by posing a credible prospect to the enemy that in committing enough forces to win he would exceed his critical risk of moving to higher levels. The first method would be the safer, but the more costly in peacetime preparation. To illustrate the second or deterrent method, NATO might provide only enough conventional forces to insure that an attack would trigger tactical nuclear war. The Soviets might still be able to win at the tactical nuclear level, but foresee a high probability that if the conflict reached this stage, it would in turn spiral into limited strategic warfare, which they would consider too costly or too liable to expand to the all-out level. In order for such spiralling to seem reasonably possible to the Soviets, the US (or NATO jointly) would have to have somewhat more than a minimum second-strike deterrent—i.e., somewhat more than the basic requirement for its own security against all-out nuclear attack—but not necessarily a maximum, first-strike force.

Intentions and Capabilities

Nuclear technology has increased the importance of *intentions*, relative to *capabilities*, in the balancing process. Intentions have always been important, of course. In the pre-nuclear balance, the balancing process was set in motion by the perception of the disturber's aggressive intent, as well as by his military capabilities and war potential. And the adequacy of balance as a deterrent rested in part on the aggressor being clear about the intentions of the states which would eventually oppose him. But both sides could be fairly sure that once the conflict was joined, all states which did participate would do so to the full extent of their military power. An important calculation for each side, therefore, concerned the balance of total capabilities.

The relation between total capabilities is still important at the level of the balance of terror—i.e., in the deterrence and fighting of all-out war. But for conflicts beginning at lower levels, the balance between overall capabilities is less important, and a new dimension has been added to the factor of intentions—namely, each side's assessment of the other's intent regarding what portion of its destructive power will be used. Each knows that the other can inflict costs far outweighing the value of any political objective if it cares to do so. Total capabilities establish the bounds of what is possible, but what is probable depends on a reciprocal assessment of wills, which in turn depends on each side's appraisal of the opponent's values at stake in each particular issue, his gambling propensities, his tendencies toward irrationality, his ideological or organizational commitments to certain responses, and his image of one's own characteristics in these respects.

Such estimates are of course highly subjective and uncertain, and the pervasive uncertainty adds an important element of stability to the overall balance of power. Each side is driven to think in terms of probabilities, and when even the smallest military action *may* eventuate in nuclear war and totally unacceptable costs, small probabilities are likely to be important. Consequently, there is considerable deterrent value in making threats which the threatener knows, and the threatened party suspects, would be irrational to carry out; if the threat increases the probability of unacceptable costs to the other side by only a few percentage points, it may be sufficient to deter.

This is to say that the existence of a "balance of power," or the capabilities requirements for balancing, can hardly be determined without attempting to look into the "mind" of the enemy. One might say that a subjective "balance of intentions" has become at least as important as the more objectively calculable "balance of capabilities."

A Concluding Comment

This article has attempted only to touch the high spots of a subject which sorely needs further theoretical analysis. International relations theory must come to terms with the weapons revolution and the logical place to start is with the balance of power concept. I have tried to show that the classical formulation is outmoded as a framework for analysis; that the modern balance of power is a multi-dimensional thing, with each dimension having different characteristics. I have been able to deal with only two broad dimensions here, but I should at least mention a third—the "balance of persuasion" or balance of capabilities to influence the internal politics of other countries—a dimension which Sigmund Neumann has picturesquely described as the "international civil war." Just as the balance of terror is the product of the revolution in weapons, the balance of persuasion is the product of the nationalist revolutions in Asia and Africa and the Soviet attempts to exploit these revolutions for its own ends. There are both supporting and competing interactions between this balance and the two military balances. It is misleading to think of the "balance of power" between the West and the Soviet bloc as a simple one-dimensional relationship in the traditional sense. To do so leads to such errors as believing that nuclear weapons have made industrial potential obsolete as a source of power, or that the criterion for security in the balance of terror is to have as many missiles as the Russians have, or that military forces and alliances are adequate responses to Russian initiative in the "balance of persuasion."

CHAPTER FOUR

Militarism and War

"War ... has at last become impossible, and those who are preparing for war, and basing all their schemes of life on the expectation of war, are visionaries of the worst kind, for war is no longer possible [and] if any attempt were made to demonstrate the inaccuracy of my assertions by putting the matter to a test on a great scale, we should find the inevitable result in a catastrophe which would destroy all existing political organizations."[1] These dramatic conclusions were written in 1899 by a European banker turned military tactician. After devoting years to the study of warfare, Ivan Bloch was convinced that the strategic, economic, and political developments of the preceding decades of the nineteenth century made any future war an impractical military operation. He died in 1902, long before World War I proved the fallacy of his thesis.

Only if we put aside such noble notions as Bloch's and discuss warfare in its proper social-psychological-political frame of reference can we begin to appreciate the significance of warfare in man's political experience. Of some 3,457 years of recorded history there have been 3,230 years of war and only 227 years of peace.[2] Warfare has been a continuous feature of politics, in premodern, inter-state relations as well as internationally. Until recent years, war has generally been acknowledged as "the method actually used for achieving the major political changes of the modern world, the building of nation-states, the expansion of modern civilization throughout the world, and the changing of the dominant interests of that civilization."[3]

[1] Ivan Stanislavovoich Bloch, *The Future of War* (New York: Doubleday and McClure, 1899), pp. ix, xi.
[2] The figures are those of Hanson W. Baldwin, military analyst of *The New York Times*, quoted in Russell Baker, "Observer," *The New York Times*, July 21, 1962, p. 18.
[3] Quincy Wright, *A Study of War* (Chicago: University of Chicago Press, 1942), I, 250.

In the first essay of this chapter, Quincy Wright argues that war should be regarded as but one of several ways that states traditionally use to resolve power conflicts. His hope is that a broader study of conflicts in general may suggest methods that will encourage a more harmonious pattern of activity among competing political groups and thus reduce reliance on coercive or purely physical techniques. "The Nature of Conflict" provides many provocative ideas concerning ways to ease tensions, although the tone of Professor Wright's concluding remarks does not suggest a scholar who is overly optimistic that future wars will be unknown in international relations.

The initial non-Western reading deals with militarism and war from the standpoint of the Chinese experience. For centuries, Europeans returning from the Far East have been tremendously impressed with the antimilitary character of Chinese society. Matteo Ricci, for example, wrote in the seventeenth century that "fighting and violence among the people are practically unheard of . . . On the contrary, one who will not fight and restrains himself from returning a blow is praised for his prudence and bravery." We have already seen in M. Frederick Nelson's article that the political philosophy of Confucianism emphasized the status of the individual in society, obedience according to that status, and the state's reliance on moral example rather than military power. The Chinese literati, confident of the efficacy of these ideas, often mentioned in their writings that "good iron is not used to make a nail nor a good man to make a soldier." Governmental leaders are said to have deplored the use of force to achieve political objectives. In his discussion of Chinese militarism, Kung-chuan Hsiao is representative of those who argue that Confucianism fostered one of the world's least aggressive empires.

Chinese history, on the other hand, is not free from strife and impressive military campaigns, so that a discrepancy exists between the theory and the facts. The military activity and the record of conquests of the Chinese empire are at least as imposing as any found among European states. Kung-chuan Hsiao dismisses too quickly these features in the annals of the Middle Kingdom. A more balanced presentation of the Chinese philosophy of warfare requires an examination of the current dispute among social scientists concerning the role and significance of the military in premodern Chinese civilization. Morton H. Fried "makes no claim to solving or settling the question," but his essay contests a basic belief of many Far Eastern experts that ancient China did not abjure force.[4]

Warfare in early Muslim society was a notably different political institution than it was in China and can be understood only after the concept

---

[4] See also John King Fairbank, *The United States and China*, rev. ed. (Cambridge, Mass.: Harvard University Press, 1958), pp. 50–51.

of the *jihād*, or holy war, has been examined. Orthodox Islamic theology imposed a duty on all free, adult, male followers of the Prophet Muḥammad who were sane of mind, physically healthy, and had sufficient financial resources to engage in a *jihād* whenever one was proclaimed by an *imām* (leader of the people). Those who participated in such campaigns were promised eternal life in paradise. The purpose of the *jihād* was to extend the area of Islam and so transform the *dār ul ḥarb* into the *dār ul Islam.*

The Western nation-state system has not known a comparable attitude toward warfare, although the Marxist theory of an ultimate Communist world does contain a number of features analogous to Muslim universalism. Majid Khadduri's article "The Islamic Philosophy of War" discusses first the classical importance of the military doctrines that governed Islam's relations with non-Muslim countries and then goes on to show how the doctrines were modified after the power of Islam declined. The Muslims' belabored modification of the *jihād* concept also serves to introduce the last selection in the chapter, Major General Nikolai Talensky's remarks concerning the Soviet philosophy of war.

The awful havoc and frightful destruction that would result from the first few hours of a full-scale missile war have been commented upon repeatedly by Western publicists; General Talensky's article was among the first public indications that Russian strategists appreciated the impossibility of a conflict between the United States and the Soviet Union. Kremlinologists considered it especially significant because the Communists, on a number of occasions, have said that a war between the blocs of states that form the two antagonistic social systems was inevitable. Faced with the realities of power politics in the Age of Missiles, Soviet military strategists seemed to be revising a time-honored, major tenet of Communist theory. Clausewitz's admonition that warfare is the continuance of state policy by other means no longer seemed a tenable position. In his article, General Talensky states that "the development of the technique of exterminating people has resulted in a situation that makes it impossible to resort to war to solve political disputes as was done throughout the history of mankind."

Is history—once again—beginning to repeat itself? As Professor Khadduri points out, after being confronted by superior military strength from the Western states, "Muslim publicists seem to have tacitly admitted that in principle the *jihād* as a permanent war had become obsolete; it was no longer compatible with Muslim interests." Perhaps modern warfare has affected the East-West struggle in an equally significant manner so that a *détente*, similar to the one that took place between the European states and the Muslim community, already has begun.

THE NATURE OF CONFLICT*

Quincy Wright

War is a species of conflict; consequently, by understanding conflict we may learn about the probable characteristics of war under different conditions and the methods most suitable for regulating, preventing, and winning wars.

In the legal sense, war has been considered a situation during which two or more political groups are equally entitled to settle conflicts by armed force. Its essence is the legal equality of the parties and the obligations of impartial neutrality by outsiders. In this sense, the Kellogg-Briand Pact and the United Nations Charter have eliminated war. Procedures have been established to determine who is the aggressor if hostilities occur, and all states have bound themselves not to be neutral but to assist the victim of aggression and to give no aid to the aggressor.

In the sociological sense, which is the sense of ordinary usage, war refers to conflicts among political groups carried on by armed forces of considerable magnitude. The street fight of two small boys, the forensic contention in a law court, the military suppression of mob violence in the state, the collision of two automobiles, and the combat of two stags are not war; but they are conflict. Perhaps an analysis of the broader concept will help better to understand the lesser.

Conflict and Inconsistency

Conflict is sometimes used to refer to inconsistencies in the motions, sentiments, purposes, or claims of entities, and sometimes to the process of resolving these inconsistencies. . . . The two meanings are not necessarily identical, because inconsistent systems of thought and action may coexist in different places for long periods of time. However, as contacts increase

* Quincy Wright, "The Nature of Conflict," *The Western Political Quarterly*, IV, No. 2 (June 1951), 193–209. Reprinted by permission. Mr. Wright is Professor Emeritus of International Relations, University of Chicago, and Professor of International Relations, University of Virginia. He is author of *A Study of War* (1942), *Problems of Stability and Progress in International Relations* (1954), and *Study of International Relations* (1955).

and the world shrinks under the influence of new inventions, such inconsistencies tend to generate processes of reconciliation or supersession and thus to constitute conflict in the second sense of the term.

The word conflict is derived from the Latin word *confligere*, meaning to strike together. Originally, it had a physical rather than moral connotation, though the English word has both. In the physical sense of two or more different things moving to occupy the same space at the same time, the logical inconsistency and the process of solution are identical. For example, the logical inconsistency of two billiard balls being in the same place at the same time is resolved by the conflict which results in their rolling to different positions.

In an analysis of conflict, as used in the sociological sense and, in accord with the etymology of the word, it seems best to limit its meaning to situations where there is an actual or potential process for solving the inconsistency. Where there is no such process, conflict does not seem to be the proper word. If used to describe mere differences or inconsistencies in societies or value systems, it may induce the belief that peaceful coexistence is impossible. Where such differences have existed violent conflict has sometimes been precipitated when none was necessary. An example may, perhaps, illustrate this terminological distinction. Islam began a career of conquest in the seventh century with the thesis that it was the only true faith and was necessarily in conflict with all other religions. This was represented by the doctrine of the *Jihad*, or perpetual war of the "world of Islam" with the "world of war." According to Majid Khadduri,

> The world of war constituted all the states and communities outside the world of Islam. Its inhabitants were usually called infidels, or better termed, unbelievers. In theory the believers were always at war with the unbelievers.

Belief in the *Jihad* induced continuous attacks by the Arabs upon the decadent Roman Empire and rising Christendom during the seventh and eighth centuries, and resulted in extensive Moslem conquests in the Near East, North Africa, and Spain. Christendom, however, reacted militantly in the Crusades of the eleventh, twelfth, and thirteenth centuries, turning on Islam with the doctrine of papal sovereignty of the world. The Ottoman Turks then took the leadership of Islam, and during the fifteenth, sixteenth, and seventeenth centuries were almost continuously at war with Christian Europe, conquering Constantinople, the Balkans, and Hungary, as well as most of the Arab countries. Turkish power then waned, and eventually the Ottoman Empire broke up into national states as did the Holy Roman Empire. Today Christian and Moslem states coexist and cooperate in the United Nations. Both the *Jihad* and the Crusades are things of the past. When, as a political measure, the Ottoman sultan, after entering World War I on the German side, proclaimed the *Jihad* on November 16, 1941, his action was repudiated by the Arab leader, Hussein Ibn Ali, of Mecca, who had entered the war on the Allied side.

Similarly, the identification of religious differences with conflict led to a century and a half of war between Protestants and Catholics in the sixteenth and seventeenth centuries, ended by the Peace of Westphalia which recognized the sovereignty of territorial states and the authority of the temporal monarch to determine the religion of his people if he wished. Since then Protestant and Catholic states have found it possible to coexist peacefully.

These bits of history suggest the question whether the inconsistency of democracy and communism makes conflict between the Western and the Soviet states inescapable. May it not be possible for communist and democratic states to coexist, even in this technologically shrinking world, as do Moslem and Christian states, Protestant and Catholic states? The answer may depend on the policy pursued by the governments or other regulatory agencies, rather than on the ideologies themselves. In 1858 Lincoln thought that, "A house divided against itself cannot stand. A government cannot endure permanently half-slave and half-free." Three years later, however, in his first Inaugural, he asserted that he had "no purpose, directly or indirectly, to interfere with the institution of slavery in the States where it exists. In your hands, my dissatisfied fellow citizens, and not in mine," he said, "is the momentous issue of civil war. The government will not assail you. You can have no conflict without being yourself the aggressor." Coexistence in the Union of diverse institutions of North and South then seemed to him possible. The Civil War occurred, and eventually emancipation was proclaimed. Some historians, however, think that emancipation could have been achieved peacefully if war had been avoided for ten years longer. They are not certain that "the inevitable conflict" really was inevitable.

Historically, radical differences of religion, ideology, or institutions have tended to induce conflict. They do not, however, necessarily do so, nor does conflict if it occurs necessarily eliminate the differences. Consequently, it is unwise to identify inconsistencies of opinion with conflict. Coexistence of inconsistent opinions may, in fact, be an essential condition of human progress. It is through the contact and competition of differing opinions and methods, and the eventual synthesis of thesis and antithesis that history is created.

Conflict and Tension

It depends on the policies of governments whether inconsistencies of social ideologies develop into conflicts, but these policies are likely to be influenced by the amount of social tension which the inconsistencies have generated. Social tension has been defined as the condition which arises from inconsistencies among initiatives in the structure of a society. Ideologies accepted by different groups within a society may be inconsistent without creating tension; but if initiatives or actions are taken by individuals or groups in accord with those inconsistent ideologies, and if these actions lead to contact, tension arises. The degree of intensity of tension tends to increase with decreases in the social distance between the groups and with increases in the amount of energy behind them. If the groups with inconsistent ideologies are in close contact, that is, if the society is closely integrated, the tension will be great. If the society is loose (as was, for example, the world society during the nineteenth century) such initiatives originating in different and widely separated nations may create little tension. It is also true that if the groups or nations within the society from which the inconsistent initiatives emerge are small and weak, tension will be less than if they are great and powerful. In the present world of decreasing social distances, initiatives emerging from such different and inconsistent ideologies as democracy and communism, respectively supported by such great powers as the United States and the Soviet Union, can be expected to cause great tension.

Tension is more likely to develop into violent conflict if it is intense and if regulatory arrangements are ineffective. The United Nations is a more effective regulatory arrangement than was the system of diplomacy of the nineteenth century, but tensions are so much greater today that serious conflict is more probable. Once conflict develops, the process by which anxiety and power accumulate in each of the conflicting groups tends to result in war.

The phenomena of inconsistency, tension, conflict, and war within a society may thus be considered distinct, but they constitute a series in which each succeeding term includes those that precede. In war, each inconsistent value system has integrated itself in order to maintain its position against the other; tensions have risen, the situation is recognized as conflict, and open violence is used or projected. Relations of logical inconsistency in social ideas or institutions are likely to generate tension, which in turn leads to conflict and frequently to war.

However, this progress is not inevitable. Social inconsistencies can coexist without tension, and tension can exist for a long time without conflict, just as conflict may be resolved without war. If regulatory procedures such as diplomacy, mediation, conciliation, consultation, arbitration, and adjudication are available and efficiently operated, then accommodation, adjustment, and settlement may be achieved at any point and the process stopped. If, however, tensions rise above a certain level, these procedures are likely to prove ineffective.

Conflict and Competition

Conflict, defined as opposition among social entities directed against one another, is distinguished from *competition* defined as opposition among social entities independently striving for something of which the supply is inadequate to satisfy all. Competitors may not be aware of one another, while the parties to a conflict are. *Rivalry,* half-way between, refers to opposition among social entities which recognize one another as competitors. Conflict, rivalry, and competition are all species of *opposition,* which has been defined as a process by which social entities function in the disservice of one another. Opposition is thus contrasted with *co-operation,* the process by which social entities function in the service of one another.

These definitions are introduced because it is important to emphasize that competition between organisms is inevitable in a world of limited resources, but conflict is not; although conflict in some form—not necessarily violent—is very likely to occur, and is probably an essential and desirable element of human societies.

Many authors have argued for the inevitability of war from the premises of Darwinian evolution—the struggle for existence among organic species from which only the fittest survive. In the main, however, this struggle of nature, is competition, not conflict. *Lethal* conflict among individuals or groups of animals *of the same species* is rare. Birds and some mammals monopolize nesting and feeding areas during the mating season and fight off intruders of the same species. Males of such polygamous species as seals, deer, and horses fight other males to maintain their harems. Social animals, such as monkeys and cattle, fight to win or maintain leadership of the group. The struggle for existence occurs not in such combats, but in the competition among herbivorous animals for limited grazing areas, and for the occupancy of areas free from carnivorous animals; and in the competition among carnivorous animals for the limited supply of herbivorous animals on which they prey. Those who fail in this competition starve to death or become victims, not of attack by their own, but by other species. The lethal aspect of the struggle for existence does not resemble human war, but rather the business of slaughtering animals for food, and the competition of individuals for jobs, markets, and materials. The essence of the struggle is the competition for the necessities of life that are insufficient to satisfy all.

Among nations there is competition in developing resources, trades, skills, and a satisfactory way of life. The successful nations grow and prosper; the unsuccessful decline. It is true that, because nations are geographically circumscribed and immovable, this competition may induce efforts to expand territory at the expense of others, and thus lead to conflict. This, however, is a product of civilization. Wars of territorial conquest and economic aggrandizement do not occur among animals of the same species or among the most primitive peoples. They are consequences of large-scale political and military organization and of legal relations defining property and territory. Even under conditions of civilization, however, it cannot be said that war-like conflict among nations is inevitable, although competition is.

Conflict and Cooperation

Lethal conflict among individuals or groups of the same species, or war in a very general sense, is not a necessary factor of either animal or human life. Most psychologists seem to be in agreement on this. However, opposition—both in the sense of conflict and of competition—is a necessary factor of human society no less important than cooperation. A society has been defined as a group manifesting sufficient cooperation internally and sufficient opposition externally to be recognizable as a unity. This definition raises the question: Can there be a *world* society unless contact is made with societies in some other planet to which it can be opposed? It is perhaps premature to say there cannot be a society existing without external opposition and manifesting itself only by the cooperation of its members to achieve common ends. It would be difficult to discover such an isolated society among either primitive or civilized peoples; but, even in such an isolated society, there would be internal opposition because a society implies that its members have interests of their own as well as common interests, and in these individual interests they not only compete but also, on occasions, conflict. . . .

Types of Conflict

As already noted, conflict can take place among different sorts of entities. *Physical conflict* by which two or more entities try to occupy the same space at the same time must be distinguished from *political conflict* by which a group tries to impose its policy on others. These two types of conflict can be distinguished from *ideological conflicts* in which systems of thought or of values struggle with each other, and from *legal conflicts* in which controversies over claims or demands are adjusted by mutually recognized procedures.

War in the legal sense has been characterized by the union of all four types of conflict. It is manifested by the physical struggle of armies to occupy the same space, each seeking to annihilate, disarm, or capture the other; by the political struggle of nations to achieve policies against the resistance of others; by the ideological struggle of peoples to preserve or extend ways of life and value systems; and by the legal struggle of states to acquire titles, to vindicate claims, to prevent violence, or to punish offenses by recognized procedures of regulated violence.

Is this identification of different sorts of conflict in a single procedure expedient? Might it not be wiser to deal with legal conflicts by adjudication; ideological conflicts by information, education, and persuasion; political conflicts by negotiation or appeal to international agencies, such as the United Nations Security Council or the General Assembly, leaving to war only resistance to armed aggression? Such discrimination is the objective of the United Nations, as it was of the League of Nations before it, the Hague system before that, and of customary international law even earlier. Practice has indicated that such a segregation of the aspects of conflict is difficult to achieve, but the effort should nevertheless be made.

Tendency of Conflict

It has been emphasized by Clausewitz that there is a tendency for conflict to become war, and for war to become total and absolute in proportion as the parties are equal in power and determination, and are unaffected by outside influences. This tendency has four aspects—the unification of policy, the garrison state, total war, and the bipolar world.

The legal claims of the state come to be conceived as inherent in the value system and way of life of the people. These claims come to be formulated as national policy, and armed forces are developed as the only certain means of achieving this policy. Policy in the legal, moral, political, and military field becomes integrated at the national level.

This integration of policy, and of military preparation to maintain it, tends to integrate the state. Public opinion and moral values, as well as economic life and the maintenance of law and order, are placed under central authority; institutions of deliberation, freedom in the formulation and expression of opinion and the exercise of individual rights, are subordinated to the demands of national policy, of military preparation, and of national loyalty. The garrison or totalitarian state emerges in which the individual is in a large measure subordinated to the group.

In such unification of the state, restraints on war tend to be abandoned. These restraints have existed because of the presence of religious, moral, aesthetic, economic, and legal opinions and interests that are independent of the government and have been influenced by similar opinions in outside countries. Once all elements of the state are united behind the national policy and the effort to achieve that policy by war, internal and external influences for moderation cannot penetrate the crust of the gigantic war machine in motion. War becomes unrestrained and total.

Integration, however, does not stop with the nation, since alliances and coalitions are formed until the entire world is drawn in on one side or the other. Absolute war is fought in a bipolar world. There are no neutrals, and the forces of the world concentrated at two strategic centers lunge at each other in unrestrained fury, each demanding total victory and the annihilation or unconditional surrender of the enemy.

This expansion of war is in fact but an aspect of the movement of conflict from the individual mind. The Constitution of UNESCO declares that wars begin in the minds of men. The psychologists assert that conflict in the individual mind is a human trait. Instead of the simple sensory-motor circuit of animals, whereby a stimulus of the senses at once induces appropriate action developed in the instincts or the experience of the animal, the circuit is interrupted in man at the seat of consciousness in the brain. Here ideal alternatives of action are set against one another, their advantages considered, and eventually a decision is made and action proceeds on the chosen course. Sometimes, however, decision fails; and the indecision gives rise to ambivalence, especially when each of the conflicting alternatives is highly charged emotionally. Such conditions are characteristic of the child who loves his mother as the source of his material comforts and yet, at the same time, hates her because she disciplines him to teach him the requirements of social life. To escape this ambivalence the child displaces his hatred upon a scapegoat—perhaps the father, perhaps a neighbor's child; but the habit of displacement to solve apparently insoluble conflicts is established. As the child becomes an adult in a local group he tends to find a scapegoat outside the group so that all can be harmony within. So with consciousness of the nation, all citizens displace their hatreds and animosities upon an external enemy who conveniently serves as scapegoat. Similarly when coalitions are formed their maintenance depends in no small degree upon displacement of all sources of conflict among the allies upon the enemy. While the United States and Russia were desperately fighting the Axis, they could displace the hatreds causing differences among them on the common enemy.

The mechanism of displacement tends to enlarge all conflicts from the individual mind to the bipolar world, and the mechanism of projection tends to augment the vigor of these conflicts. Once group conflict develops, each group is stimulated by its anxieties about the other group to build its armaments and to prepare for stategic action. Its own preoccupation about the favorable conditions of attack is projected upon its antagonist. It sees every move of that antagonist as preparation for attack. This stimulates its own preparation. The enemy similarly projects his own aggressive dispositions, armaments mount, and eventually war emerges.

The tendency toward the expansion and intensification of war is further developed by the rational pursuit of balance of power politics. Each of two rivaling great nations seeks allies to maintain the balance, and smaller nations seek protection of one or other of the great. The number of uncommitted powers declines. Finally, all power in the world is gathered about one or the other pole. Once the world is bipolarized, each center of power anticipates war and begins to calculate the influence that time is having on its relative power position. There is a strong urge for the power against which time is running to start the fight. This may entail risk, but the risk may be greater if hostilities are postponed. Thus, psychological and political factors conspire to extend, enlarge, and integrate conflicts, and to precipitate war.

Methods of Conflict

Conflict may be carried on by methods of coercion or persuasion. The former usually involves violence and has the character of physical conflict; the latter need not involve violence, though violence may be utilized as a method of persuasion, and is characteristic of political, ideological, and legal conflict.

In employing purely coercive or physical methods of conflict, each party may seek to destroy the other, to control him, or to occupy his territory. In war, the destruction or disorganization of the enemy's armed forces, communications, and sources of supply; the capture of his materiel and the imprisonment of the personnel of his forces; and the driving of the enemy from strategic points or from productive territory and the occupation of that territory are operations of this character, constituting what may be called the military front in war. These methods are also used by governments in conflict with criminals and by international organizations in operations of collective security.

Noncoercive or moral methods of conflict involve efforts by each party to isolate the other, to persuade him to change his policy, ideology, or claims, or to defeat him in accordance with the rules of the game. In war successful efforts to cut off the enemy's external trade and communications, to create an opinion opposed to him in other countries and governments, and to deprive him of allies, make for his isolation. Such efforts constitute the economic and diplomatic fronts in the war. Military methods may also contribute to such isolation—such as naval blockade and the destruction of the instruments of external trade and communication.

Persuasion may be conducted by propaganda utilizing symbols to influence the minds of the enemy's armed forces, his government and his civilian population. In war, propaganda constitutes the psychological front. Persuasion is, of course, used in many types of conflict other than war, such as diplomatic conversations, political campaigns, and parliamentary debates.

In a certain sense, however, all methods of war, unless the total destruction of the enemy's population as well as his power is contemplated, are aimed to persuade the enemy's population and government. The object of war is the complete submission of the enemy. It is assumed that military methods aimed to destroy or control his armed forces and occupy his territories, economic measures designed to starve his population and reduce his resources, and diplomatic measures designed to destroy his hope of relief or support will, when sufficient, induce the enemy government and population to change their minds and submit to whatever terms are demanded.

Defeat means formal abandonment of effort by the losing party to the conflict. It implies that all parties to the conflict have accepted certain rules and criteria by which victor and vanquished can be determined. In games such as chess, bridge, football, and tennis defeat is thus conventionalized, although in some, such as football, the conventions may permit coercive methods resembling war, but with less violence. Chess is a highly conventionalized war in which available forces, strategies, and tactics are strictly regulated by the rules. War itself may have a conventional character. Rules of war may prohibit certain kinds of action, and custom may even decree that forces or fortified places ought to surrender in certain circumstances even though such action is not physically necessary. War among primitive peoples often has a highly conventional character not unlike a game; and in the wars of the *Condottiere* in fifteenth-century Italy and the sieges of the eighteenth century, war was highly conventionalized in Europe and regulated so as to moderate losses. In most wars, the formalities of surrender instruments, armistices, and peace treaties register defeat and victory symbolically, usually after the application of military, economic, diplomatic, and psychological methods have persuaded one side that further resistance is hopeless. The degree of formality, regulation, and symbolic representation in conflicts varies greatly from games to total war. However, the extent to which war has been conventionalized at certain periods indicates possibilities of limitation and avoidance of the trend toward absolute war by means of rational considerations and suitable social organization.

Under suitable conditions, war might be decided by highly intelligent generals without any bloodshed. Each would calculate the best utilization of materials and manpower, the best strategy and maneuvers of armed forces both for himself and the enemy, each assuming—as in playing a game of chess—that the other would similarly calculate and would follow the plan most in his own interest. According to such calculations, victory for one side and defeat for the other might be certain, and the defeated would surrender without any hostilities. However, it is highly improbable that war will ever be so conventionalized that incalculable factors like courage, morale, faulty intelligence, accidents of weather, and new inventions can be eliminated. The party whose defeat seems certain by logical calculations may yet believe it can win because of these factors, and so will not surrender without a trial of strength unless indeed the disparity in strength is very great as in interventions by a great power in the territory of a very weak power. In the course of time, such disparity may be presented by the United Nations in its operations of collective security or international policing; but, as the Korean episode indicates, the United Nations cannot yet be certain of overwhelming power against a dissident member. Even national federations cannot always muster sufficient power to discourage rebellion, in which case their policing operations assume the character of war—as witness the American Civil War.

Consideration of the variety of methods by which conflict is conducted suggests that appraisal of national power or capacity to win wars cannot be based on any simple analysis. Capacity to win allies and persuade enemy and neutral opinion by propaganda is no less important than capacity to create a powerful war potential including the command of large armed forces. Capacity to invent and to produce, which depends upon a high development of science and technology, is no less important than capacity to plan the strategy of campaigns and tactics of battle. Perhaps most important in statecraft is the capacity to analyze conflicts, to distinguish the important from the unimportant aspects, to view the world as a whole, to appreciate the influence of time and opinion, and to synthesize this knowledge in order to forward the interests of the nation and of the world without resort to violent methods, which often destroy more than they create and which settle fewer conflicts than they initiate.

Solution of Conflicts

None of the methods by which conflict is carried on necessarily ends the conflict—unless, indeed, the conflict is completely conventionalized as in a game. Even total defeat in war may not remove the causes of conflict, and after a time the defeated may revive and renew the conflict.

A conflict is solved by *definitive acceptance* of a decision by *all* parties. In physical conflicts where all but one party are totally destroyed such decisions may be absolute; but if the conflict concerns ideas, policies, or claims, the words "definitive," "acceptance," and "all" have to be taken relatively. The rejected ideas, policies, or claims may be presented again. A decision may be accepted in a different sense by different parties. Finally, the direct parties to a controversy may not be the only parties interested. In the modern situation of wide spread interdependence and general vulnerability to military and propaganda attacks from distant points, solutions of a dispute may not stand unless accepted by many states and groups in addition to the formal litigants. . . .

There are four ways in which social conflicts can be relatively solved: (1) by negotiation and agreement resulting in settlement or adjustment in accord with the will of all the parties; (2) by adjudication and decision in accord with the will, perhaps guided by legal or moral principles, of an outside party; (3) by dictation or decision in accordance with the will of one party to the conflict; and (4) by obsolescence through agreement to disagree which may in time, as new issues arise, sink the conflict into oblivion and result in a settlement according to the will of no one. It may be that while negotiation and obsolescence are least likely to result in speedy and definitive decisions, yet, for that very reason, they may be most suitable for dealing with controversy among the nations and alliances of the international community. In practice, settlement by dictation usually involves violence; and while it brings about social change and settles some conflicts, at least for the time, it is likely to precipitate new ones. Adjudication in the form of arbitration and judicial settlement has been used in international affairs; but has, on the whole, proved capable of settling only controversies in which both parties base their claims on formal principles of law and in which vital interests, such as national power and survival, and policies supported by widespread and intense public opinion, were only slightly involved.

With these considerations in mind, it is well for those responsible for the foreign policy of a nation in the presence of any conflict to ask in what degree decision is desirable, and to adjust the methods employed to conclusions on that point.

Conflict and Civilization

This discussion should indicate that conflict is a complicated subject and presents complicated problems to individuals, group leaders, and statesmen. Conflict is related to competition and to cooperation, but differs from both. There are many types of conflict—physical, political, ideological, and legal—but there is a tendency for conflict to become total and absolute, and to split the community of nations into halves which would destroy one another in absolute war. The shrinking of the modern world under the influence of new means of communication and transport, and the increasingly destructive methods of warfare culminating in the airborne atomic bomb, have augmented this tendency, and have made war ominous for the future of civilization.

Conflict is carried on by many methods—coercive and noncoercive—and there are various procedures for settling conflicts; but among large groups no final decision of most conflicts is likely to be absolute, and it is perhaps undesirable that it should be.

It may be suggested that all champions of civilization, particularly of the American type should earnestly and hopefully search for means to obstruct the natural tendency of conflict under present-day conditions to integrate policies, to centralize authority both geographically and functionally, to bipolarize the world, and to precipitate absolute war between the poles. It is difficult to question the existence of that tendency manifested in two world wars and in the present "cold war." It is possible to describe the psychological, technological, sociological, and political factors which account for this tendency, but it is difficult to stem the tide. Nevertheless, the effort to do so is called for by our culture and may be required for the salvation of our civilization. It is worth recalling that, when faced by conditions resembling those of today, most civilizations have begun a fatal decline ending in death to be followed, after a period of dark ages, by a new civilization. Since our civilization, differing from others, is worldwide, and therefore without the roots of new civilizations on its periphery, the situation may be more ominous.

The object of such efforts should be to diffuse conflicts by increasing the number of centers of initiative. Overcentralization is dangerous. Many small conflicts are less serious than one great conflict. . . .

It may also be that a zone of states manifesting different patterns of nationalism, and reluctant to follow blindly, the leadership either of the United States or of the Soviet Union can in time establish third, fourth, and fifth forces in the world thus multiplying centers of initiative between the two great poles and providing the conditions for a more stable equilibrium of power and a more effective international organization.

Conflicts can perhaps be analyzed and certain of their aspects dealt with by nonviolent methods, thus weakening some of the urge toward unified policies and total war. Perhaps, also, a more careful examination of the roots of social and political conflict in the individual mind will suggest methods of education in personal decision-making which, when widely practiced, will moderate the tendency to displace hatreds and project aggressive impulses upon scapegoats. Such education of the kind attempted by UNESCO, but up to this time rather ineffectively, might reduce the ultimate springs from which great conflicts arise.

Undoubtedly wider appreciation of the complexity of most international conflicts, of the inevitability and desirability of some conflict in the world, of the value of a broad spirit of toleration in our complex world, and of the possibilities of coexistence of divergent cultures, systems, ideologies, and policies, may offer effective obstacles to the development of the fatal tendency toward a new world war.

THE CHINESE PHILOSOPHY OF WAR: THE TRADITIONALISTS' ARGUMENTS*

Kung-chuan Hsiao

China had no knowledge of international law and international relations, in their strictly modern sense, until the latter part of the nineteenth century. But, long before that time, she had developed independently a conception of international relations which is at once humanitarian in its sentiment and peaceful in its intention. She had produced no Vasquez, nor Ayala, nor Grotius to define the rights of war between states, but she had produced enough sages to discover the great truth that it never pays, and it is never right to wage a war of aggression against any state. The best exponents of this truth are to be found in the Confucian and Mohist schools, although all ancient thinkers... upheld the ideal of universal peace.

... the conception of international war found no place in Confucian political philosophy. The Confucians taught a doctrine of universal love and regarded virtue and benevolence as the fundamental principles of all good government. A virtuous king could rectify the mind and win the hearts of the people entirely through the influences of education or his own ex-

* Kung-chuan Hsiao, *China's Contribution to World Peace* (Chungking, China: China Institute of Pacific Relations, 1945), pp. 35–41, China Council Series No. 1. Reprinted by permission of the publisher, Institute of Pacific Relations. Kung-chuan Hsiao is Former Professor of Political Science, Nankai University, Tientsin, and Former Professor of Political Science, Yenching University, Chengtu. He is author of *Political Pluralism* (1927), *History of Chinese Political Theory,* and *China's Contribution to World Peace* (1945).

emplary conduct. So great was the moral force thus exerted that even persons living in the remotest regions would willingly place themselves under his rule. The use of force and compulsion was necessary only when some persons proved themselves incorrigible. This necessity, however, was created not by a failure of governance, but by a defect in the natural endowment of these persons. For men, according to Confucius, were unequal in their individual capacities. Those above the average could comprehend the higher values of life, whereas those below the average could never appreciate them. The former needed little instruction, whereas the latter were not amenable to it at all. Education had its greatest influence upon those who stood between these two extremes, and compulsion was the only effective means of preventing the incorrigibles from wrong doing. Criminal punishment, therefore, was an indispensable auxiliary method of government. It was to be employed sparingly, but it could not be dispensed with.

Like private individuals, the ruler of a state or the head of a feudal house could be bad beyond moral persuasion. But as such an offender could not be punished like a private individual, it was the proper function of the emperor to send a punitive force to the state or house concerned to deal out imperial justice. The *Chou Li* [*Constitution of Chou*] enumerates nine circumstances under which such an expedition should be made, one of these being "injuring the virtuous and harming the people." We can easily see that a war in this sense is no war at all; it is, as the *Sayings of the States* puts it, "an extensive punishment employing armor and weapons."

But even this sort of war should be avoided whenever peaceful means were available. For instance, an ancient chronicler recorded in the third section of the *Book of History* that the Sage-Emperor Yü led a punitive force against Yu Miao, the chieftain who refused to obey imperial commands and acted contrary to reason and virtue. After an ineffective siege of thirty days, Yü took the wise counsel of one of his ministers and withdrew his army. The emperor then spread far and wide his enlightened virtue; in three score and ten days the Yu Miao went to the imperial court and paid their homage! Indeed, so confident were the Confucians of the efficacy of moral force that some of them went so far as to hold that when a virtuous ruler had to resort to force, his very virtue would paradoxically render the actual use of force unnecessary. Mencius, for one, believed that "a human-hearted king was without opponents." The explanation is not far to seek. For when a benevolent king sent a punitive expedition against some tyrannical ruler, the oppressed people would certainly be very happy to welcome their liberators and refuse to fight them.

It would not be a mistake, therefore, to hold that the Confucians were pacifists, not merely because they were opposed to war, but because they never recognized the right and necessity of war. Or, to state it more precisely, they never had the conception of war in the true sense of the word.

But living in an age when incessant wars of annexation broke out all over the country, the Confucians could not refrain from voicing their condemnation of such acts of violence. Confucius himself was unequivocal in this condemnation. Duke Ling of Wei once indicated his wish to learn from Confucius the art of arranging soldiers in battle. Confucius replied curtly that he had heard of the peaceful and ceremonial meetings between states, but he had never made a study of matters concerning the army. Mencius echoed this condemnation, but in a more severe tone. "When two states went to war in contending for a piece of land," he said, "the men killed in battle covered the fields; when they went to war in contending for a city, the men killed in battle filled up the city. That was tantamount to devouring human flesh in a thirsty pursuit of land. Death is hardly an adequate punishment for such a crime. Therefore those who are expert in waging wars should justly suffer the penalty of death."

While Mencius vehemently denounced aggressive war on moral grounds, Mo Tzǔ condemned it unconditionally on utilitarian principles. Mo Tzǔ endeavored to make it clear that war is a risky business which never pays its cost. The following passage is typical. "Suppose," he said, "soldier hosts arise. If it is in winter it will be too cold, and if in summer it will be too hot. So it should be done neither in winter nor in summer. But if it is in spring it will take people away from sowing and planting, and if in fall it will take them away from reaping and harvesting. Should they be taken away in any of these seasons, innumerable people would die of hunger and cold. And, when the army sets out, the bamboo, arrows, plumed standards, house tents, armor, shields and sword hilts will break and rot in innumerable quantities and never come back. Again with the spears, lances, swords, poniards, chariots and carts: these will break and rot in innumerable quantities and never come back. Innumerable horses and oxen will start out fat and come back lean, or will die and never come back at all. And innumerable people will die because their food will be cut off and cannot be supplied on account of the great distance of the roads, while other innumerable people will get sick and die from constant danger, the irregularities of eating and drinking, and the extremes of hunger and over-eating. Then the army will be lost in large numbers or in its entirety; in either case the number will be innumerable." If it is argued that war brings fame and additional possessions to the conqueror, Mo Tzǔ's retort is "when we consider the victory as such, there is nothing useful about it. When we consider the possessions obtained through it, it does not even make up for what has been lost."

Mo Tzŭ, too, sometimes appealed to moral principles. In one of the chapters of the *Mo Tzŭ*, we encounter the following story: Kung Shu Pan, a noted mechanical inventor of the time, had completed the construction of Cloud-ladders (*Yün-t'i*) for the state of Ch'u, and was going to attack Sung with them. Mo Tzŭ heard of it and set out from Lu, arriving at the capital of Ch'u after a journey of ten days and nights. When he saw Kung Shu Pan, the following conversation ensued:

> Kung Shu Pan inquired: "What is your pleasure, Sir?"
>
> Mo Tzŭ replied: "Some one in the North had insulted your humble servant. I wish to procure your assistance to kill him."
>
> Seeing that Kung Shu Pan was offended by this request, Mo Tzŭ said: "Allow me to offer you ten pieces of gold."
>
> Kung Shu Pan declared: "My principles forbid me to commit an act of homicide."
>
> Mo Tzŭ rose, bowing twice and said: "Permit me to explain. I heard in the North that you have constructed Cloud-ladders and are going to attack Sung with them. Has Sung done any wrong at all? Moreover, the state of Ch'u possesses land in excess and is deficient in population. Now to sacrifice what is insufficient in mortal contest for what is already superfluous can hardly be regarded as wise. To attack a state which has done no wrong can hardly be said to conform to the principle of benevolence. Failure to protest against the injustice of this action can hardly be regarded as loyal (to your sovereign). To protest without success can hardly be regarded as firm (in your will). Your principles forbid you to kill one man but allow you to slaughter whole armies; this can hardly be regarded as conversant with the logic of analogy."
>
> Kung Shu Pan was thus convinced of his mistake, and the two agreed to bring the matter up to the king.
>
> Mo Tzŭ said: "Suppose there is a man who abandons his own richly adorned carriage and desires to steal the shabby wagon of his neighbor, who relinquishes his own elegant bestments and desires to steal the coarse jacket of his neighbor, and who foregoes his own tasty fare of millet and meat and desires to steal the unpalatable food of his neighbor, what sort of fellow would this man be?"
>
> The King replied: "Surely he must be a person with a pathological tendency toward stealing."
>
> Mo Tzŭ said: "Well, the territory of Ch'u measures five thousand *li*, whereas that of Sung a mere five hundred. These remind me of the ornamented carriage and the shabby wagon. Ch'u has the marshes of Yün-meng, full of valuable animals such as the rhinoceros and the deer; she is in possession of rivers Kiang and Han, in which fishes, turtles and alligators abound. It is one of the wealthiest of states under the sun. Sung does not even have pheasants, hares and silver carps. These remind me of the tasty fare and the unpalatable food. Ch'u has all sorts of useful trees, pine, catalpa, *nan-mu,* and camphora. Sung has no tall trees at all. These remind me of the elegant vestments and coarse jacket. In short, your humble servant is of the opinion that in deciding to attack Sung, Your Majesty bears a close resemblance to the above-mentioned person."

Numerous other instances may be cited, but the above suffice to show the pacifist tendency of ancient Chinese political philosophy. Later writers inherited this tradition and the Chinese people in general, consciously or unknowingly accepting the teachings of their ancient instructors, have become one of the most peace-loving peoples of the world. . . .

But we must not think that the Chinese idea of peace is merely passive or negative. Far from it. For behind the anti-war theories of the Confucians and Mohists there stood a positive ideal of world order. The Confucians, especially, had developed a theory of *Wang-tao* or "the Kingly Way" which was the concrete embodiment of the principle of human-heartedness. It contrasts sharply with *Pa-tao* or "the Way of the Feudal Lord," a government by means of force and in the interest of the ruler. According to Mencius, "he who, using force, makes a pretense at virtue, is a *Pa* . . .; he who, using virtue, practises human-heartedness, is a King." The superiority of the latter over the former is obvious. "When one subdues men by force, they do not submit in their hearts, (and submit outwardly only because) their strength is insufficient. When one subdues men by virtue, in their hearts' core they are pleased and sincerely submit. . . ."

Hsün Tzŭ similarly exalted the Kingly Way and deprecated the Way of the Feudal Lord in these words:

The disciples of Confucius, and even immature menials, were ashamed to talk about the five *Pa*. Why was this the case? Because they (the five *Pa*) did not have a just doctrine of government; . . . and they did not satisfy people's minds. Their course of action was well-calculated; they used judgment in seeing who worked and who was lazy; they carefully accumulated their resources; they prepared instruments of war; they were able to overturn their enemies. They conquered through a deceitful heart. They glossed over their contentiousness by an appearance of yielding the precedence to other; they relied on an appearance of benevolence to enable them to tread the path of profit seeking. They are heroes of the small-minded man. . . .

But the true Kings were different. They were most worthy and could therefore save the degenerate; they were most powerful, and could therefore bear with the weak; in war they could certainly have imperiled the weak, but they were ashamed to fight them. They modestly achieved refinement and displayed it to the whole world; then oppressive states became peaceful and changed of themselves. They only punished the dangerous and violent. Hence punishment was used very rarely by the Sage-King.

This distinction between the two ways of government made by Mencius and Hsün Tzŭ was maintained by almost all Confucian scholars of later times, and the ideal of the Kingly Way became the fundamental political outlook of the Chinese people. It is a decidedly un-Machiavellian ideal which trusts in the efficiency of peaceful means in dealing with the people and puts faith in love and virtue. Chinese thinkers held the vision of a world order in which all states lived peacefully and righteously, under the moral direction of a Sage-King. The realization of *Wang-tao* would give rise to a *Pax Sinica,* a world united harmoniously by the tie of universal love and enlightened virtue. It is unlike the *Pax Romana* which had its foundation in military power. It reminds us somewhat of the *Monarchia* of Dante, the rule of the world by one prince for the sake of peace. The form of this world order is antiquated, but the spirit underlying it contains an element of eternal value which no men of any generation can afford to reject....

THE CHINESE PHILOSOPHY OF WAR:
A DISSENTER'S HYPOTHESIS*

Morton H. Fried

Spurred by contemporary events, there is an increasing demand in social science for materials on and analyses of the cultures of the Far East. Within the past decade there has been a gradual accumulation of publications dealing with the sociological investigation of the Orient, especially of China. Within such a vast area and working with societies of such large populations and long-recorded histories, the task of the interpreter is a difficult one. It is to be expected that there will be many areas of disagreement which will require special and intensive study. The subject of the present paper is precisely such a problem.

With the recent publishing of H. H. Gerth's translation of the *Konfuzianismus und Taoismus* of Max Weber, a very popular concept of the nature of Chinese society will no doubt be reinforced: that in the China of the last twenty centuries the positions of highest status, exclusive of those held by the sovereigns and their close kin, have been those occupied by literary men and that the soldier, even the high ranking military officer, has been a despised figure. The conception, which by no means originated with Max Weber, is associated with a number of corollary positions which have achieved widespread though uncritical acceptance. Since they have attracted investigators in the field of personality and culture, their in-

* Morton H. Fried, "Military Status in Chinese Society," *American Journal of Sociology,* LVII, No. 4 (January 1952), 347–357. Reprinted by permission of The University of Chicago Press. Mr. Fried is Professor of Anthropology, Columbia University, and author of *Readings in Anthropology* (1959).

corporation into present-day research may lead to serious error. These views are three: that the Chinese nation is nonmilitaristic; that Chinese interpersonal relationships are devoid of physical violence; and that Chinese personality is nonaggressive. The social scientist who tries to find in these statements a reflection of modern events either is thrown into confusion or takes refuge in the belief that aggressive personalities and militarism are new to China, brought either by the West in the nineteenth century or induced by the more recent interaction with the Soviet Union.

Max Weber's view of the social inferiority of Chinese military officers was explicitly stated in a chapter on the literati which was made available in English in a translation by Gerth and [C. Wright] Mills. Weber wrote that "the military were just as despised in China as they were in England for two hundred years, and that a cultivated literary man would not engage in social intercourse on an equal footing with army officers." This assertion is supported by reference to a single item reported in the *Peking Gazette* in 1894.

Sociologists writing before and after Weber's analysis of Chinese society have expressed similar concepts. Writing on the eve of the Chinese Nationalist revolution, E. A. Ross stated: "Feeling the closing jaws of the vise ... Chinese patriots are making the army the national pet in order to raise the despised calling of the soldier." More recently a textbook in sociology predicted changes in the Chinese pattern of nonviolence and asserted that violence in China was something "only of recent years." In a work analyzing the changing familial norms of China, Marion Levy provides one of the latest statements of this kind:

Soldiers have for centuries been considered the lowest rung of Chinese society. The present Chinese government has been at some pains to change this conception, as have the Chinese Communist groups. The latter seem to have had the more success along these lines, but by and large the Chinese still aver that "good iron is not used for nails; good men do not become soldiers."

In the works of anthropologists similar declarations are generally made in terms of a professed Chinese contempt for violence. At times, however, explicit statements assert a pattern of Chinese disparagement of the military. Weston LaBarre, for example, writing on character structure in the Orient, remarked: "The Chinese are not *militaristic*. ... The soldier in the long span of Chinese history until the fall of the Manchu dynasty in 1912, has been looked down upon with a disenchantment bordering on contempt."

Even among Sinologists there is a lack of unanimity, and the few specialists who have turned their attention to the status of military personnel have been interested in special periods of history rather than in generalization. The most characteristic position of the specialists is that such statements as those cited above are true but must be qualified or completely altered for their own periods of specialization or areas of greatest interest.

Actually, then, the problem of the status of military personnel in Chinese society may be seen as a set of three questions. (1) What is and has been the actual position of the military in Chinese society? (2) If there is a marked difference between the actual conditions of status in Chinese society and the idealized conceptions of that status, how is this difference to be explained? (3) Why have Western analysts adopted the view of military inferiority and what is the history of this conception in Western social science?

The present paper is an attempt to answer in brief detail the first of these questions. Another paper is in process on the second question. The third problem is one for students with special interest in the history of Western thought. It is not unimportant, since for many of the French rationalists the most enlightened country in the world was thought to be China. The belief in Chinese antimilitarism certainly must have contributed to this conception. . . .

High Military Status as a Permanent Feature of Chinese Culture

. . . well accepted is the view that prior to the conquests of Ch'in, or the establishment of Han (third century B.C.), China was dominated by military officials. What is neglected is the military tradition of the two-thousand-year period from the time of Ch'in to the coming of the West.

To attempt to abridge that vast span of time for presentation in this paper would be to produce a ludicrous image. The available histories of China are crammed with the details of wars, battles, and military intrigues. The names of the great men and women of Chinese history include a high percentage of persons who gained their reputations through fierce combat. Imperial lines were most often begun by warriors rather than by politicians, and the descendants of Imperial ancestors frequently prided themselves on their military accomplishments. At times, the highest praise of a ruler might be couched in terms of martial prowess.

There is evidence that at least once in the course of Chinese history military titles were in such good standing that the government resorted to their sale in order to refurbish a depleted treasury. The data are not clear, but it seems possible that the government resorted to the sale of the military titles only after failing to arouse public interest in a similar sale of civil titles.

High-ranking military men had at least the prestige of the foremost scholars. One of the most literary of the emperors, Ch'ien Lung of the Ch'ing Dynasty, included an illuminating vignette of the great Ming general Hsü Ta in his *History of the Ming Dynasty*. Not only does the short sketch bespeak the reverence of an emperor for a warrior long dead but it tells us that "on the day of his return to court, without pomp, with a single carriage, he went to his own house and there graciously received the literati and conversed with them." For that matter, men of originally literary training sometimes ended with military commissions, at times as active warriors, occasionally performing their letters for military commanders.

During the Ch'ing Dynasty and before, soldiers when not fighting sometimes had the opportunity of becoming farmers on lands which, though originally granted under special restricted title, often became freehold in the course of two or three generations. Such lands were extensive enough to warrant separate classification as a major category in the tax system. As a source of wealth in many parts of China, as the fountainhead of the financial success and high status of innumerable gentry families, the military land grants should not be underrated. In the community studied by the author there were a large   number of prominent gentry who were descended from military officers of the Ch'ing Dynasty. Similar observations were made in Yunnan Province by Fei and Chang:

> The ancestors of the "lord" were only ordinary persons until his great-grandfather became a military officer in the Tsing Dynasty. The officer at this time acquired more than 100 *mow* of land. His son, grandfather of the "lord," became a military commander in Hunan, acquired more than 300 *mow* of land, and built a large temple and also the large house now occupied by the family in the village. No one knows, at present, how the grandfather, as a simple military officer, was able to accumulate such wealth; but the big estate is evidence of his success and reinforces the traditional idea of how wealth is acquired in the village.

The security of military identification also prompted masquerade on the part of civilians. Thus, in the salt trade on the Huai River, merchants of the Ch'ing Dynasty often flew banners from the masts of their craft in order to "mislead people into thinking they were military ships."

The Ch'ing legal code prescribed heavy penalties for persons who pretended without warrant to be military personnel.

Cultural Evidence of Military Status

Those who present the view of the status inferiority of the military frequently do so in terms of the proverb, "Good iron is not made into nails; good men should not become soldiers." Yet, the case should not be permitted to rest there, for proverbs of the opposite twist are common. At times the homilies stress the equality of civil and military functionaries, as in the saying, "Civil government tranquilizes a state; military rule settles a kingdom." Or, "First politeness (*li*), then weapons." Some proverbs unite civil and military talents to get the perfect man, as in "military, literary, his talents are complete."

Other types of proverbs stress the importance of military prestige, such as, "A great general has everywhere an awe-inspiring reputation." A final example: "To rush on the foe at the point of a spear is the work of a truly brave man; and the scholar who can move heaven and earth is wonderfully talented." The continuity of military tradition within a family line is reflected in the saying, "From a general's home come generals." The most popular version of this proverb is: "From a general's home come tigers (brave sons)."

Chinese literature, whether the short story, novel, or play, is frequently devoted to portrayals of military situations and characters. The prevalence of violent themes and martial heroes is incompatible with the myth of military inferiority, Chinese pacifism, and nonaggression. . . .

Banditry and Rebellion

The concept of military inferiority is not in harmony with empirical observation of Chinese behavior, and it creates inconsistencies in an evaluation of Chinese history. Two elements which have always been functional parts of Chinese culture are particularly incomprehensible if one accepts the idea that soldiers are despised. These are the capacity of the Chinese for revolt and the tendency for dispossessed persons to form local bands with military organization and seek their fortunes through banditry. There is a decided relationship between the two, as well as a connection with the institution of the secret society, which underlies so much of Chinese political organization. The dividing line between bandits and rebels, on the one hand, and rebels and victorious revolutionists, on the other, is not always clear. Almost up to the moment of its last continental resistance, the Kuomintang called the Chinese Communists "bandits." At present, the Chinese Communists call such groups of Nationalist troops as may be met on the mainland "bandits." In the T'ang Dynasty, when bandit groups felt strong enough to challenge the central government for control of a region, they would take the designation *i-ping*, "Righteous Troops." . . .

At times the government legalizes the status of a group of bandits, and bandit chiefs sometimes become ranking military officers. In T'ang times bandit leaders in control of definite territories adopted official military titles and sometimes took royal titles. The prestige which a group of out-laws might enjoy is portrayed in an idealized and romantic way in the novel *All Men Are Brothers,* in which the 108 heroes are all fugitives from the injustice of corrupt officialdom. Several of the militant heroes of this novel are described as originally being scholars and graduates.

Conclusions

This paper has attempted to demonstrate that a popular conception of the nature of Chinese society, a conception which apparently has been uncritically borrowed from the ideology of a small segment of Chinese society, the literati, is faulty and unwarranted. The recent publication of a work by Max Weber threatens to reinforce this view of the status in-feriority of the military in China. Since this concept is often used as the basis for generalizations involving other aspects of Chinese culture, social structure, and social psychology, it has been important to present a sum-mary of some of the more evident facts in the case.

We have alluded to a mass of historical, biographical, and sociological data which reveals that military status, far from being low or despised, has frequently enjoyed the highest rating. This version of the position of mili-tary personnel is more in accord with the facts of Chinese culture, agree-ing with such normally inconsistent factors as the frequent preoccupation with war and rebellion, the prominence of military events and characters in art and literature, and the importance of military supernaturals in the pantheon. Applied to contemporary affairs, it necessitates a re-evaluation of the often conjectured sudden rise of militarism in China, which is seen as a diffusion from the West. It will be seen that what the Occident has contributed to the present Chinese scene, new weapons and some new concepts of military organization, does not include the martial spirit. What the West has done is to act to intensify those conditions in China which have previously been associated with turmoil and military activity—the population has increased, the accumulation of property in the hands of few has been accelerated, and, a most important new factor, the market for locally produced commodities such as silk and homespun fabric has been sharply curtailed through competition with outside nations.

It should be emphasized that neither military nor civil status has been unconditionally ascendant during the past two millenniums in China's history. The two have been related in various ways; at times competing with one or the other dominant, at times harmoniously interacting. To un-ravel the ups and downs of this relationship would be to move into the very dynamic of Chinese culture itself.

COMMENT

Shu-ching Lee

A point-by-point refutation of the author's assertions would take another paper of the same length, if not longer, to do the job. However, the following remarks may suffice. He personally observed in China the common practice of lavishing special favors upon soldiers and that "relationships between civil and military personnel favored the military." These observations were undoubtedly true. Why did the author not go on to mention that Chiang Kai-shek is a trained professional soldier and that most of the governors of China's twenty-odd provinces under Chiang's rule were military generals, not to mention the once numerous warlords. The author further observed that bureaucratic residences in the town he studied protected themselves by posting on the doors notices which bore only the personal seals of high military officials. The author may be pleased to know that this practice was also common under the Nationalist rule, often the faculty dormitory of the National Southwest Associated University at Kunming during the war years had to resort to this means of protection. These notices indicate, as every Chinese can testify, nothing but the direction from which intrusion and molestation had come—to be exact, the soldiery. Since the mercenary with his gun was beyond the control of civil authorities, to post protective warnings bearing their names would be pointless. From this very evidence, it is apparent that ordinary citizens, who had no connection with officialdom and could not secure such military notices to post on their doors, were actually living at the mercy of ill-disciplined and unprincipled soldiers. Is that not enough to arouse the populace to disparage the soldier?

Military status in Chinese history may have been higher and lower as situations changed; a threatening barbarian invasion, for instance, might enhance the prestige of the military. (The Confucian scholar who openly praised the soldiery was Lu Yu, a great poet of the southern Sung.) And the chaos of civil strife might also place a number of military generals in high civil posts. But these facts do not warrant a generalization that the military has always enjoyed a status higher than, or even equal to, that of the literati. On the whole, the hardship and misery of the soldier's life are inadequately emphasized, and his chance of making a fortune through military service is grossly exaggerated. On one occasion, the author, strangely, regards the military colonization system as a means by which soldiers may acquire land to become farmers. It must be pointed out that land assigned to military colonization has been negligible in history and almost nonexistent in contemporary China. Proverbs, novels, and theatrical materials were cited as cultural evidences, most of which seem to be either irrelevant or insignificant in actuality; yet, the voluminous Confucian teachings, historical records, and writings of literature, which bear distinctly on antiwar, antimilitary character, the author ignores. . . .

In a sound sociological study of military status in China, the author has to tackle effectively the following problems upon which the unfavorable rating of the military rests (let us temporarily overlook the recent political change): (1) Who constitute the soldiery? It is a well-established fact that the literati are mainly recruited from the landowning gentry, whereas the military, especially the mercenaries, from the poor and illiterate peasantry, and, therefore, the former hold a higher status. (2) What is the general behavior of an ordinary soldier? If he behaved not otherwise than as described in the popular song cited by the author, or even worse, he cannot but be despised. (3) What is the psychological orientation of the common people toward the military and literati? Would a peasant prefer to see his son go to school for study or join the army for drill, if he could afford to do either? He would probably choose the former. Unless the author can refute all these commonly accepted facts, he may lead the Western readers to further confusion.

REJOINDER
Morton H. Fried

The arguments of Dr. Lee are familiar to one who for several years has followed discussions of the status of the military in China with Chinese friends of the literati. Their basic error is the insistence on a single-track approach to Chinese culture and society; the sort of thing which is implicit in such a statement as "the intelligentsia, the bearer of culture." The use of the term "culture" in contemporary social science explicitly denies the concept that culture is a monopoly of certain classes or specific societies. This is very much to the point, for the article in question does not deny the existence within Chinese society of groups or classes which regard the military as inferior, but questions the application of their particular ideology to the total society.

Humbly accepting Dr. Lee's criticism of my knowledge of Chinese scholarship, it nevertheless seemed necessary to air and interpret various data which could not be reconciled with the current belief in Chinese military inferiority. In this matter, it is of interest that Dr. Lee's criticisms seem more *ad hominem* than substantive, emotional rather than objective. My observations on military status in contemporary China are indorsed by Dr. Lee but are interpreted by him as new and deviant. Further, in noting the abuse of military power, Dr. Lee asks the moral and rational question whether such abuse is not enough to "arouse the populace" against the soldier? Such a technique does not seem conducive to the sort of "genuine sociological study" Dr. Lee requests. Again, in this issue Dr. Lee obviously takes "ordinary citizens" as largely synonymous with scholar-gentry, an assumption which is all too usual but quite unwarranted.

The use of literary materials to clarify the question of military status is disparaged by Dr. Lee. This is unfortunate. Documents of an antimilitary nature were little used by me because their concepts are the basis of the present general belief and are widely appreciated. Since, however, it is a function of the social scientist to understand or explain cultural manifestations, it seemed legitimate to ponder the meaning of military symbolism in so much Chinese literary and artistic production. If the major locus of such symbolism is among the peasantry, it cannot be explained away by denying the peasants' culture.

Dr. Lee admits that "military status in Chinese history may have been higher and lower." This thesis may be familiar to him, but it is not well known in the West. The basic point of the paper seems to be accepted, though questioned in detail.

The writer makes no claim to solving or settling the question of Chinese military status. He has introduced certain materials which conflict with prevalent views and has done so primarily for the consideration of Western scholars. The author enthusiastically supports the call for a more intensive study of the problem and hopes that Dr. Lee may find time to elaborate his criticisms and present them in a space compatible with the weight of the subject.

THE ISLAMIC PHILOSOPHY OF WAR*

Majid Khadduri

The state which is regarded as the instrument for universalizing a certain religion must perforce be an ever expanding state. The Islamic state,

* Majid Khadduri, War and Peace in the Law of Islam (Baltimore: Johns Hopkins Press, 1955), pp. 51–66. Reprinted by permission. Majid Khadduri is Professor of Middle East Studies, School of Advanced International Studies, Johns Hopkins University; author of War and Peace in the Law of Islam (1955), Independent Iraq, 1932–1958 (1960), and Modern Libya (1962); and coeditor of Law in the Middle East (1955).

whose principal function was to put God's law into practice, sought to establish Islam as the dominant reigning ideology over the entire world. It refused to recognize the coexistence of non-Muslim communities, except perhaps as subordinate entities, because by its very nature a universal state tolerates the existence of no other state than itself. Although it was not a consciously formulated policy, Muhammad's early successors, after Islam became supreme in Arabia, were determined to embark on a ceaseless war of conquest in the name of Islam. The jihād was therefore employed as an instrument for both the universalization of religion and the establishment of an imperial world state. The mission of Islam was rapidly and successfully carried out during the first century of the Islamic era—although the peaceful penetration of Islam continued—and the empire extended over a large portion of the Old World and became as large as the Roman Empire.

But the expanding Muslim state, not unlike other universal states, could not extend *ad infinitum*. The hitherto victorious Muslim warriors were defeated in the West at Tours (A.D. 732) and in the East found they could not proceed further than the Indian borders. Thus the wave of Muslim expansion, strong as it was, could not complete the Sun's circle; it imperceptibly subsided where it reached its utmost limits at the Pyrenees and the Indus. The Muslim (world) state consequently did not correspond to the then known world. Outside it there remained communities which the Muslim authorities had to deal with, though in theory only temporarily, throughout all the subsequent history of Islam.

The world accordingly was sharply divided in Muslim law into the dār al-Islām (abode or territory of Islam) and the dār al-ḥarb (abode or territory of war). These terms may be rendered in less poetic words as the "world of Islam" and the "world of War." The first corresponded to the territory under Muslim rule. Its inhabitants were Muslims, by birth or conversion, and the communities of the tolerated religions (the dhimmīs) who preferred to hold fast to their own cult, at the price of paying the jizya (poll tax). The Muslims enjoyed full rights of citizenship; the subjects of the tolerated religions enjoyed only partial rights, and submitted to Muslim rule in accordance with special charters regulating their relations with the Muslims. The dār al-harb consisted of all the states and communities outside the world of Islam. Its inhabitants were often called infidels, or, better, unbelievers.

On the assumption that the ultimate aim of Islam was world-wide, the dār al-Islām was always, in theory, at war with the dār al-ḥarb. The Muslims were required to preach Islam by persuasion, and the caliph or his commanders in the field to offer Islam as an alternative to paying the poll tax or fighting; but the Islamic state was under legal obligation to enforce

Islamic law and to recognize no authority other than its own, superseding other authorities even when non-Muslim communities had willingly accepted the faith of Islam without fighting. Failure by non-Muslims to accept Islam or pay the poll tax made it incumbent on the Muslim state to declare a jihād (commonly called "holy war") upon the recalcitrant individuals and communities. Thus the jihād, reflecting the normal war relations existing between Muslims and non-Muslims, was the state's instrument for transforming the dār al-ḥarb into the dār al-Islām. It was the product of a warlike people who had embarked on a large-scale movement of expansion. Islam could not abolish the warlike character of the Arabs who were constantly at war with each other; it indeed reaffirmed the war basis of intergroup relationship by institutionalizing war as part of the Muslim legal system and made use of it by transforming war into a holy war designed to be ceaselessly declared against those who failed to become Muslims. The short intervals which are not war—and these in theory should not exceed ten years—are periods of peace. But the jihād was not the only legal means of dealing with non-Muslims since peaceful methods (negotiations, arbitration, and treaty making) were applied in regulating the relations of the believers with unbelievers when actual fighting ceased.

The Muslim law of nations was, accordingly, the product of the intercourse of an ever-expanding state with its neighbors which inevitably led to the development of a body of rules and practices followed by Muslims in war and peace. The practices followed by the Arabs before Islam in their intertribal warfare were regarded as too ungodly and brutal, because they were motivated by narrow tribal interests. Islam abolished all war except the jihād and the jurist-theologians consciously formulated its law subordinating all personal considerations to *raison d'état,* based on religious sanction.

The Meaning of Jihād

The term jihād is derived from the verb jāhada (abstract noun, juhd) which means "exerted"; its juridical-theological meaning is exertion of one's power in Allah's path, that is, the spread of the belief in Allah and in making His word supreme over this world. The individual's recompense would be the achievement of salvation, since the jihād is Allah's direct way to paradise. This definition is based on a Qur'ānic injunction which runs as follows:

O ye who believe! Shall I guide you to a gainful trade which will save you from painful punishment? Believe in Allah and His Apostle and carry on warfare (jihād) in the path of Allah with your possessions and your persons. That is better for you. If ye have knowledge, He will forgive your sins, and will place you in the Gardens beneath which the streams flow, and in fine houses in the Gardens of Eden: that is the great gain.

The jihād, in the broad sense of exertion, does not necessarily mean war or fighting, since exertion in Allah's path may be achieved by peaceful as well as violent means. The jihād may be regarded as a form of religious propaganda that can be carried on by persuasion or by the sword. In the early Makkan revelations, the emphasis was in the main on persuasion. Muḥammad, in the discharge of his prophetic functions, seemed to have been satisfied by warning his people against idolatry and inviting them to worship Allah. This is evidenced by such a verse as the following: "He who exerts himself (jāhada), exerts only for his own soul," which expresses the jihād in terms of the salvation of the soul rather than a struggle for proselytization. In the Madīnan revelations, the jihād is often expressed in terms of strife, and there is no doubt that in certain verses the conception of jihād is synonymous with the words war and fighting.

The jurists, however, have distinguished four different ways in which the believer may fulfill his jihād obligation: by his heart; his tongue; his hands; and by the sword. The first is concerned with combatting the devil and in the attempt to escape his persuasion to evil. This type of jihād, so significant in the eyes of the Prophet Muḥammad, was regarded as the greater jihād. The second and third are mainly fulfilled in supporting the right and correcting the wrong. The fourth is precisely equivalent to the meaning of war, and is concerned with fighting the unbelievers and the enemies of the faith. The believers are under the obligation of sacrificing their "wealth and lives" (Q. LXI, 11) in the prosecution of war.

The Jihād as Bellum Justum

War is considered as just whether commenced and prosecuted in accordance with the necessary formalities required under a certain system of law, or waged for justifiable reasons in accordance with the tenets of the religion or the mores of a certain society. In Islam, as in ancient Rome, both of these concepts were included in their doctrine of the *bellum justum* since a justifiable reason as well as the formalities for prosecuting the war were necessary. In both Islam and ancient Rome, not only was war to be *justum*, but also to be *pium*, that is, in accordance with the sanction of religion and the implied commands of gods.

The idea that wars, when institutionalized as part of the mores of society, are just may be traced back to antiquity. It was implied in the concept of vendetta as an act of retaliation by one group against another. In the *Politics*, Aristotle refers to certain wars as just by nature. The Romans instituted the *jus fetiale*, administered by a *collegium fetialium* (consisting of twenty members, presided over by *magister fetialium*), embodying the proper rules of waging war in order to be just. In medieval Christendom, both St. Augustine and Isodore de Seville were influenced in their theory of just war by Cicero. St. Thomas Aquinas, who was acquainted with Muslim writings, formulated his theory of just war along lines similar to the Islamic doctrine of the jihād. St. Thomas and other Medieval writers influenced in their turn the natural law theories of the sixteenth, seventeenth, and eighteenth centuries. Grotius, the father of the modern law of nations, developed his system under the impact of the natural law theory of just war, and his ideas remained predominant until the end of the eighteenth century. Although the doctrine of war during the nineteenth century was by far less influenced by natural law than in previous centuries, the concept of just war reappeared after the First World War in the form of a doctrine of outlawing war, save that against an aggressor.

Recurring as a pattern in the development of the concept of war from antiquity, it assumed in Islam a special position in its jural order because law and religion formed a unity; the law prescribed the way to achieve religious (or divine) purposes, and religion provided a sanction for the law.

In Muslim legal theory, Islam and shirk (associating other gods with Allah) cannot exist together in this world; it is the duty of the imām as well as every believer not only to see that God's word shall be supreme, but also that no infidel shall deny God or be ungrateful for His favors (ni'am). This world would ultimately be reserved for believers; as to un-believers, "their abode is hell, and evil is the destination." The jihād, in other words, is a sanction against polytheism and must be suffered by all non-Muslims who reject Islam, or, in the case of the dhimmīs (Scrip-turaries), refuse to pay the poll tax. The jihād, therefore, may be defined as the litigation between Islam and polytheism; it is also a form of punish-ment to be inflicted upon Islam's enemies and the renegades from the faith. Thus in Islam, as in Western Christendom, the jihād is the *bellum justum*.

In Islam, however, the jihād is no less employed for punishing poly-theists than for *raison d'état*. For inherent in the state's action in waging a jihād is the establishment of Muslim sovereignty, since the supremacy of God's word carries necessarily with it God's political authority. This seems to be the reason why the jihād, important as it is, is not included—except in the Khārijī legal theory—among the five pillars of Islam.[1] The reason is that the five pillars are not necessarily to be enforced by the state; they must be observed by the individuals regardless of the sanction of authority. The jihād, in order to achieve *raison d'état*, must, however, be enforced by the state. In the technical language the five pillars—the basic articles of the faith—are regarded as individual duties (farḍ 'ayn), like prayer or fasting, which each believer must individually perform and each is held liable to punishment if he failed to perform the duty. The jihād, on the other hand—unless the Muslim community is subjected to a sudden attack and therefore all believers, including women and children, are under the obligation to fight—is regarded by all jurists, with almost no exception, as a collective obligation of the whole Muslim community. It is regarded as farḍ al-kifāya, binding on the Muslims as a collective group, not individually. If the duty is fulfilled by a part of the community it ceases to be obligatory on others; the whole community, however, falls into error if the duty is not performed at all.

The imposition of the jihād duty on the community rather than on the individual is very significant and involved at least two important implications. In the first place, it meant that the duty need not necessarily be fulfilled by all the believers. For the recruitment of all the believers as warriors was neither possible nor advisable. Some of the believers were needed to prepare food and weapons, while the crippled, blind, and sick would not qualify as fighters. Women and children were as a rule excused from actual fighting, although many a woman contributed indirectly to the war effort.

In the second place, the imposition of the obligation on the community rather than on the individual made possible the employment of the jihād as a community and, consequently, a state instrument; its control, accordingly, is a state, not an individual, responsibility. Thus the head of the state can in a more effective way serve the common interest of the community than if the matter is left entirely to the discretion of the individual believer. Compensation for the fulfillment of such an important public duty has been amply emphasized in both the authoritative sources of the creed and in formal utterances of public men. All of them give lavish promises of martyrdom and eternal life in paradise immediately and without trial on resurrection and judgment day for those who die in Allah's path. Such martyrs are not washed but are buried where they

---

[1] The five pillars or religious obligations of the Koran are (1) ablutions before prayer, (2) prayer, (3) fasting in the month of Ramadan, (4) a pilgrimage to Mecca at least once in the lifetime of every believer, and (5) almgiving. See Carl Brockelmann, *History of the Islamic Peoples*, trans. Joel Carmichael and Moshe Perlmann (New York: G. P. Putnam's Sons, 1947), pp. 39–43—Ed.

fall on the battlefield, not in the usual type of grave, after washing in a mosque. It is true that a promise of paradise is given to every believer who performs the five basic duties, but none of them would enable him to gain paradise as surely as participation in the jihād.

The Jihād as Permanent War

War, however, was not introduced into Arabia by Islam. It was already in existence among the Arabs; but it was essentially a tribal war. Its nature was peculiar to the existing social order and its rules and procedure were thoroughly integrated as part of the sunna. Since the tribe (in certain instances the clan) was the basic political unit, wars took the form of raids; mainly for robbery or vendetta (tha'r). This state of affairs had, as observed by Ibn Khaldūn, developed among the Arabs a spirit of self-reliance, courage, and co-operation among the members of the single tribe. But these very traits intensified the character of warfare and rivalry among the tribes and created a state of instability and unrest.

The importance of the jihād in Islam lay in shifting the focus of attention of the tribes from their intertribal warfare to the outside world; Islam outlawed all forms of war except the jihād, that is, the war in Allah's path. It would, indeed, have been very difficult for the Islamic state to survive had it not been for the doctrine of the jihād, replacing tribal raids, and directing that enormous energy of the tribes from an inevitable internal conflict to unite and fight against the outside world in the name of the new faith.

The jihād as such was not a casual phenomenon of violence; it was rather a product of complex factors while Islam worked out its jural-doctrinal character. Some writers have emphasized the economic changes within Arabia which produced dissatisfaction and unrest and inevitably led the Arabs to seek more fertile lands outside Arabia. Yet this theory—plausible as it is in explaining the outburst of the Arabs from within their peninsula—is not enough to interpret the character of a war permanently declared against the unbelievers even after the Muslims had established themselves outside Arabia. There were other factors which created in the minds of the Muslims a politico-religious mission and conditioned their attitude as a conquering nation.

To begin with, there is the universal element in Islam which made it the duty of every able-bodied Muslim to contribute to its spread. In this Islam combined elements from Judaism and Christianity to create something which was not in either: a divine nomocratic state on an imperialistic basis. Judaism was not a missionary religion, for the Jews were God's chosen people; a holy war was, accordingly, for the defense of their religion, not for its spread. Christianity on the other hand was a redemptive and, at the outset, a non-state religion. Even when it was associated with politics, the Church and state remained apart. Islam was radically different from both. It combined the dualism of a universal religion and a universal state. It resorted to peaceful as well as violent means for achieving that ultimate objective. The universality of Islam provided a unifying element for all believers, within the world of Islam, and its defensive-offensive character produced a state of warfare permanently declared against the outside world, the world of war.

Thus the jihād may be regarded as Islam's instrument for carrying out its ultimate objective by turning all people into believers, if not in the prophethood of Muḥammad (as in the case of the dhimmis), at least in the belief in God. The Prophet Muḥammad is reported to have declared "some of my people will continue to fight victoriously for the sake of the *truth* until the last one of them will combat the anti-Christ." Until that moment is reached the jihād, in one form or another, will remain as a permanent obligation upon the entire Muslim community. It follows that the existence of a dār al-ḥarb is ultimately outlawed under the Islamic jural order; that the dār al-Islām is permanently under jihād obligation until the dār al-ḥarb is reduced to nonexistence; and that any community which prefers to remain non-Islamic—in the status of a tolerated religious community accepting certain disabilities—must submit to Islamic rule and reside in the dār al-Islām or be bound as clients to the Muslim community. The universalism of Islam, in its all-embracing creed, is imposed on the believers as a continuous process of warfare, psychological and political if not strictly military.

Although the jihād was regarded as the permanent basis of Islam's relations with its neighbors, it did not at all mean continuous fighting. Not only could the obligation be performed by nonviolent means, but relations with the enemy did not necessarily mean an endless or constant violent conflict with him. The jihād, accordingly, may be stated as a doctrine of a permanent state of war, not a continuous fighting. Thus some of the jurists argued that the mere preparation for the jihād is a fulfillment of its obligation. The state, however, must be prepared militarily not only to repel a sudden attack on Islam, but also to use its forces for offensive purposes when the caliph deems it necessary to do so.

In practice, however, the jihād underwent certain changes in its meaning to suit the changing circumstances of life. Islam often made peace with the enemy, not always on its own terms. Thus the jurists began to reinterpret the law with a view to justifying suspension of the jihād, even though temporarily. They seem to have agreed about the necessity of peace and the length of its duration. When Muslim power began to de-

cline, Muslim publicists seem to have tacitly admitted that in principle
the jihād as a permanent war had become obsolete; it was no longer compatible with Muslim interests. The concept of the jihād as a state of war
underwent certain changes. This change, as a matter of fact, did not
imply abandonment of the jihād duty; it only meant the entry of the obligation into a period of suspension—it assumed a dormant status, from
which the imām may revive it at any time he deems necessary. In practice,
however, the Muslims came to think of this as more of a normal condition
of life than an active jihād.

The shift in the conception of the jihād from active to dormant war
reflects a reaction on the part of the Muslims from further expansion. This
coincided with the intellectual and philosophical revival of Islam at the
turn of the fourth century of the Muslim era (tenth century A.D.), when
the Muslims were probably more stirred by the controversy between
orthodoxy and rationalism than by fighting Byzantine encroachments on
the frontiers. To certain Muslim thinkers, like Ibn Khaldūn (d. 1406), the
relaxation of the jihād marked the change in the character of the nation
from the warlike to the civilized stage. Thus the change in the concept
of the jihād was not merely an apologia for weakness and failure to live
up to a doctrine, but a process of evolution dictated by Islam's interests
and social conditions.

THE SOVIET PHILOSOPHY OF WAR*

Nikolai Talensky

A correct understanding of the socio-political and military-strategic
character of war and its perspectives has always been of the utmost importance. The ruling classes of every state, resorting to war as an instrument of policy, must have clearly in mind the forms which hostilities will
take and the conditions necessary for victory, and at least the basic outlines of post-war perspectives in the event of victory or defeat. Any
neglect of this theoretical and practical problem has always been severely

* Nikolai Talensky, "On the Character of Modern Warfare," *International Affairs*
(U.S.S.R.), No. 10 (October 1960), pp. 23–27. Nikolai Talensky is a Major General in
the Soviet Army and a professor at the Voroshilov Higher General Staff Military
Academy. He is considered one of the most famous and influential military theoreticians on the Soviet General Staff.

dealt with by history. The First and Second World Wars are instructive in this respect. Their characters and consequences proved to be far different from those anticipated by the imperialist Powers which prepared and unleashed them. . . .

Marxism-Leninism teaches that the character of a war, its methods and forms of conduct depend upon socio-economic conditions and the development of military technology as a derivative of the general development of the productive forces of society. In our times, phenomenal social changes—the victory and storming advance of the Socialist system, the disintegration of colonialism, sharp restrictions in the sphere of imperialist influence—are combined with a tremendous leap forward in the development of productive forces—mastery of nuclear energy and man's reach into outer space. All this is reflected in the military field.

The technological revolution in the military field has created weapons of destruction which are a thousandfold more powerful than their predecessors. Should the imperialists be permitted to unleash a war in the future, rocket-nuclear weapons will predominate as the basic means of mass destruction.

The destructive force of such weapons has been widely publicized in the press as follows:

An American 20 megaton thermo-nuclear device exploded in March 1954 had a radius of destruction of 9 miles and a radius of heat effect—up to 14 miles. According to the calculations of the American scientist Dr. Libby, the total area contaminated in a thermo-nuclear explosion of such magnitude could cover 95,000 sq. miles. There are data indicating that one 10 megaton bomb is 5 times more powerful than all bomb loads released over Germany during the war, and 100 times greater than those dropped on Japan.

According to American estimates, a nuclear bomb attack on the 50 biggest U.S. population centers, in which reside almost one-half of the country's population, would result in the loss of 15–20 million persons killed and 20–25 million injured. A 10 megaton bomb exploded over the center of New York would result in 3 million dead out of the 4 million working and living in this area. The rest would be injured.

J. D. Bernal, in his book *World Without War*, offers the following estimates of probable losses in regions of various population density. The explosion of a 10 megaton bomb in urban areas (density 20,000 persons per sq. mile) would kill 10 million persons; in industrial areas (density 1,000 persons per sq. mile)—1.5 million persons; and in agricultural areas (100 persons per sq. mile)—150 thousand persons. In addition, losses resulting from radioactive fall-out would amount in industrial countries to 4 million persons; and in agrarian countries to 400 thousand persons.

The dropping of a 50 megaton bomb would increase these losses from one and a half times to twice over. Modern thermo-nuclear weapons make it possible to devastate vast territories completely and literally to wipe entire nations from the face of the earth.

On the supposition that the area devastated by a thermo-nuclear device (bomb or rocket warhead) of 10–20 megatons would amount to 270 sq. miles, a country like the United States (excluding Alaska) could be wiped off the face of earth with 8,500 such devices. But even such a number would not be required since strikes at the key strategic, economic and political centers would require only a fraction of such weapons. Added to this, dangerous radioactive contamination could be created by a few hundred, and in some cases, even by a few dozen bombs.

It is quite clear that in the event of war, nations with smaller territories and denser population could be wiped out by a few dozen thermo-nuclear bombs. The British military expert Liddell Hart estimates that 5–10 hydrogen bombs would be sufficient to destroy all the principal industrial centers of Britain.

If one takes into account that the present store of nuclear weapons of all types already runs into the thousands, then the lethal character of modern rocket-nuclear warfare becomes crystal-clear. To destroy all living and devastate all non-living things in Europe, including mountains, woods and tundra, no more than 15,000 thermo-nuclear bombs of the above-mentioned force would be necessary to contaminate this area with radiation, and no more than 500 bombs would be needed to devastate the territory of all the countries of the aggressive NATO bloc with all U.S. bases.

Such is the destructive force of thermo-nuclear devices, which may be delivered as warheads of powerful ballistic rockets or airborne bombs. The force of atomic, as distinct from thermo-nuclear bombs or rocket warheads, is less; nonetheless it is of colossal magnitude. The atom bomb comparable to that dropped on Hiroshima (20 kilotons), classified as a "tactical" atomic weapon, is capable of laying waste an area up to 17 sq. miles. The explosion of such a bomb in an urban area would result in up to 200,000 killed; in industrial areas, up to 10,000; and in the country-side, up to 1,000. One "tactical" atomic bomb of a maximum caliber with an explosive force of 500 kilotons is capable of devastating an area of 250 sq. miles and claiming the following number of victims: in urban areas, up to one million killed; in industrial areas, up to 50,000 and in the country-side, up to 5,000. It should be borne in mind that such bombs are "employed" in NATO tactical exercises.

Such is the real destructive power of modern atomic armaments. It should be emphasized that the major means of delivering these weapons to target is now the ballistic missile. . . .

What are the consequences of such a radical leap forward in the development of modern means of warfare? What is the influence of rocket and nuclear weapons in warfare—its character, methods and forms?

The first and major conclusion to be drawn is that war conducted with rocket and nuclear weapons would be an exceptionally destructive one. Undoubtedly, warfare conducted with such weapons would suck the entire world into its wake. Not a single country involved in such a war would escape the ensuing crushing, devastating blows. Should the countries of the aggressive North Atlantic pact unleash a war against the U.S.S.R. and the entire Socialist camp, it would lead to the total devastation of almost the entire territory of Europe and North America which will inevitably become a major theater of war. Countries in other continents which took part in the war would also suffer cruelly.

This war would differ sharply in form and content from all preceding wars. In the wars of previous epochs, the main blows were directed against the armed forces in the theater of hostilities. In a rocket and nuclear war, the main and most destructive blows would be directed against the major economic and political centers and against strategic targets in the heart of a country. War with conventional weapons in frontier areas would be of an auxiliary nature and its role, particularly at the beginning and the middle of a war, would be of secondary importance.

Rocket and nuclear warfare, even without the use of chemical and bacteriological weapons, would lead to the annihilation of entire nations and the devastation of their lands. Vast areas would be contaminated by lethal concentrations of radiation. According to the most conservative estimates, the number of human lives lost in a rocket and nuclear war taking place in the probable main theater, populated by approximately 800 million people, would amount to 500–600 million people. And this is a minimum figure.

But a global war, and in the present circumstances there can be no other, would embrace a considerably greater territory. The British Air Vice-Marshal Kingston-McCloughry, reflecting the views of the most aggressive circles, writes:

"It is inevitable that the boundary of the geographical area of NATO and SHAPE presents our nations with difficult problems. In war it is clear that the present artificial limits of NATO's responsibilities would become meaningless. It is equally clear that the free world defence organization and strategy should be extended to cover the whole world." Translated from diplomatic language into plain English, this means that the imperialist aggressors are seeking to broaden considerably the scale of warfare, which unavoidably increases losses.

However, the total losses from rocket and nuclear warfare are not completely reflected in the estimated losses resulting from the actual impact of the rocket or bomb, blast and light radiation. Radioactive fall-out would result in hundreds of thousands and even millions of square miles of land being rendered lethal for long periods. Indeed, such areas would be scorched and poisonous deserts. An especial danger of radioactive fall-out is that the area depends only on meteorological conditions. Consequently, death from radioactive fall-out threatens not only people in warring countries, but also the entire population of our planet. Radioactive fall-out from experimental explosions of only a few thermo-nuclear devices (1955 data) spread out over 200 million square miles. Various estimates give losses due to radioactive fall-out as not less than one-third of losses caused by blast and light radiation. Domestic animals would also be killed and food reserves contaminated.

"It was evident even earlier, from the results of the tests of the hydrogen bombs," writes J. D. Bernal, "that any serious war, even without long-range missiles, would result in such contamination of the atmosphere, water, and earth of this world as to make the continuation of any kind of civilized life impracticable. All would suffer in some degree or other from radiation sickness, and even those who survived that—not only human beings, but also the animals and plants they lived on—would be exposed to genetic damage of a degree never before found in the history of this earth."

Geneticists have not, as yet, said the final word on the question of the possible genetic consequences of nuclear warfare. There is no doubt, however, that the danger of harmful genetic consequences is at present underestimated rather than overestimated.

Not to see the dangers of rocket and nuclear war is harmful and to underestimate them is criminal. The world wars unleashed by the imperialists seriously undermined capitalism as the previously dominant social system. There is no doubt that in the event of a new war capitalism will succumb completely. But does this mean that the sacrifices of war, however heavy, are justified? This is a harmful, anti-humane point of view.

The world population would be reduced by one-half as a result of a new global war. Moreover, the most active, capable and civilized portion would be wiped out. One should also remember that the material and technological basis for life would be destroyed. Thermo-nuclear weapons would destroy plants and factories, devastate fields and orchards, destroy means of transportation and communication, almost all buildings. Libraries, institutes and museums would fall into ruin: humanity would be thrown back and its way to Communism would become immensely longer. . . .

In the recent past, a country that was superior to its adversary as regards size of its armed forces and quality of their technical equipment could confidently count on victory. Moreover, the losses of the victor were usually less than those of the defeated country. Thus we have the typical example of colonial wars in which the military superiority of the colonial Powers was so much greater that detachments consisting of a few dozen or a few hundred soldiers were able to conquer entire countries. In preparing for war, the general staffs would nicely calculate the correlation of forces and the means necessary for the struggle and, if they tackled their task objectively, could assess fairly closely the probability of success and the extent of losses.

In the case of warfare with nuclear weapons, the picture is radically different. The destructive power of nuclear weapons is so great that even if this weapon were used in small numbers against a more powerful enemy the losses inflicted would be very heavy. Many foreign writers recognize that the stockpiles of nuclear weapons have reached a "saturation level" that makes it possible to strike simultaneously at all the most probable strategic targets.

Some assert that with the present "stage of development of the weapons of war, any further increase in the destructive power of weapons no longer yields important strategic advantages." Under such conditions, it is incorrect to assume that a surprise mass attack could lead to winning a war without destruction being wreaked upon the aggressor. The "saturation level" of nuclear weapons, their disposition, and methods of using them are at present such that the attacked country would always be left with sufficient nuclear means to inflict a counterblow of sufficient proportions to cause tremendous losses and destruction.

And so nuclear weapons have been developed to such a point of destructive power that limits of the conception of them as absolute weapons have already been surpassed. "Of even greater, cataclysmic potency," writes Kingston-McCloughry, "the hydrogen weapon could bring devastation to humanity, and, in theory at least, could provide a single unit capable of fracturing the earth itself." Together with this, the accumulated reserves of nuclear weapons and the future possibilities of their increasing are such that a basic change has been brought about in the hitherto existing conception of the theory of war.

The idea of winning a war by a surprise blow, and of preventive war, under conditions of "atomic abundance," as they say in the West, has been advanced by certain zealous NATO military theoreticians. This is also a speculative publicity stunt calculated to mislead people and maintain an atmosphere of tension.

Nuclear weapons are not the only means of mass destruction in a future war. Thus, advances in rocket techniques may radically increase the military effectiveness of chemical and bacteriological weapons, whose development in the West is proceeding intensively. From time to time, articles appear in the West on the "humane" character of chemical weapons and on the advantages of biological weapons, which strike at people but do not result in material destruction. They say that an attacking country using these means is better able to protect itself than when nuclear weapons are used, and so on. Such lucubrations are usually inspired by yearning for an "easy" war which would be "safe" for the aggressor, but a war of this type is now a thing of the past.

As the fatal danger of a large-scale nuclear war became evident, Western theoreticians began more and more to advocate the possibility of limited or local wars. The purpose of this ideological diversion in the military sphere is clear. Unwilling to renounce preparations for a new aggressive war, the imperialists are seeking less dangerous forms. At the same time, they are striving to mislead the people, who realize the disastrous consequences of an all-out nuclear war and are resolutely fighting against it. In advocating local or limited wars, the imperialists seek to hold on to a weapon for suppressing the national-liberation struggle of the colonial and semi-colonial peoples.

The press of the Socialist countries and progressive Western writers have thoroughly unmasked the true nature of the propaganda for such a war. It has been shown that local and limited wars under present conditions would be a prelude to an all-out rocket and nuclear war, a way for unleashing war.

The proponents of the theory of limited warfare often refer to the experience of past ages when most wars were relatively limited in character. Such arguments, however, cannot withstand serious criticism. Limited wars were possible under entirely different economic, political and strategic conditions. As a rule, the restricted scale of these wars was due to the lack of sufficient strength and means to wage them.

With the transition of capitalism to its imperialist stage, world wars became the major form of warfare. Wars that were limited in scale were in effect either a prelude to a world war or what might be considered a concluding phase of the latter. "When Defense Department spokesmen assert, as they have repeatedly done, that nuclear war can be limited, I feel very strongly that they should be challenged..." writes R. Lapp, U.S. atomic scientist. "... confining the bomb to a local battlefield would be exceedingly difficult."...

R. Osgood, the American author of the book *Limited War*, notes that ". . . the danger of unintentional total war lies not only in such direct provocation but also in the possibility of a limited war gradually growing out of control." At the same time, he does not conceal that "the deliberate limitation of war assumes a conception of the relation between power and policy that is, in many ways, antithetical to American ideas and predisposition in foreign relations—so antithetical, in fact, that a sound strategy of limited war implies a basic revision of the traditional American approach to war."

Underlining the groundlessness of the idea of limited warfare under present conditions Bernal writes:

"So long as the potential for total destruction is there, the tendency to use it to redress the balance of the side temporarily worsted in limited warfare is likely to be overwhelming. At any rate, no one is prepared to trust that this temptation will be resisted: even the staunchest advocates of limited warfare demand the maintenance simultaneously of the whole apparatus for all-out inter-continental warfare as well. In other words, they wish to reduce the ill effects of war by duplicating the means required to carry it out." And: "Much of the force behind the argument for limited war stems from the belief that it would be possible for the Western Powers to use nuclear weapons in conditions when the other side had not got them or would not use them."

The development of the technique of exterminating people has resulted in a situation that makes it impossible to resort to war to solve political disputes as was done throughout the history of mankind. A rocket and nuclear war is dangerous not only for the side subject to attack, but suicidal for the aggressor.

It is our opinion that, in terms of military technology, war as an instrument of policy is outliving itself. But this, obviously, does not in the least exclude the possibility that an aggressor can still unleash war, as the advancement of military technology, taken alone, cannot serve as a guarantee of peace on earth. The conclusion that war today is not fatally inevitable is based chiefly on an analysis of the *social and political conditions* which have emerged in the world.

The classics of Marxism-Leninism have clearly demonstrated that historically war is of a transient nature, belonging to societies of class exploitation. War is alien to Socialist society by its very nature. Socialism and war are incompatible. Hence, the victory of Socialism throughout the world will, so to speak, automatically eliminate war.

However, a large part of the world is still dominated by capitalism, which is accustomed to solving its class problems by recourse to war.

Can wars be eliminated under these conditions, and can this weapon be wrenched from the hands of the imperialist aggressors?

The resolutions of the 20th and 21st congresses of the C.P.S.U., the Declaration of Communist and Workers' Parties, and the Peace Manifesto give the well-founded elucidation that under present conditions war is not inevitable, the outbreak of war can be prevented, peace can be safeguarded and consolidated. This magnificent idea has enormously intensified the efforts of the broad masses in the struggle for peace and armed them with a clear perspective.

If the forces of imperialism were to succeed in dragging the world into a new war, it would be a horrible catastrophe. This should be remembered. But not in order to be seized with hopeless despair, to submissively throw up one's hands and reconcile oneself to "fate." This should be kept in mind in order to struggle more stubbornly and perseveringly for the scrapping of all armament, for outlawing war from human society, for peace throughout the world.

PART THREE

THE ADJUSTMENT OF
POWER CONFLICTS

CHAPTER FIVE

Diplomacy

Countless wits have displayed their satirical skill by depreciating diplomacy and those who practice it. One unknown pundit, frequently quoted, said that "when a diplomat says yes he means perhaps; when he says perhaps he means no; and when he says no he is no diplomat." An observation by C. L. Sulzberger of *The New York Times* belongs in future compendiums of such quips. "There are, in diplomacy, four cardinal rules," he says. "Rule one is always keep the initiative. Rule two is always exploit the inevitable. Rule three is always keep in with the outs. And rule four is never stand between a dog and a lamppost."[1]

It is one thing to chuckle over these remarks, but quite another to accept them as attesting to the actual significance of diplomacy and diplomats. Throughout history, diplomacy has been the first technique used to resolve political disagreements or reduce power conflicts among states. Many writers have undertaken to explain the hallmarks of the art of diplomacy, but few have done so with greater preciseness and more lasting significance than François de Callières, whose early-eighteenth-century treatise, *On the Manner of Negotiating with Princes,* has been called "the best manual of diplomatic method ever written."[2]

The several excerpts included here from de Callières's book survey from the standpoint of a traditionalist the agency through which states seek to attain their foreign-policy goals and describe the nature of the diplomatic process, its value in international politics, and the personal virtues that should be possessed by those conducting negotiations. In contrast to the authors of earlier books about diplomacy, who emphasized the need for deceit and duplicity, de Callières believed that honesty,

---

[1] *The New York Times,* May 27, 1957, p. 30.
[2] Harold Nicolson, *The Evolution of Diplomatic Method* (London: Constable & Co., Ltd., 1954), p. 62.

reason, and straightforward methods reduce best the pressures that arise in the conduct of official relations between governments. Unfortunately, many students of international affairs continue to believe that Machiavellian cunning is the principal prerequisite of the successful practitioner of diplomacy; we have included de Callières's article to help dispel such a shortsighted—however prevalent—notion.

The two selections that follow consider Chinese and Islamic diplomacy. Before the beginning of its intercourse with Western states in the late eighteenth century, China had no diplomatic activity in the sense of two sovereign entities dealing with each other on the basis of equality. Western-style diplomatic negotiations were unknown to the Celestial throne. China's neighbors appeared in Peking as barbarian states, bringing tribute and paying homage to the emperor. These well-regulated visits served two main functions. First, China reaffirmed its superior role in the Confucian state system. By coming to the Middle Kingdom, the barbarian state publicly acknowledged its subservient political and cultural position. Second, the mutual exchange of gifts that took place between the Son of Heaven and the visiting dignitaries promoted commercial intercourse between China and the various tributary states. J. K. Fairbank and S. Y. Têng explain how premodern Chinese diplomacy became a mechanism to reinforce the preeminence of the Middle Kingdom with the barbarous regions of the empire.

The early Muslim caliphs used the practices and principles of diplomacy quite differently. They considered diplomacy a function of the permanent war between their religious community and the non-Muslim states. Military commanders of the dār ul Islām negotiated with rulers from the dār ul ḥarb concerning the acceptance or rejection of Muslim sovereignty. If the fighting was inconclusive, precise terms of an armistice were fixed and prisoners of war exchanged. Classical Muslim diplomacy cannot be examined apart from the Muslim dream of world domination.

After experiencing a number of crushing military defeats, the Muslim leaders realized that their inter-state system had to be reexamined; the doctrine of the jihād needed to be reinterpreted, and Muslim statesmen had to reconcile themselves to a less bellicose outlook. Peaceful coexistence with the West became the only rational political alternative. A new period in European-Muslim relations, which called for a quite different type of diplomacy, had begun.[3]

Muhammad Hamidullah's essay "The Islamic Tradition of Diplomacy"

[3] See Majid Khadduri, "Islam and the Modern Law of Nations," *American Journal of International Law*, L, No. 2 (April 1956), 358–372, and *War and Peace in the Law of Islam*, pp. 238–250.

describes something of the origin and early use of diplomatic practices both during and immediately following the reign of Muḥammad. It presents additional evidence to Sir Harold Nicolson's belief that "diplomacy is neither the invention nor the pastime of some particular political system, but is an essential element in any reasonable relation between man and man and between nation and nation."[4] The contrast offered by the premodern Chinese theory of unequal state intercourse and the diplomacy formulated by the Muslims suggests reasons why later Islamic empires had less difficulty than the Middle Kingdom in adjusting to classical European diplomacy.

Concluding the chapter is Lord Vansittart's entertaining yet forceful article in which he longs for a return of the past. He castigates the West for failing to appreciate the purpose, methods, and significance of classical-style diplomacy. He laments the fact that the totalitarian states have destroyed the traditional process of negotiating. The Soviet Union is the object of his greatest scorn, for he believes that Soviet statesmen have introduced techniques and activities in their international practices that make today's Cold War diplomacy an empty exercise. Diplomacy, he concludes, "may come to its own again in modern dress ... but ... it can never regain world-wide acceptance, so long as the New Barbarians hold sway."

[4] Sir Harold Nicolson, *Diplomacy*, 2nd ed. (London: Oxford University Press, 1950), p. 14.

THE METHODS AND OBJECTIVES OF DIPLOMACY*

François de Callières

The art of negotiation with princes is so important that the fate of the greatest states often depends upon the good or bad conduct of negotiations and upon the degree of capacity in the negotiators employed. Thus monarchs and their ministers of state cannot examine with too great care the natural or acquired qualities of those citizens whom they despatch on missions to foreign states to entertain there good relations with their masters, to make treaties of peace, of alliance, of commerce or of other

* François de Callières, *On the Manner of Negotiating with Princes*, trans. A. F. Whyte (Boston, Houghton Mifflin Company, 1919), pp. 7–18, 109–113. Reprinted by permission of the publisher, Constable & Co., Ltd., London. François de Callières (1645–1717) was a French diplomat. During the reign of Louis XIV, he was Secretary to the Cabinet of the king.

kinds, or to hinder other Powers from concluding such treaties to the prejudice of their own master; and generally, to take charge of those interests which may be affected by the diverse conjunctures of events. Every Christian prince must take as his chief maxim not to employ arms to support or vindicate his rights until he has employed and exhausted the way of reason and of persuasion. It is to his interest also, to add to reason and persuasion the influence of benefits conferred, which indeed is one of the surest ways to make his own power secure, and to increase it. But above all he must employ good labourers in his service, such indeed as know how to employ all these methods for the best, and how to gain the hearts and wills of men, for it is in this that the science of negotiation principally consists.

It causes me no surprise that men who have embarked on this career for the sake of titles and emoluments, having not the least idea of the real duties of their post, have occasioned grave harm to the public interest during their apprenticeship to this service. These novices in negotiation become easily intoxicated with honours done in their person to the dignity of their royal master. . . . This happens above all to those who are employed by a great monarch on missions to princes of a lower order, for they are apt to place in their addresses the most odious comparisons, as well as veiled threats, which are really only a mark of weakness. Such ambassadors do not fail to bring upon themselves the aversion of the court to which they are accredited, and they resemble heralds of arms rather than ambassadors whose principal aim is ever to maintain a good correspondence between their master and the princes to whom they are accredited. In all cases they should represent the power of their own sovereign as a means of maintaining and increasing that of the foreign court, instead of using it as an odious comparison designed to humiliate and contemn. These misfortunes and many others, which are the result of the lack of capacity and of the foolish conduct of many citizens employed by princes to deal with public affairs abroad, occasioned in me the belief that it is by no means impertinent to set down some observations on the manner of negotiating with sovereigns and with their ministers, on the qualities necessary for those who mean to adopt the profession of diplomacy, and on the means which wise princes will take to secure a good choice of men well adapted at once to the profession of negotiation and to the different countries where they may be sent. But before I take my subject in detail it is perhaps well that I should explain the use and the necessity for princes to maintain continual negotiation in the form of permanent embassies to all great states, both in the neighbouring countries and in those more distant, in war as well as in peace.

To understand the permanent use of diplomacy and the necessity for continual negotiations, we must think of the states of which Europe is composed as being joined together by all kinds of necessary commerce, in such a way that they may be regarded as members of one Republic and that no considerable change can take place in any one of them without affecting the condition, or disturbing the peace, of all the others. The blunder of the smallest sovereigns may indeed cast an apple of discord among all the greatest Powers, because there is no state so great which does not find it useful to have relations with the lesser states and to seek friends among the different parties of which even the smallest state is composed. History teems with the results of these conflicts which often have their beginnings in small events, easy to control or suppress at their birth, but which when grown in magnitude became the causes of long and bloody wars which have ravaged the principal states of Christendom. Now these actions and reactions between one state and another oblige the sagacious monarch and his ministers to maintain a continual process of diplomacy in all such states for the purpose of recording events as they occur and of reading their true meaning with diligence and ex- actitude. One may say that knowledge of this kind is one of the most im- portant and necessary features of good government, because indeed the domestic peace of the state depends largely upon appropriate measures taken in its foreign service to make friends among well-disposed states, and by timely action to resist those who cherish hostile designs. There is indeed no prince so powerful that he can afford to neglect the assistance offered by a good alliance, in resisting the forces of hostile powers which are prompted by jealousy of his property to unite in a hostile coalition. . . .

It is not necessary to turn far back into the past in order to understand what can be achieved by negotiation. We see daily around us its definite effects in sudden revolutions favourable to this great design of state or that, in the use of sedition in fermenting the hatreds between nations, in causing jealous rivals to arm against one another so that the *tertius gaudens* may profit, in the formation of leagues and other treaties of vari- ous kinds between monarchs whose interests might otherwise clash, in the dissolution by crafty means of the closest unions between states: in a word, one may say that the art of negotiation, according as its conduct is good or evil, gives form to great affairs and may turn a host of lesser events into a useful influence upon the course of the greater. Indeed, we can see in diplomacy thus conducted a greater influence in many ways upon the conduct and fortunes of mankind than even in the laws which they themselves have designed, for the reason that, however scrupulous private man may be in obedience to the law, misunderstandings and conflicts of ambition easily arise between nations, and cannot be settled by a process of law but only by a convention between the contending parties. It is on the occasion of such conventions that diplomacy plays a decisive part.

It is thus easy to conclude that a small number of well-chosen negotiators posted in the different states in Europe may render to their sovereign and their state the greatest services; that a single word or act may do more than the invasion of whole armies because the crafty negotiator will know how to set in motion various forces native to the country in which he is negotiating, and thus may spare his master the vast expense of a campaign. Nothing can be more useful than a timely diversion thus set on foot.

It is also of high interest to all great princes that their negotiators should be of such character and standing as to act appropriately as mediators in the disputes between other sovereigns and to produce peace by the authority of their intervention. Nothing can contribute more to the reputation, the power, and the universal respect of a monarch, than to be served by those who themselves inspire respect and confidence. A powerful prince who maintains a constant system of diplomacy served by wise and instructed negotiators in the different states of Europe, and who thus cultivates well-chosen friendships and maintains useful sources of information, is in a position to influence the destiny of neighbouring foreign states, to maintain peace between all states, or to pursue war where it is favourable to his design. In all these concerns the prosperity of his plans and the greatness of his name depend first and last on the conduct and qualities of the negotiators to whom he entrusts his services. . . .

The functions of a minister despatched on a mission to a foreign country fall into two principal categories: the first to conduct the business of his master, and the second to discover the business of others. The first of these concerns the prince or his ministers of state, or at all events those deputies to whom are entrusted the examination of his proposals. In all these different kinds of negotiation he must seek success principally by his straightforward and honest procedure, for if he attempts to succeed by subtlety or by a sense of superiority over those with whom he is engaged he may very likely deceive himself. There is no prince or state which does not possess some shrewd envoy to discern its real interests. And indeed, even among people who seem to be the least refined, there are often those who know their own interests best, and follow them with the most constancy. Therefore the negotiator, no matter how able he may be, must not attempt to teach such persons their own business, but he should exhaust all the resources of his mind and wit to prove to them the great advantage of the proposals which he has to make.

An ancient philosopher once said that friendship between men is nothing but a commerce in which each seeks his own interest. The same is true or even truer of the liaisons and treaties which bind one sovereign to another, for there is no durable treaty which is not founded on reciprocal advantage, and indeed a treaty which does not satisfy this condition is no treaty at all, and is apt to contain the seeds of its own dissolution. Thus the great secret of negotiation is to bring out prominently the common advantage to both parties of any proposal, and so to link these advantages that they may appear equally balanced to both parties. For this purpose when negotiations are on foot between two sovereigns, one the greater and the other the less, the more powerful of these two should make the first advance, and even undertake a large outlay of money to bring about the union of interests with his lesser neighbour, for his own self-interest will show him that he has really the greater object and the larger advantages in view, and that any benefits he may confer or subsidies which he may grant to his weaker ally will be readily repaid by the success of his designs. Now, as we have said, the secret of negotiation is to harmonise the interests of the parties concerned. It is clear that if a negotiator excludes the honest and straightforward method of reason and persuasion, and adopts on the contrary a haughty and menacing manner, then obviously he must be followed by an army ready to invade the country in which he has put forth such provocative claims. Without such a display of force his claims will fall to the ground, even though by advantageous arguments they might have prevailed with the prince whom he addressed, and who might have accepted them had they been proposed in a different manner. When a prince or a state is powerful enough to dictate to his neighbours the art of negotiation loses its value, for then there is need for nothing but a mere statement of the prince's will; but when there is a balance of force an independent prince will only decide to favour one of the two parties of a dispute if he discerns advantages to himself and good results to the prosperity of his realm.

A prince who has no powerful enemies can easily impose tribute on all neighbouring Powers, but a prince whose aim is self-aggrandisement and who has powerful enemies must seek allies among the lesser states in order to increase those friendly to him; and if possible he should be able to prove his power by the benefits which an alliance with him can confer upon them. Therefore the principal function of the negotiator is to bring about a harmonised union between his master and the sovereign to whom he is sent, or else to maintain and increase existing alliances by every means in his power. He must labour to remove misunderstandings, to prevent subjects of dispute from arising, and generally to maintain in that foreign country the honour and interests of his prince. This includes the protection and patronage of his subjects, assistance to their business enterprises, and the promotion of good relations between them and the subjects of the foreign prince to whose court he is accredited. He must always assume that there is no prince nor state in the world which does not desire to avoid a condition of crisis, and that those princes who love to fish in troubled waters will never lack the means to stir them up, but that the storms which such men conjure up are apt to overwhelm them, so that the wise negotiator will do all he can to avoid giving provocation, and will conduct himself in such a manner that no one will be able to impute reckless motives to him.

His second function being the discovery of all that is happening at court and in the cabinet, he should first of all take steps to learn from his predecessor all that he knows regarding the state of affairs in the country to which he is about to proceed and to acquire from him those hints and suggestions which may be of use. He should take up the friends and acquaintances left behind by his predecessor, and should add to them by making new ones. It would be no bad practice in this matter to imitate the established rule of the Venetian Republic, which obliges an ambassador returning from a foreign court to render a detailed account in writing of the country, both for the information of the public and for the instruction of his successor at the embassy. The diplomatists of Venice have drawn great advantage from this practice, and it has been often remarked that there are no better instructed negotiators in Europe than those of Venice.

THE CHINESE TRADITION OF DIPLOMACY*

J. K. Fairbank and S. Y. Têng

Chinese foreign policy in the nineteenth century can be understood only against its traditional Chinese background, the tributary system.

* J. K. Fairbank and S. Y. Têng, "On the Ch'ing Tributary System," Harvard Journal of Asiatic Studies, VI (1941), 135–144. Reprinted by permission of the editor of the Harvard Journal of Asiatic Studies. J. K. Fairbank is Professor of History, Harvard University, and author of China's Response to the West (1954), Trade and Diplomacy on the China Coast (1954), and The United States and China (rev. ed., 1958). S. Y. Têng is Associate Professor of History, Indiana University, and author of Japanese Studies on Japan and the Far East (1961) and Historiography of the Taiping Rebellion (1962).

This system for the conduct of foreign relations had been directly inherited from the Ming dynasty (1368–1644) and modified to suit the needs
of the Manchus. As a Confucian world-order in the Far East, it continued
formally in existence until the very end of the nineteenth century, and
was superseded in practice only gradually, after 1842, by the British
treaty system which has until recently governed the foreign relations of
Siam, Japan, and other states, as well as China. The Chinese diplomatic
documents of a century ago are therefore really unintelligible unless they
are studied in the light of the imperial tributary system which produced
them.

The ramifications of this vast subject, in political theory, in international trade, and in diplomacy, have been explored by a few pioneer
scholars... Studies of the tributary system in the Ch'ing period are
less numerous; relatively little effort has been made to link the sorry
Chinese foreign policy of the nineteenth century with the great tradition
which lay behind it. . . .

The present article attempts a preliminary survey of the tributary system as it developed under the Ch'ing dynasty of the Manchus (1644–
1912). . . . Before proceeding to the presentation and analysis of this
material, we offer below a brief explanatory discussion of the function of
tribute in the Chinese state, which may serve to pose further problems
for research.

For purpose of analysis it may be pointed out (1) that the tributary
system was a natural outgrowth of the cultural preeminence of the early
Chinese, (2) that it came to be used by the rulers of China for political
ends of self-defense, (3) that in practice it had a very fundamental and
important commercial basis, and (4) that it served as the medium for
Chinese international relations and diplomacy. It was, in short, a scheme
of things entire, and deserves attention as one historical solution to problems of world-organization.

Behind the tributary system as it became institutionalized in the Ming
and Ch'ing periods lay the age-old tradition of Chinese cultural superiority over the barbarians. Continuously from the bronze age, when Shang
civilization first appears as a culture-island in North China, this has been
a striking element in Chinese thought, perpetuated by the eternal conflict
between the settled agrarian society of the Yellow River basin and the
pastoral nomads of the steppe beyond the Wall, as well as by the persistent expansion of the Chinese to the south among the tribes whose
remnants are now being absorbed in Yunnan and Kweichow. From this
contact with the nomads of the north and west and with the aborigines of
the south, the Chinese appear to have derived certain basic assumptions
which may be stated as follows: first, that Chinese superiority over the

barbarians had a cultural rather than a mere political basis; it rested less upon force than upon the Chinese way of life embodied in such things as the Confucian code of conduct and the use of the Chinese written language; the sign of the barbarian was not race or origin so much as non-adherence to this way of life. From this it followed, secondly, that those barbarians who wished to "come and be transformed," and so participate in the benefits of (Chinese) civilization, must recognize the supreme position of the Emperor; for the Son of Heaven represented all mankind, both Chinese and barbarian, in his ritual sacrifices before the forces of nature. Adherence to the Chinese way of life automatically entailed the recognition of the Emperor's mandate to rule all men. This supremacy of the Emperor as mediator between Heaven and Earth was most obviously acknowledged in the performance of the kotow, the three kneelings and nine prostrations to which European envoys later objected. It was also acknowledged by the bringing of a tribute of local produce, by the formal bestowal of a seal, comparable to the investiture of a vassal in medieval Europe, and in other ways. Thus the tributary system, as the sum total of these formalities, was the mechanism by which barbarous non-Chinese regions were given their place in the all-embracing Chinese political, and therefore ethical, scheme of things.

This general theory is of course familiar to the most casual student of Chinese history, and yet the realities of the situation are still a matter of dispute. In the intercourse between the Chinese state and the barbarians, commercial relations became inseparably bound up with tributary. Trade was conducted by barbarian merchants who accompanied the tributary envoy to the frontier or even to the capital; sometimes it was conducted by the members of the mission itself. That tribute was a cloak for trade has been a commonplace ever since merchants from the Roman orient arrived in China in 166 A.D. claiming to be envoys of Marcus Aurelius. Thus Benedict de Goez, crossing Central Asia in the year 1604, describes the "sham embassies" of the merchants from the western kingdoms who "forge public letters in the names of the kings whom they profess to represent" and "under pretence of being ambassadors go and offer tribute to the Emperor." Innumerable other examples could be cited wherein tribute, in the minds of the tribute bearers, was merely a formality connected with trade; at Macao and Canton, indeed, the Europeans in their concentration upon the substance of commerce eventually forgot all about the formality which theoretically still went with it.

This economic interpretation, however, is made from the point of view of the barbarians. The motivation of the Court is a different matter.

The argument that the tributary system was developed by the Court chiefly for political defense has been succinctly stated by Dr. T. F. Tsiang:

Out of this period of intense struggle and bitter humiliation [the eleventh and twelfth centuries], the neo-Confucian philosophy, which began then to dominate China, worked out a dogma in regard to international relations, to hold sway in China right to the middle of the nineteenth century. . . . That dogma asserts that national security could only be found in isolation and stipulates that whoever wished to enter into relations with China must do so as China's vassal, acknowledging the supremacy of the Chinese emperor and obeying his commands, thus ruling out all possibility of international intercourse on terms of equality. It must not be construed to be a dogma of conquest or universal dominion, for it imposed nothing on foreign peoples who chose to remain outside the Chinese world. It sought peace and security, with both of which international relations were held incompatible. If relations there had to be, they must be of the suzerain-vassal type, acceptance of which meant to the Chinese acceptance of the Chinese ethic on the part of the barbarian. . . .

It must not be assumed that the Chinese Court made a profit out of . . . tribute. The imperial gifts bestowed in return were usually more valuable than the tribute . . . Chinese statesmen before the latter part of the nineteenth century would have ridiculed the notion that national finance and wealth should be or could be promoted by means of international trade. On China's part the permission to trade was intended to be a mark of imperial bounty and a means of keeping the barbarians in the proper state of submissiveness. . . .

Thus we might conclude that trade and tribute were cognate aspects of a single system of foreign relations, the moral value of tribute being the more important in the minds of the rulers of China, and the material value of trade in the minds of the barbarians; this balance of interests would allow mutual satisfaction and the system would continue to function. From this it might be concluded further that the tributary system really worked in reverse, the submission of the barbarians being actually bought and paid for by the trade conceded to them by China. But this last is an over-simplification which runs counter to the whole set of ideas behind the system, and it also overlooks the interesting possibility, which deserves exploration, of an imperial economic interest—for instance, in the silk export trade. In short it seems impossible at present to make more than one generalization: that the tributary system was a framework within which all sorts of interests, personal and imperial, economic and social, found their expression. Further study should reveal an interplay between greed and statecraft, dynastic policy and vested interest, similar to that in other great political institutions.

One untouched aspect of the system is its functioning as a diplomatic medium. Since all foreign relations in the Chinese view were ipso facto tributary relations, it followed that all types of international intercourse, if they occurred at all in the experience of China, had to be fitted into the tributary system. Thus Chinese envoys were sometimes sent abroad to spy out the enemy or to seek allies, and foreign envoys came and conducted negotiations at the capital, all within this framework. . . .

[S]everal things stand out [from an examination of the tributary system]. Relations between the Son of Heaven and his tributaries were on an ethical basis, and hence reciprocal. The tributaries were submissive and reverent, the Emperor was compassionate and condescending. These reciprocal relationships required formal expression. Presentation of tribute was a ritual performance, balanced by the forms of imperial hospitality and bestowal of imperial gifts. Hence the great importance of ceremonies, so complicated that they must be practiced under guidance beforehand. The detailed regulations given at length in official Chinese works might fruitfully be compared with the feudal and ecclesiastical ceremonies of medieval Europe.

But, as in European experience, very practical results were achieved within this cloak of ritual. Mourning for the dead being a major ceremony in the Confucian life, the Emperor could properly send his envoys abroad on the death of a foreign ruler, at just the time when it was desirable to have information as to the new ruler and perhaps exert pressure upon affairs in the foreign state. Tuan Ch'ên, in going to offer condolences to the Hsiung-nu, incidentally took an army with him. Bestowal of an imperial seal upon a new ruler has obvious analogies to the recognition of new governments practiced in the West. Diplomatic courtesies of a sort were extended to tributary envoys, who traveled by government post and received state burial if they died in China. Other comparisons can be made to show that the tributary system functioned, among other things, as a diplomatic medium. The fact that the normal needs of foreign intercourse could be met in this egocentric manner tended to perpetuate it, and made any other system seem impossible. Hence the fatal tenacity with which the Manchu Court in the modern period tried to solve its foreign problems through the ancient tributary mechanism.

THE ISLAMIC TRADITION OF DIPLOMACY*

Muhammad Hamidullah

Instances of envoys temporarily sent to foreign Courts, and of secret agents posted in foreign countries, exist from time immemorial in human

* Muhammad Hamidullah, *Muslim Conduct of State*, 3rd ed. (Lahore, Pakistan: Muhammad Ashraf, 1954), pp. 143–154. Muhammad Hamidullah is author of *Le Prophète de l'Islam* (1959).

annals. Thus, no wonder if both these kinds of persons are found in Muslim history as early as the time of the Prophet. . . .

As self-sufficiency and self-dependence grew less and less, giving place to interdependence regarding necessities and luxuries of life, States were prompted to have greater international intercourse, commercial as well as political. Classical Arabic literature on diplomacy is very scant. . . . Questions of commercial intercourse has attracted even less attention of classical authors.

I have not yet made any profound study of the commercial agents in foreign countries. My tentative conclusion is that intrepid traders have been used to go to foreign countries before their own State had any diplomatic relations with them. In olden times, trade caravans used to stay in a country for longer periods than now. The local chiefs appointed what are known as the *Hunarman, Shahbandar,* and *Malik-ut-tajjār* in order to regulate the affairs and disputes of foreign traders. These developed into European consuls, during the Crusades. And thus permanent commercial agents came into existence long before permanent political agents and envoys.

The Prophet himself took the initiative of giving impetus to trade and commerce even at the expense of State income. Thus it was that he abolished all inter-Provincial customs duties within the realm, and the many treaties concluded by him with tribes submitting to his authority expressly stipulate that. Foreign trade, however, remained subject to the usual tithe or whatever percentage was stipulated for by express treaties and conventions between States. The treaty for levying a tithe on the traders of Manbij (Hierapolis) is said to be the first of its kind in the time of 'Umar. The words *tariff* and *douane* or cognate words in European languages, borrowed from Arabic, have a history in themselves. There is an implied reference in the writings of ash-Shaibānīy that sometimes the goods for trade belonging to minors or women were exempt in Islamic territories from customs duties. Again, goods of less value than 200 drachmas belonging to a person were customs-free. Abū-Yūsuf records an interesting correspondence exchanged between 'Umar and his governor, Abū-Mūsā-al-Ash'arīy:

Al-Ash'arīy wrote: Some traders of ours go to non-Muslim territory where they are subjected to tithes. 'Umar replied: Levy thou also on theirs as they levy on Muslim traders.

Although Abū-Yūsuf has known dumping and "famine on account of the excess of goods," he still believes in free trade, and quotes the injunctions of the Prophet not to interfere with prices.

As for diplomatic relations and representations, we have mentioned that at first they were not maintained on a permanent basis. In his *A Short History of the Saracens*, Ameer 'Ali says, however:

When the provincial governors became the feudatories of the empire, and the sovereignty of the Caliph dwindled into more or less effective suzerainty, the confidential messengers were turned into legates of the Pontiffs, and acted as his resident agents in the Courts of Nīshāpūr, Merv, Mosul. Damascus, etc. Like the Papal legates, in the later mediaeval times in Europe, they accompanied the sovereigns to whom they were accredited in their military marches. We find them not only in the camps of Alp Arsalān and Malik Shāh, but also in those of Nūr-ud-Din Maḥmūd and Saladin, ever active and sometimes meddlesome; occasionally as under the later Ayūbids, reconciling contending princes, and settling fratricidal strifes . . .

Each sovereign on his side maintained a commissary called Shaḥna at the Pontifical Court, charged with the duty of keenly watching the moves of the game on the part of his rivals, for the struggle for predominating influence over the source of all legitimate authority was as great at Baghdād as in Papal Rome. Shahnas were usually stationed, besides the capital, in places like Wāsit, Bussorah, Tikrit, etc.

In an appendix, the same author says:

The Abbaside sovereigns frequently employed a special envoy to transact confidential business with neighbouring potentates. The office was called the Niẓām-ul-Haḍratain.

After the destruction of Baghdād by Mongols in 656 H., there is apparently another gap in the history of permanent embassies in Islamic countries; there were no permanent ambassadors at that time even in Europe.

Reception of Envoys

In the time of the Prophet, whenever a foreign envoy or delegation came, we find there was a sort of Master of Ceremonials who instructed the guests previous to their reception by the Prophet in the local formalities. The envoys sometimes disregarded them. There are many incidents in the time of 'Umar when the Muslim envoys disregarded certain local formalities in foreign courts, especially prostration, and caused umbrage.

The Prophet, when in Madīnah, used to receive foreign envoys in the Great Mosque where the Pillar of Embassies still commemorates the place. The Prophet and his Companions are said to have usually put on fine dress at the time of the ceremonial reception of envoys. . . .

Envoys generally presented gifts from their senders to the ruler to whose court they were accredited. Such things went to the State treasury.

The wife of the Caliph 'Umar once received, in return for her gift, a gift from the wife of the Emperor of Constantinople, but the Caliph likewise confiscated it in favour of the general exchequer, and only the value of the original gift of the Caliphline was given her. There are cases of the Prophet accepting the gifts of foreign potentates and using them in his official capacity—and there was no private capacity of his as is testified to by his dictum that he could not be inherited from, and whatever he possessed would go to the general exchequer.

The envoys, too, received gifts from those to whom they were sent. The Prophet is recorded to have willed on his death-bed that his successor should award gifts to envoys as he himself used to during his lifetime. The Prophet once gave an envoy from 'Umān 500 drachmas, at another occasion gold and silver girdles, and at other times other things, sometimes more, sometimes less, according to individual cases. It is generally admitted that, if a Muslim envoy received a gift on the part of foreign rulers, etc., that would go to the State coffers.

The envoys are officially entertained. There were several large houses in Madīnah, in the time of the Prophet, specially meant for foreign guests. ... No wonder when the Prophet took special pains personally to entertain the envoys of Abyssinia, for it was in this country that he had found a most friendly State even when he was in extreme danger in Mecca in the early days of his mission. Generally speaking, envoys were treated corresponding to their personal position and that of their sender.

Privileges of Envoys

Envoys, along with those who are in their company, enjoy full personal immunity: they must never be killed, nor be in any way molested or maltreated. Even if the envoy, or any of his company, is a criminal of the State to which he is sent, he may not be treated otherwise than as an envoy. The envoys of the impostor Musailimah provide good law to whom the Prophet had said: Had you not been envoys, I would have ordered you to be beheaded.

Envoys are accorded full freedom of prayer and religious rites. The Prophet allowed the delegation of the Christians of Najrān to celebrate their service in the very Mosque of the Prophet. Muslim historians mention as a curiosity that these Christians turned their faces towards the East and prayed.

Envoys may only in extraordinary cases be detained or imprisoned. So, the Prophet detained the plenipotentiaries of Mecca until the Muslim ambassador detained in Mecca returned safe to Ḥudaibīya where the Prophet was camping.

The property of the envoys is exempt from import duties in Muslim territory if reciprocated. So, ash-Shaibānīy says, if the foreign States exempt Muslim envoys from customs duties and other taxes, the envoys of such States will enjoy the same privileges in Muslim territory; otherwise they may, if the Muslim State so desire, be required to pay ordinary dues like foreign visitors.

Peaceful Settlement of International Differences

The object of diplomacy is peaceful solution of international questions and promotion of harmony between different States. It is immaterial whether the differences between States are legal or political or otherwise. We are concerned here only with the modes of their settlement, which are of various kinds:

1. The first and the simplest kind is mutual negotiation. This is done through permanent or special and extraordinary envoys. This need not be discussed in any detail.

2. Conciliation, mediation and good offices. By these different terms we understand third parties, friends to both the contending States serving as channels for mutual negotiation and tendering friendly suggestions and advice to bring the disputants to an amicable settlement of their relations. Ibn-Hishām records that in the year 1 H. the first, or at least one of the first expeditions the Prophet despatched against the caravans belonging to the city-state of Mecca—then at war with Islam—was headed by Ḥamzah, who encountered the enemy near the seacoast of Yanbūʿ. Abū-Jahl was leading the enemy party. A fight was imminent but Majdīy-ibn-ʿAmr, who was an ally of both the States, Muslim as well as Meccan, intervened with mediations; and both the detachments parted from each other quietly. We may also refer to the case of Ubaīy-ibn-Salūl, who, although a Muslim subject, in his capacity as an old ally of the Jewish tribe of Qainuqāʿ, interceded with the Prophet on their behalf, and the Prophet granted him his request.

3. The third and the most important kind is arbitration. This means the determination of a difference between two States through the decision of one or more umpires chosen by the parties. The most important case in the time of the Prophet is the arbitration as to the treatment to be meted out to the Jewish tribes of Banū-Quraiẓah after their capitulation on the condition that a certain person should decide their lot. The Prophet accepted it, and carried out the arbitral award fully. Another case, rather complicated, is the following. The tribe of Banū'l-ʿAnbar, a branch of the Tamīmites of Eastern Arabia, was politically independent and at the time of the incident under discussion had not yet embraced Islam. His-

torians report that, owing apparently to lack of rain in its own territory, it came to the territory of the tribe of Khuzāʿah (which was Muslim and lived inside the Islamic State) for purposes of grazing. When the tax collector, sent by the Prophet, came to this region, he exacted from the ʿAnbarites same tax as from Muslim citizens. They opposed it with arms, and the tax collector had to flee to Madīnah. The Khuzāʿites thought it prudent to ask their troublesome guests to quit the territory, which they did. Some days later, when they were still on the march, the detachment sent by the Prophet overtook them, made some prisoners and returned to Madīnah while the rest of the ʿAnbarites escaped all pursuit. Not long after, a delegation of the ʿAnbarites came to Madīnah, and was persuaded to embrace Islam. Then they spoke about their kinsmen who were made prisoners of war by the punitive expedition. The Prophet would have strictly been within his rights if he had refused any clemency for acts committed before their conversion, yet he made a gesture: he left the matter in the hands of one of the members of the delegation, and said whatever award he would give would be executed. This arbitrator decided that half of the prisoners should be freed gratuitously and the rest should be liberated on payment of customary ransom for prisoners of war. The famous arbitration between ʿAlīy and Muʿāwīyah is another classical example, the document containing the terms of reference in this case having come down to us *in toto*. The question was who should succeed to the Caliph ʿUthmān who had been murdered. ʿAlīy being elected by the people of Madīnah, and Muʿāwīyah, who was governor of Syria, contending its validity and himself standing as a candidate. The arbitrators had agreed among themselves that both ʿAlīy and Muʿāwīyah should be deposed, and that the Muslim community should elect a Caliph anew. Accordingly at the fixed time and place the arbitrators came to deliver their award. First the nominee of ʿAlīy pronounced that he deposed both ʿAlīy and Muʿāwīyah so that a new Caliph might be elected and the Muslim community once more united. After him stood the arbitrator nominated by Muʿāwīyah, who said that the nominee of the other party had no right to decide except for his own client; and that he, the nominee of Muʿāwīyah, however, would not depose his client; on the other hand he confirmed him in his position. As the arbitrators had no agreed award, ʿAlīy did not feel himself bound by the award and he did not abide by it. Civil wars would have again ensued had not ʿAlīy been assassinated by an anarchist. In an interesting passage, Abū-Yūsuf says what applies admirably to the case of ʿAlīy:

If the parties agree on two arbitrators ... who differ in the award, it is void, except when both the parties agree to accept the award of one of them.

If only one party agrees to the award of one of the arbitrators and not the other, the arbitration is void. If each of the parties agrees to the award of one of the arbitrators, the arbitration is void.

According to Abū-Yūsuf, the following categories of people are not fit to be selected as arbitrators, viz., Muslims punished for scandalizing respected ladies, minors, women, slaves, blind people, the immoral, men of suspected or notoriously bad conduct, Muslims who are prisoners in the hands of the other party to arbitration, Muslim traders in the territory of the other party, Muslim subjects of the other non-Muslim party, be he in his own home or even in the Muslim camp. According to our author an arbitrator must be:

A man of insight in affairs, orthodoxy in religion, eminence and trust among the Muslims, and profound knowledge of law is preferred and aimed at in this matter. And those whose evidence is not accepted in court, should not be selected to arbitrate in such affairs.

Abū-Yūsuf also maintains that a non-Muslim subject, too, is not eligible to the honour of arbitership, but his opinion has not found favour with other jurists. For al-Kāsānīy is explicit that a non-Muslim subject can be accepted as arbitrator, and the trend of his argument bears little doubt that, according to him, even neutral non-Muslims may be accepted as arbiters.

Abū-Yūsuf says that awards to the effect of maintaining status quo, futile in themselves, are void and are equivalent to saying: We do not accept arbitership. So, too, awards for returning Muslims into the subjection of non-Muslims are void. He is so emphatic on the point that, according to him, if the other party to the arbitration had brought to the Muslim camp Muslim prisoners, slaves of Islamic faith, and Muslim subjects of the other non-Muslim party, these will not be allowed to return to the non-Muslim territory, for "the arbiteral award does not allow the return of Muslims to belligerent and infidel territory." But his opinion is not shared by other jurists on the higher authority of the practice of the Prophet who expressly consented to return Muslims under the treaty of Ḥudaibīyah. If for the death of the arbitrators or disagreement between them, an arbitration fails, status quo must be restored and no undue advantage be taken of the other party's sense of security and consequent carelessness.

DIPLOMACY IN THE MISSILE AGE*

Lord Vansittart

In the days when politeness was a tradition, and tradition counted, demands for the recall of diplomatists were unknown save in rare cases of extreme provocation or impropriety. (The expulsion of Lord Sackville from the United States was not really deserved.) Now removal of Ambassadors or Chargés d'Affaires is continually demanded on the flimsiest pretext, and subordinates are simply thrown out in 48 hours. (I have often urged that we should all retaliate more formidably; Communist missions are much more useful to them than ours in Totalitaria are to us.) The excuse for this insolence is usually some stale and fantastic taradiddle on the theme of espionage, which is worked to death like much else by the Cominformants. The simplest conversation with a local citizen is sufficient to start the insanity, which invariably ends in manifold liquidations.

Here it should be stated parenthetically as a quite small cause of disrespect that Ambassadors have been multiplied beyond sense or recognition to gratify *amour propre*. Before 1914 only the Great Powers had Ambassadors, and these had both rank and power. Now they are increasingly mere mouthpieces; they have lost stature, and braided lightweights have not gained it.

Diplomacy would, however, have changed even without this minor metamorphosis. It is a commonplace that the Iron Curtain exists not only to prevent its inmates from knowing anything of the outside world, but also to bar all understanding from unwelcome but inevitable intruders, which is the totalitarian conception of even the most diplomatic infidel. Here we get nearer to the real causes of the decline in diplomacy during the second quarter of the twentieth century. For, until the First German War at least, diplomatists who knew well the peoples and languages of the countries where they were posted were thought to be an asset to both

* Robert Gilbert Lord Vansittart, "The Decline of Diplomacy," *Foreign Affairs*, XXVIII, No. 2 (January 1950), 178–188. Copyright 1950 by the Council on Foreign Relations Inc., New York, and reprinted by permission. Robert Gilbert Lord Vansittart served from 1902 to 1941 as Chief Diplomatic Adviser to the Foreign Secretary of H. M. Government. He is author of *Bones of Contention* (1945) and *Lessons of My Life* (1943).

parties. They were always useful in maintaining good relations; they were often exceedingly popular, and the governments to which they were accredited were loath to let them go. Indeed foreign requests for prolongations of their appointments were sometimes embarrassing. Sometimes they—for instance Herrick—acquired the popularity without acquiring the tongue.

The past put a premium on courtesy. Wherever they went—mainly without let or hindrance—sane diplomatists tried to absorb as much as possible for their real purpose—peace, which they much enjoyed. Contrast this with the real policy of Totalitaria, which is the deepening and widening of ignorance. There is a deliberate aim to get rid of western diplomatists who know the language or nature of the country where they are stationed. There are many cases where this has been the sole reason for expulsion. The change is fundamental.

Here again I must diverge for a moment to complete the picture, and to add in fairness that often where a government had evil intentions its diplomatic representatives were kept in ignorance, the better to play their parts; or sometimes, knowing, they protested. There were bad men in the business, like Holstein, but the novelesque Machiavellis were the exception, not the rule. To the same order of ideas belongs the dramatized cliché of the mid-nineteenth century that "a diplomatist is an honest man paid to lie by his country." With the advent of Nazism and Communism, alike state conspiracies, most of their representatives were involved.

Thus we come to the main cause for the decline of diplomacy; and it will only be fully apparent when we look at its operation from the other end—that is, the composition, activities and purposes of the Communist staffs in foreign capitals. This is a matter to which I have amply drawn attention in the House of Lords, in the hope of making the democracies realize the total nature of the change before it is too late.

The change resides in this. The old diplomacy mainly existed to maintain good international relations. When it failed, its job was done and it packed up—"asked for its passports," or more prosaically took a train— for then war had come in spite and not because of it in most instances. Enough official papers from the last century are now available to prove the truth of this assertion. Take, for example, the desperate efforts made to deter Germany from the last two of her five wars. In 1914 both Lichnowsky and Mensdorff did what little they could to milden their evil governments. Broadly speaking, the real charge that can be made against the old diplomacy is that, though sometimes tough or provocative, it was mostly too suave and honeyed on the part of the intending aggressor, too patient and conciliatory on the part of the aggressed. The second tendency issued in appeasement.

Nowadays the diplomacy of an increasing part of the world is thoughtfully calculated to create and maintain *bad* relations. This, of course, is done in no mere *Schadenfreude* or spirit of spite. Bad relations with western democracies and capitalist countries are an article of faith, an accepted condition for the survival of Totalitaria. The successful Communist statesman is therefore he who ensures the permanence and intensity of this condition. So the missions of the Cominform are largely stocked with persons who make no pretense of practising diplomacy as previously defined, but are employed solely for hostile propaganda, sabotage, subversion and espionage. I have plenty of evidence and illustration for which I have no space here, and which indeed are unnecessary to demonstrate so notorious a truism.

To revert again to the old diplomacy, espionage was not usually practised from embassies, though they were often the victims of it. They were generally kept apart from such compromising activities—at least by the cautious or respectable Powers. An occasional Military Attaché was mentioned in a scandal like the Dreyfus case. The diplomatic body was, however, practically never involved in such hullabaloos as those now fabricated by ubiquitous secret police disguised in the combinations and permutations of infinite initials. Erstwhile spy-stories rarely attained publicity; when they did there was something in them, but gentlemen in knee-breeches and decorations were seldom implicated. (Of legitimate information they naturally obtained as much as possible.) Sardou's famous play, "Les Pattes de Mouche," often acted in Britain and the United States under the title of "Diplomacy," was a joke in the profession. (Abel Hermant's "La Carrière" was great fun.) Communist diplomatic missions, on the contrary, are everywhere up to the eyes in spying, and "make no bones" about it, though they protest loudly and *pro forma* when detected.

Espionage, however, is only the beginning of the mischief. Sabotage is an even surer way of ensuring the ideal of bad relations, because it is more widely felt. Totalitarian diplomacy now practises two kinds of sabotage, both of which are directed by its missions. The first, of course, is technical preparation for the event of war. The second is the "softening" or undermining of the countries with which war is contemplated. It is essential for the Soviet "Day" that these should first be economically weakened or ruined. The most favored methods are the "unofficial" and "rolling" strikes; but there are many other means of fomenting political disloyalty through industrial disaffection. The details of the technique do not concern us here; the point is that they are a function of the new diplomacy. The old might well turn in its grave. By these openly flaunted means a maximum of resentment is attained by Soviet diplomacy and its satellites. It all sounds like madness, but there is a tireless method in it.

The next activity is more insidious and equally novel, though its advent has been more gradual. It is openly to persuade as many people as possible, in the country whose hospitality is accepted, to hate and revile their own land. This is by far the best way to ensure bad relations. It is achieved partly by Communist press and radio from without, but also by local agencies for publicity which take orders and subsidies from the Cominform through Communist embassies and legations), and finally by forming and financing "Friendship Societies" to cover the knaves who recruit the fools.

All this leads logically to the next step in the decline. Under the old school, immunity was limited to the diplomatic staff. There were considerable doubts whether it even extended to the consular personnel. Certainly no one would ever have thought of extending the claim to any other body. Such a course would have been impossible, and anyhow it would not have paid, for it would have lowered the status of the greatly self-esteeming plenipotentiaries.

With the vicious extension of the province of diplomacy has come a corresponding exaggeration of the claim for immunity. When all sorts of rogues are part of the machinery, all sorts of devices must be thought up to cover them. The process began in the greatly overstaffed Communist trade agencies—thin concealment indeed, seeing the small trade done by them. Now it has reached the press agencies, and has just produced a *cause célèbre,* which may find its place in international law, if any such thing is preserved in the future—a doubtful hypothesis.

The Soviet Government keeps Tass agencies everywhere for disseminating propaganda. Hitherto these have enjoyed no more privilege than any other undiplomatic body. But recently the London office of Tass brought a foul charge against a most worthy and distinguished exile. He tried to bring a libel action, and Tass at once bolted for cover. It produced to the British court a certificate from the Soviet Ambassador affirming that the news agency is an organ of the Soviet Government. The British court felt bound to accept the certificate. By this trick the agency has hitherto avoided prosecution. I say "hitherto," for I do not mean to let the decision stand unchallenged, and shall attack it when Parliament reassembles. I have already obtained from the Lord Chancellor a public admission that the claim is wholly unprecedented. Just think of the consequences were such a pretension conceded! Any foreign fount of malevolence would then be a law unto itself; there would be no conceivable bound to privilege, which would need only a small further stretch to cast its mantle over espionage as well. Even the most disreputable gangsters would thus be an official part of the new diplomacy. It is typical of the times that such a monstrosity as this Ambassadorial testimony should have been put forward at all. It must be brushed aside, and that gesture also will be symptomatic of a growing disregard for envoys.

Of old, as aforesaid, we diplomatists lived together in apparent comity for enjoyable lapses of time. Even in periods of friction there was some semblance of *esprit de corps*. We were rival practitioners of the same honorable trade. All this is changed. Nowadays these accumulated and exploited elements of discord amount to a state of permanent bad temper. I sometimes think that the degradation of the language of diplomacy is even more sinister than the debasement of its performance. There is a smell of the jungle about these dense growths of words, which smother old conceptions like voluble creepers.

Diplomacy has passed through every phase in its short life, for it only began in the last few centuries, and grew up late. It started with covenants secretly arrived at, less because anyone was ashamed of their contents than because they were of no interest to an illiterate and uninfluential public. The old methods have proved to be no more obnoxious than the new. Similarly, the balance of power, after having been first an ideal and then a punch-bag, is now being practised again and not mentioned by name—which is perhaps sensible, seeing that "human notions are few, not far between."

In the twentieth century, however, President Wilson had a brain-wave. He dreamed of "open diplomacy," and of "open covenants openly arrived at." That really sounded like something. Only after unhappy experience was it discovered that preliminary negotiation cannot profitably be conducted in the open. This glimpse of the obvious was generously assisted by the well-informed activities of the press and by the embarrassing antics of national propaganda and self-advertisement. Wilson was sagely crying for the moon. All right, said some, let us compound for open covenants secretly arrived at. Alas, great chunks of humanity were morally indisposed even to this check on their way to the abyss. The Nazis and the Communists in their *amours* begat a clutch of secret treaties much worse than any that had gone before.

The world of optimists, or even meliorists, thought again, and tended to content itself with a diplomacy which could produce decent treaties "any old how." In consequence it got some rather indecent ones after much indecent bickering. The Allies, still so-called, concluded—a verb as inept as the noun—the treaties with Italy and the other ex-satellites, which contained many grave errors and stood no chance of observance, as I pointed out at the time. We have since discovered that the new diplomacy affords no possibility of concluding a German treaty at all; and this is just as well, when we consider the total perfidy of Totalitaria. It is one of history's little jokes that the authors of the Treaty of Versailles were blamed for drafting it in six months. We may be sorry for the Austrians, but even if their desire for a treaty be fulfilled, it will also be an unjust one, which would compromise the little country's prospect of economic survival, and even of territorial integrity. King Log being withdrawn, King Stork may return. No treaty is certainly better than a bad one. I understand this to have been the view of the American representative. I certainly concur in it. I have no wish to see Austria either ruined or reinvaded. In any case even a good treaty would not be kept by the Soviets. The futility of treaties is, however, another matter, which would require a chapter, or even a book, to itself. I will not dwell on it here, beyond observing that all endeavor of diplomacy in treaty-making is stultified by the habitual treaty-breaking of modern despotism.

We have reached the paradox that the decline of diplomacy has synchronized with the increasing equipment of its exponents. The great Ambassadors of the nineteenth century were sometimes not particularly clever men; sometimes they were not even particularly well educated, and owed their positions to favor. I saw at close quarters some who survived into the twentieth. Few of them would have had the least chance of withstanding an examination in any modern sense; but they did their work with authority, partly because there was no organized attempt to prevent them. In the period preceding theirs, an Ambassador's authority was even greater: he sometimes initiated policy and enjoyed considerable latitude, owing to lack of communications. As these improved, Ambassadorial status dwindled to that of mere executant of a policy decided not even in Foreign Offices but in Cabinets.

In complete contrast with a school as extinct as the dodo, our young men today are trained, perhaps overtrained, for a vanishing future, and tested and accoutred with all specialized ingenuity, some of it—in our case—sometimes a little silly. "Too clever by half," my Victorian nurse used to say. Their intellectual attainments greatly, and rightly, exceed those deemed essential in the zenith of diplomacy when the wheels of procedure crunched over the gravel, not always easy going but good enough for carriage folk. Now the surface is made for speed, but the road is usually blocked. Simultaneously the traffic has increased. The staffs of missions have been multiplied tenfold. And all this apparatus has been brought into play in an era which offers less hope for it. The negotiators of the Austrian treaty re-formed, dissolved, returned, mulled over their texts, till they knew them and each other by heart. Nothing happened year after year. Such treaties as have been landed lie instantly in fragments, and all protests are vain. These goings-on would have been deemed impossible in an age less efficient and more affable.

Diplomacy, with all its failings—it had many because it was far too much a class affair, and power politics are never pretty—was an instrument of civilization. It is being paralyzed, but only in common with other previously accepted amenities. It was one of the many veils in which we had sought to soften the outlines of the real harshness of human nature and existence. Now veils have gone out of fashion. I have "done" many conferences in my life, but never went into one without some hope of a fairly quick result. No one could say the same today. Results are often not expected, and often not even desirable, while the technique of negotiation is equally often transformed into a brawling match.

A gallant and pernickety veteran, who had risen to a colonelcy in the First War Against the Germans, immediately volunteered for the Second, and was duly invalided out. Describing his experiences in his club, he said: "My dear fellow, you really can't think what it's like *this* time! The smell . . . the noise . . . and . . . the *people!*" The comment is less applicable to the battlefield than to the conference chamber, for all its newfangled facilities of earphones and automatic translations.

It may be said that this applies only to the representatives of half mankind. There is no reason why the other half should not behave itself. Part of our species is being conducted by sedulous apes back to the treetops, where it cannot exist; but the rest of *Homo sapiens* can live up to its lightly assumed title. That is perfectly true. And it isn't—not perfectly. We cannot get away from "the noise . . . and the people" of the Iron Curtain leaders so long as we have to meet them in the United Nations or in any more of these shy-making Big Fours—the Apotheosis of Avoirdupois. The pace of a troop was proverbially regulated by the slowest horse; the tone of a conference is set by its noisiest delegation. Diplomacy could flourish only so long as there was a loose, tacit and general agreement to behave *more or less* like gentlemen. There was no snobbery in the notion—only an instinctive recognition of our own limitations. The code was quite vague, and we never used the term "gentlemen's agreement" until it had become anathema to use the word gentleman in any other sense. It survived for a while like an appendix in the diplomatic body. From the moment when the behavior of rowdies became a constant feature, the old body was plainly moribund—for good or evil. We may hope for "somehow good," but the adverse balance is thus far incontestable.

One kind of old diplomacy did cling on until the end of the war; but it was the dubious sort known as personal. From distant days to the present, Very Important Persons have kept up intimate and important correspondences. Then it was time to go, and they mostly took their personal archives with them, salving their public consciences by underlining the word Private in the top left-hand corner. Some valuable material vanished in this way. Only a man as unearthly as Edward Grey kept and left his "private" correspondence in its official place. There is no positive harm in getting off the record, unless the exchanges become unduly secretive, as they sometimes do. Subordinates may then err through ignorance of vital passages between superiors. In general we may say that it is natural for the great to be on epistolary terms—within limits.

Unhappily, and mechanically, those limits extend themselves. From having their private post offices, the great pass easily to having their private postmen. Thus a rival Foreign Office was run by Lloyd George: it consisted of Lord Lothian. As liaison between Curzon and Lloyd George I had the uneasy task of trying both to contend and cooperate with it. Very Important Persons comprehensibly like to count on a reliable body of assent. They mean to pursue a policy: why weaken themselves by doubts and contradictions? The term yes-men is unnecessarily harsh—indeed unfair—because most henchmen are sincerely fascinated by their chiefs. Thus Chamberlain too had his supporter, Sir Horace Wilson, and the Foreign Office was again overshadowed. As Chief Diplomatic Adviser I saw Chamberlain only thrice in three years, and never once alone. What could be more understandable? He knew that I disagreed with his views. Unhappily neither Lothian nor Wilson had experience of Europe. Nor, for that matter, had Harry Hopkins. Yet it seemed as natural to his patron that he should be sent to cope with Stalin as it seemed natural to Chamberlain that Halifax should go to Berlin and Berchtesgaden under the amateurish cover of a hunting exhibition.

The V.I.P.'s often love to get rid of experts (which was easier of yore, when there weren't many anyway) and to indulge in a little—which becomes a lot of—diplomacy "on their own." I fully understand the taste, but—all passion spent—condemn it because it is apt to be attended by favoritism and incompetence. There is something restricted and restraining about an expert, which makes him look narrow to the wide-eyed; and since

> "les oreilles des grands
> Sont souvent de grandes oreilles,"

he is sometimes compelled, if he has any guts, to adopt the governess touch, which is unfair to him. There is something at once humble and superior about an expert—a trying combination. Consequently some antagonism may arise on *both* sides. But I do comprehend the recurrent itch of the Big Boys (Fours or better) to give rein to their untrammelled inspirations; and it was good entertainment when one day at the Peace Conference M. Clemenceau flared up, and threw out all his own experts plus everyone else's. A little personal diplomacy was impending. Arthur

Balfour's chief interest in Lloyd George—and a fascinating one too—was wondering, in his own words, what the Little Man would do next.

In modern times personal diplomacy was much favored by both Churchill and Roosevelt, who loved to carry on negotiations free from "interference." This predilection was facilitated, and in part necessitated, by war; but such courses are always apt to go too far and to produce errors which might be avoided, given better opportunities for briefing. When it came to personal diplomacy with Stalin, the results were more unfortunate, and to East Europe ruinous. The deals at the expense of Poland and China were as immoral as anything in the ages preceding Ostensible Enlightenment, and were only put over by the weight of unparalleled authority. I do not suppose that there have been many further temptations to personal diplomacy with the Kremlin.

The practice is an essay in omniscience, and it is only sometimes successful, because everyone needs advice. *Nemo sapit omnibus horis* was translated by Mr. Carter of "The Dolly Dialogues": "Everyone has been in love at least once." He should have added, "in love with himself." There is nothing new in a tendency which has long roots, but it has grown considerably as the century wears on—perhaps the right expression.

Another modern habit greatly increasing of late is "popular diplomacy." Of course there is really no such thing, just as there is no "popular democracy." There are either democracy and diplomacy without epithets or there are not. In this case the device is an attempt to bypass the governments concerned by appealing over their heads to their people. This has developed into a pernicious usage, and some may point to the fact that the United States virtually started it in the First World War. The answer is that it would have come about anyhow. President Wilson hoped to curtail hostilities by addressing himself to the German people. Most commentators greatly overestimate the effect of this legitimate manœuvre in wartime. I am not among them. The Germans fought both their great wars to the bitter end. In any case when Wilson later attempted the same tactics with the Italians, the results were admittedly disastrous.

Since then the Totalitarians, in complete control of all their means of communication, have taken over and insensately developed the method. I have already enumerated the nefarious uses for which Communist missions really exist. For true diplomatic considerations they might as well not be there, and we of the democracies might *almost* as well have no representation in Moscow, though there are a few faint arguments for maintaining it in satellite countries. Communist radio is Communist diplomacy, and it has defeated its own ends. While the bellowings go crescendo, the fruits are in marked diminuendo, for no Soviet spokesman seems to have a middle register.

The method is already past its peak, but it has forced itself back upon the democracies by making them resume and improve Wilson's initiative. In the ungraceful German metaphor, we have to do a bit of "howling with the wolves." Here also the effect is small, because so few of the enslaved peoples are able to hear the B.B.C. or the Voice of America owing to jamming and the shortage of receivers. Still we rightly plug along in this duplicate diplomacy; my only comment is that we do not exploit it with sufficient punch and virility. We may as well "make the best of a bad job."

"Everything flows," though not to the pacific. We have lost the belief in automatic progress, and diplomacy is for the nonce among the casualties, through no fault of genuine democracy. It outlasted the parallel practitioners of the League, and could well have coexisted with the United Nations, had they not suffered from trichinosis. It has only wilted under Communist hot air. It may come to its own again in modern dress; indeed it has never fallen into disuse among civilized peoples. But, in common with other advantageous growths, such as Justice, it can never regain worldwide acceptance, so long as the New Barbarians hold sway. We had better make up our minds to that, and conduct ourselves accordingly.

Harold Nicolson calls the life of his father, Lord Carnock, "a study in the Old Diplomacy." There was something to be said for it. Some will say: "Not much." Having experienced both old and new I reply: "More than can be said for its successor."

CHAPTER SIX

International Law
and the Peaceful Settlement of Disputes

The late Professor James Brierly once noted that "international law is a subject on which anyone can form an opinion intuitively, by using what we sometimes miscall our common sense, and without taking the trouble to inquire first of all what the facts about it may be."[1] Some men who have taken the pains to examine the nature of international law consider the subject an academic humbug, a product solely of Western scholarship that has no real significance in world affairs. Others believe that only man's shameful shortsightedness prevents him from employing the hoary norms of international law in order to stop the endemic power struggles among sovereign states. The selections in this chapter reveal that the facts are neither as cynical as indicated by the first point of view nor as rosy as indicated by the other.

The initial article is extracted from a paper delivered by Baron S. A. Korff in July 1923 to the then recently formed Academy of International Law at The Hague. Apropos of such an occasion, he outlined the role that law has played in world politics, partially answering the argument of those who believe that the failure to establish a universal legal order in the last century dooms international law to a permanent impotence. The unflagging efforts of Western statesmen and scholars to develop an effective code of rules to fix the rights and duties of states is cause for guarded optimism. "A very interesting point to remember," Baron Korff believes, "is the fact that all through the ages, international law keeps steadily its basic characteristics, notwithstanding the great changes that take place all over the world. This seems to be another strong proof that

---

[1] James Leslie Brierly, *The Basis of Obligation in International Law and Other Papers* (London: Oxford University Press, 1958), p. 306.

international law is an inherent corollary of civilization and invariably comes with any cultural development." *Ubi societas ibi est jus.*

Precisely what gains have been made in the development of a law of nations since Grotius published *De Jure Belli et Pacis* in 1628? What role can realistically be assigned to international law in governing the relations of sovereign states? These are the two main questions that Lord McNair seeks to answer in his article "The Place of Law and Tribunals in International Relations." Those who are overly enthusiastic champions of the rule of law, and who dismiss as unimportant or temporary the inherent limitations of the judicial and arbitral processes, will find a wealth of ideas in this selection that should help to clarify their thinking.

One of Britain's most distinguished jurists, Arnold Duncan Lord McNair masterfully examines the factors that limit the judicial and arbitral processes, whose essence "is to declare the law, including reasonable developments of it, and to state the existing rights and duties of the parties." He then presents a thesis that is all too frequently ignored: "To change the law and the existing rights and duties of the parties for the purpose of settling a dispute is foreign to the judicial or arbitral process, and involves quite different functions, namely, the legislative or the executive function, or a combination of both."

The concern to establish an international law has not been restricted to the West. The Muslims formulated a code to govern their inter-state relations that must be included under the rubric of international law. The great English historian Edward Gibbon believes that had the Muslim armies been successful at Tours, the Koran and not the Bible would have been taught at Oxford and Cambridge.[2] If he is correct, it is also true that the Muslim law of nations (*al-siyar*) today would be studied and followed in all Western capitals. Majid Khadduri, in the third article of this chapter, describes the Muslim legal system, which was based on the Prophet's teachings, alien from Christian principles, and developed to meet an inter-state political pattern quite unlike the West's. Students of comparative international relations should not overlook the points of similarity between the two sets of norms.

The problem of differing international legal systems is also the theme of Oliver J. Lissitzyn's essay, but he is concerned with the present period. Are Western-developed international-law norms considered obsolete by the newly independent countries of Asia and Africa? What view do the Soviet Union and its allies entertain concerning the law of nations; what role would they assign to these norms in the conduct of foreign affairs?

---

[2] Edward Gibbon, *History of the Decline and Fall of the Roman Empire;* quoted in Majid Khadduri, *War and Peace in the Law of Islam* (Baltimore: The Johns Hopkins Press, 1955), p. 52.

In "International Law in the Missile Age," Professor Lissitzyn offers his carefully balanced conclusions to these questions. A world-wide public order is not about to be inaugurated, he believes; but there is no reason for pessimistic resignation to chaos. "Both universal and particular international law may be expected to grow in scope and complexity as the volume and variety of transnational activities increase," he concludes, and so recalls the earlier article by Baron Korff.

AN INTRODUCTION TO THE HISTORY OF INTERNATIONAL LAW*

Baron S. A. Korff

The Ancient World

For a long time writers on international law took it for granted that the subject of their studies was a relatively recent product of modern civilization, and that the ancient world did not know any system of international law. If we go back to the literature of the nineteenth century, we can find a certain feeling of pride among internationalists that international law was one of the best fruits of our civilization and that it was a system which distinguished us from the ancient barbarians. Some of these writers paid special attention to this question of origins and endeavored to explain why the ancient world never could have had any international law.

As time went on, however, and modern historical investigations were constantly and persistently digging deeper into the past ages, this theory had to be considerably altered and finally discarded. Many interesting studies have appeared, some concerning Greece, others relating to more ancient times, but all of them bringing to light a whole mass of material which confirms the exact opposite point of view, namely, that the ancient world knew very well the meaning of international relations and was making use of an elaborate system of institutions, well developed and firmly established. . . . These results may be summed up in a short sentence: as soon as there developed a cultural center of a certain level of civilization,

* Baron S. A. Korff, "An Introduction to the History of International Law," *American Journal of International Law*, XVIII, No. 1 (January 1924), 246–259. Reprinted by permission. Baron S. A. Korff was a Professor of Political Science, School of Foreign Service, Georgetown University, Washington, D.C., and author of *Russia's Foreign Relations during the Last Half Century* (1922).

a state of some prominence, there grew up simultaneously relations with the outside world that soon took the shape of a whole system of institutions. In other words, such a system was the necessary consequence of any civilization and was as old as human culture in general. One matter of importance must be remembered in this connection: the ancient peoples of Asia or Africa were well acquainted with international relations and law. Further, there is another striking consequence: the careful analysis of these relations of different ancient civilizations reveals a remarkable similarity in their main lines of development. Take, for example, the history of ambassadorial missions, the question of extradition of fugitive criminals, the protection of certain classes of foreigners, and, above all, the sanctity of international contracts. In the growth of all these institutions identical principles prevail everywhere, in Sumer or Thebes, in Nineveh or Athens, and down to Rome.

The explanation of the mistake of our teachers of the nineteenth century is a very simple one. They were not acquainted with the history of the ancient civilizations. In their time that branch of historical research was hardly started; most facts concerning those bygone ages were absolutely unknown. Martens or Wheaton, Laurent or Coleman Phillipson, thus invariably commenced their detailed investigations with the Treaty of Westphalia, 1648. Today they seem dilettante, naïvely convinced that international law was a product of modern times only. New horizons have been opened to us, new vistas have been disclosed into the past ages, that compel us to change our point of view and accept new methods of research. . . .

Thus, under the influence of these new studies, our point of view concerning the historical development of international relations and law has necessarily but drastically changed. We know now that it is not *our* civilization that created these institutions, but that *every* civilization possessed whole systems of them; that they are first a necessary product of social life, and secondly, that they had everywhere many traits in common and do not belong exclusively, as was formerly supposed, to Europe. It is to be regretted that these first attempts have not yet been followed by a general treatise drawing attention to the modern historical investigations of ancient epochs and showing the gradual growth of institutions of international law and of their great and guiding principles.

The fact that the fundamental principles of international intercourse always were and are even in our day identical all over the world proves their inward, potential strength and vitality. But at the same time this also justifies the theory that international law is a necessary consequence of any civilization.

If we glance at the contents of those ancient systems of international law, we easily become aware of two things. First, that in this domain there always existed a distinct predominance of moral ideas or conceptions; those moral ideas conquer and subdue brute force and firmly control it. Secondly, that the fundamental principles are not so many in numbers. Among them the most important one is the principle of international obligations, the sanctity of the international contract, binding the state or nation, king or people. Another one concerns the establishment of channels of communications between two or several states and governments, growing into a law of embassies, with moral and legal guarantees for ambassadors and envoys from one country to another.

Thus gradually became established and mutually recognized certain ways of international behavior, certain customs and usages, relating in particular to war and its conduct. The binding force of all these international obligations has remained exactly the same since the times of Rameses or Murdoc, Pericles and Cicero, to those of Napoleon, George V of England or the Tsars of Russia. The mere fact of neighborly cohabitation creates moral and legal obligations, which in the course of time crystallize into a system of international law. In other words, the latter grows up and develops in exactly the same way *outside* of the state, as legal institutions form and crystallize *inside* the state—from the mere fact of the social life of man.

We must mention, however, one important exception. At certain historical periods one civilization or one people seem to develop so rapidly and outgrow their environment to such an extent that their relations with the outside world are no longer normal; their acquired superiority in many respects weighs heavily over their neighbors.

This leads to two conclusions, namely, that a certain principle of equality is of the essence of international relations and law; and further, that when such a state of equality does not exist, international relations acquire certain unusual characteristics. We find examples of such exceptional historical periods in the history of Greece and more so in Rome. Surrounded by "barbarians," neither Greece nor Rome could acknowledge the principle of equality, and in consequence their international relations possessed some very special traits. This explains, incidentally, why the writers of the nineteenth century were partly right when they pointed out the absence in Rome of normal international relations. They were wrong, however, in exaggerating this and denying the existence of any international law at all.

The other point concerning the principle of equality has a much greater theoretical value. It implies that international relations thrive and international law crystallizes normally only in those epochs when there existed simultaneously two or several states or nations possessing more or less equal cultural standards. Only among relatively equal states does the sanctity of international obligations, which, as we saw, is the moral foundation of all international law, find a guaranteed existence and recognition. Egypt, for instance, had Babylonia as partner; in the case of Greece, we see the existence of inter-state relations and federations. . . .

One more point should be mentioned concerning this ancient epoch. The system of international law of those days found its sanction in religion. Law and religion were invariably closely bound together. According to the conception of the ancients, they belonged to the same domain of morals. Every treaty or agreement, every institution involving an international obligation, had its counterpart in some sort of religious sanction. The outward expression of this we find in religious formulas or ceremonies, meant to impress the people and bind the kings and their governments. Most prominent in this respect was the rôle played by the religious oath, taken by the contracting Powers at the conclusion of an obligation. The force and stability of international agreements by these means were perhaps even better guaranteed than in our times. They certainly were in no way less effective or less binding than in the succeeding periods of the history of civilization. . . .

Conclusion

[W]e can infer that international law is as old as human civilization in general, and that it is really a necessary and unavoidable consequence of any civilization. Modern historical research goes far into the ages without having yet discovered the primeval start of human culture; the latter seems to recede constantly further back and with it the beginnings of international obligations. Further, a very interesting point to remember is the fact that all through the ages, international law keeps steadily its basic characteristics, notwithstanding the great changes that take place all over the world. This seems to be another strong proof that international law is an inherent corollary of civilization and invariably comes with any cultural development. It lifts the international institutions above questions of race, nationality or religion, showing and proving unmistakably their all-human qualities. They grow up gradually from custom and usage, similar to any other rule of law, but with this difference, that usually the rule of law develops *inside* the body politic, while international law grows up *outside* the state, binding the latter nevertheless in exactly the same way as an individual is bound by the rule of law in the state.

From ancient times too the system of international law, equally as at present, covers two fields, the time of peace, when it chiefly develops under the influence of commercial relations, and the time of war, when by custom it grows up among belligerents. In both cases the essence of the system is identical, namely, the *mutual recognition of obligations* and the reciprocal observance of certain customs or usages. The antiquity of these institutions in either field cannot now be questioned. As a matter of fact, some of the more ancient civilizations have had better developed ideas of international intercourse than the civilizations of later periods!

The fundamental principle of international relations has been constantly and everywhere the same, consisting in the *mutual recognition of the sanctity of international obligations and contracts*. It never made any difference whether such obligations were considered as binding the impersonal state or its chief representative, the king and ruler. In ancient times these two ideas, of state and ruler, were usually identical; and, just as today, the most difficult question seems to have been the one of sanctions. It was not easy at any time to bind the powerful states or conquering monarchs and make them keep their international contracts. Still, antiquity possessed perhaps better guarantees than more recent epochs in the great strength of religious obligations and in the fear of the wrath of gods, which was much more real than in later days.

The second no less important historical principle of international law was the recognition of the necessity of having regularly established *channels of intercourse*, through which the different international obligations and agreements had to be contracted and established. These channels and means of communication are also of the greatest antiquity; they are found at all times and among all civilizations. In creating these channels, usually called embassies, the states or rulers were bound first of all to recognize them on the principle of reciprocity; secondly, they were forced to respect them, establishing mutual guarantees for the safe conduct of international relations, which invariably grew into systems of mutually recognized immunities and privileges (like the idea of the personal immunity of envoys or ambassadors).

Finally, out of such a mutual recognition of international obligations there grew up unavoidably a third important principle, the idea of a certain equality among the transacting and contracting states or rulers. And, though at times, as in the case of Rome, there seem to have existed exceptions to this general rule, they do not disprove the theory and can be easily explained from the historical point of view by the tremendous advance in culture that the Roman state took in comparison with the surrounding world. Such epochs as the Roman were certainly exceptions. In normal times international relations developed among relatively equally civilized peoples, and thus always bore the unquestionable stamp of cultural and legal equality. It is only in the nineteenth century that this fundamental principle somehow gets lost under the influence of the diametrically opposed idea of the hegemony of the great Powers.

THE PLACE OF LAW AND TRIBUNALS IN INTERNATIONAL RELATIONS*

Lord McNair

I have not time to say much about the history of the development of international justice. Without going into its pre-history one can say that modern arbitration begins with the Jay Treaty between Great Britain and the United States of 1794. Throughout the nineteenth century the process of international arbitration developed in frequency and received a great impulse from the famous *Alabama* arbitration at Geneva of 1871-2, which disposed of a number of disputes between Great Britain and the United States of America arising out of the American Civil War. This event captured the popular imagination because it was the first occasion on which two great States had agreed to refer to arbitration disputes which, in the language of those days, touched their vital interests and honour, and had indeed brought them to the brink of war. This arbitration, in which Great Britain was the loser and paid the sum of three million sterling, then a very considerable amount, gave a great stimulus to what our grandfathers called "the Peace Movement," and there is no doubt that it was one of the factors responsible for the establishment of the Permanent Court of Arbitration at The Hague in 1900 and the Permanent Court of International Justice in 1920.

In this movement from 1794 onwards Great Britain and the United States of America have been the principal promoters.

In 1946 the International Court of Justice—the supreme judicial organ of the United Nations—succeeded the Permanent Court of International Justice, which was for technical reasons wound up in 1946 at the same time as the League of Nations which had established it. But for all substantial and practical purposes these two Courts are one. Their Statutes

* Arnold Duncan Lord McNair, *The Place of Law and Tribunals in International Relations* (Ludwig Mond Lecture) (Manchester, England: Manchester University Press, 1957), pp. 2–20. Reprinted by permission. Arnold Duncan Lord McNair is former President of the International Court of Justice (1952–1955) and, since 1959, has been President of the European Court of Human Rights. He is author of *Legal Effect of War* (3rd ed., 1948) and *Law of Treaties* (2nd ed., 1961).

are almost identical. The present International Court occupies the same building as the Permanent Court, took over its staff, and constantly cites the Judgments and Advisory Opinions of the Permanent Court as if they were its own.... Thus the power to give Advisory Opinions on a question of law at the request of the General Assembly or the Security Council of the United Nations forms an important part of the jurisdiction.

Then there is the Permanent Court of Arbitration at The Hague which dates from 1900 and was brought into being by the Hague Convention for the Pacific Settlement of Disputes of 1899. To a large extent this Court has been replaced by the Permanent Court of International Justice and its successor, and it has only dealt with one case since 1932. Nevertheless, there are reasons why it should remain in existence and it costs practically nothing. It is really a piece of machinery for the facilitation of arbitration available to States which for one reason or another prefer to refer a dispute to it rather than to the International Court. There are no permanent arbitrators; they are nominated by the parties when a case arises. The law administered by it is, for all practical purposes, the same as that administered by the International Court. It is a mistake to think that arbitration as a process is any less legal, or any more discretionary, than adjudication by the International Court. The most important case dealt with by the Hague Court of Arbitration is the *North Atlantic Coast Fisheries* dispute between Great Britain and the United States of America in 1910.

In addition it not infrequently happens that two Governments will refer a dispute to a single arbitrator or to an arbitral tribunal of three or more arbitrators which they create themselves, and without making use of the machinery of the Hague Court of Arbitration....

After this very brief outline of the existing international tribunals and some of the cases with which they have dealt, I return to the factors which impose certain limitations upon recourse to the judicial or arbitral process as a means of settling international disputes. I shall call those factors:

1. *intrinsic*, that is, arising from the essential nature of the judicial or arbitral process;

2. *personal*, that is, arising from the personality of the litigant; and

3. *jurisdictional*, that is, arising from the requirement of consent to the jurisdiction.

Let us begin with the *intrinsic nature* of the judicial or arbitral process as a means of settling disputes. The first thing—and this applies both to national and international tribunals—is to understand what is the function of a court of law and what is not. It is the function of a court of law to resolve *legal* disputes—not disputes which are political or economic or religious. Take the case of an industrial dispute in England on the subject of an adequate wage or decent working conditions. In so far as those matters are regulated by statute or agreement, as in some cases they are, there is a legal dispute, or at any rate a legal element in the dispute, and a court will be able to interpret and apply the statute or agreement and to say that the employers or the workers are right in their contention and give judgment accordingly. But suppose that there is no statute or agreement regulating the matter and the employers and workers are in conflict because the workers think that their wages ought to be increased and the employers say that they cannot afford to increase them. That is not a legal dispute, though there may be power under some statute to refer it to a tribunal of enquiry. It is really an economic dispute—a dispute as to the respective shares which capital and management and labour ought to receive in the profits of an industry.

Consider the case of disputes between States. One State may accuse another of a breach of a treaty binding upon them both, or of a breach of customary international law, such as a denial of justice to the subject of the claimant State by the courts of the defendant State, or a violation of the territorial sovereignty of the claimant State by the public ships or public aircraft or armed forces of the defendant State. Those are legal disputes. But let us look at some political or economic disputes. Consider the immigration of population from certain European States to certain American States, which has been one of the features of the past two or three centuries and particularly of the past hundred years, and is now subject to a good deal of restriction and control by the receiving States. Suppose that a European State were to contend that the immigration quotas fixed by the American State operate harshly upon it either by discriminating against it in favour of other States or by preventing it from exporting its surplus population and thus causing acute unemployment, the only answer that an international tribunal could give is that the American State as an independent State has a legal right to admit or exclude aliens at its discretion and to discriminate between the subjects of this or that foreign State at will. Thus reference to an international tribunal could not solve this dispute; the tribunal could not apply political or economic considerations; it could only state what the law is—which everyone knew beforehand.

On the other hand, if the European State and the American State were parties to a treaty, bilateral or multilateral, which contained agreed provisions as to quotas of immigrants and cognate matters, then to that extent the parties have by their treaty converted political and economic considerations into legal rights and duties and a court has a better chance of solving the dispute.

Again, let us suppose that State A complains that State B, by imposing a tariff which virtually excludes certain of the manufactured products of

State A, is killing some of State A's important industries and producing widespread unemployment and suffering. In the absence of a relevant commercial treaty between States A and B, that is a political or economic dispute and a legal tribunal has no power to settle it.

Thus it is, I hope, clear that when one says that an international court can only deal with legal disputes what is meant is that, although the source of the dispute and the incidents giving rise to it may be political or economic or religious, the court can do no more than state the relevant law and declare the existing legal rights and duties of the parties, and has no power to change them. Moreover, it may often happen that a judicial or arbitral decision on the basis of existing law instead of solving a dispute can even aggravate it by "high-lighting" the existing rights and duties of the parties.

From these instances it will be apparent that it is the function of a court of law, either national or international, to deal with legal disputes and, in doing so, to declare the existing legal rights and duties of the parties before it and not to change those rights and duties in the particular direction desired by one of them, because the change of the rights and duties of the parties is not a judicial function. Most disputes between States arise not because of any conflict of opinion as to their legal rights and duties but because one of them can no longer tolerate the *status quo* and considers that circumstances have arisen in which their legal rights and relations should be changed.

In this respect there is a real difference between a dispute between two citizens or groups of citizens of the same State and a dispute between two States. Let us suppose that in England a group of citizens contend that this or that legal provision ought to be changed; for instance, that land should or should not be capable of being compulsorily acquired for this or that purpose, or that the period of national service should be twelve months instead of twenty-four; the courts of law can do nothing but Parliament can deal with the situation by changing the law. In the international sphere, that is, between States, there is no legislature or executive which can change the law and their legal relations, because they are equal and sovereign or independent States.

Here we touch the crucial problem of international relations, namely, to find some machinery for the purpose of bringing about changes in the *status quo ante* by peaceful means—changes in the law or in territory or in the enjoyment of natural resources or other changes. The relations of the international community can no more remain stereotyped than can the relations of individuals and groups within a national community. So long as the international community consists of sovereign, that is, independent States, their relations can only be lawfully modified by consent. Suppose, for instance, that Great Britain wanted the right for her aircraft to fly across the territory of a foreign State in order to reach a certain destination and that foreign State declined to permit such flights, as it would be lawfully entitled to do if Great Britain and that foreign State were not parties to a reciprocal treaty permitting aerial navigation across their respective territories. There would be a dispute. What would be the use of referring that dispute to a court? The Court could only declare the law and decide in favour of the foreign State. On the other hand, within a State, Parliament, or the Executive acting in pursuance of an Act of Parliament, would be able to secure for the public a right to fly over any territory belonging to that State under proper conditions.

I shall not attempt to offer you suggestions for the solution of this crucial problem of peaceful change. That is another story. But I must point out that the remedy cannot be found in the process of judicial settlement or arbitration. Some international disputes occur in which there is a legal question that is capable of being isolated or abstracted from a mixed dispute. In such cases the reference of that legal question to judicial or arbitral courts may be helpful to the solution of the political dispute. For instance, in the long-standing dispute between the Assembly of the United Nations and the Union of South Africa regarding the status of the formerly German South-West Africa of which the Union became the mandatory in 1920, the Assembly has on three occasions exercised its right to request the International Court to give an Advisory Opinion on a question of law, and has obtained those Opinions, but the dispute has not yet been solved.

Before leaving the limitations upon international adjudication which spring from the intrinsic character of the judicial or arbitral process, two points of subsidiary importance require attention. The first is the attempt to enlarge the functions of a court by conferring upon it a power to do justice not merely according to law but according to equity. (By way of parenthesis, I may point out that the word "equity" as used in this connection has nothing to do with that part of English law which was developed by the Court of Chancery and is now regarded as the province of the Chancery Division, though in fact it can be invoked in any of the Divisions of the High Court. This English equity was originally conceived of as the discretionary power of the Chancellor to modify the rigour of the common law or to supplement its defects.) The Statute of the Permanent Court of International Justice, and now of the International Court, has, since its adoption in 1920, contained in Article 38 an interesting reference to equity. Paragraph 1 of that Article directs the Court to decide disputes "in accordance with international law," and, for that purpose, to apply treaties, customary international law, the general principles of law recognized by civilized nations, and, as subsidiary sources, judicial decisions and the writings of highly qualified lawyers. Paragraph 2 is as follows:

This provision (that is, paragraph 1) shall not prejudice the power of the Court to decide a case *ex aequo et bono,* if the parties agree thereto.

What does this expression *ex aequo et bono* mean? Can we find here that enlargement of the powers of the International Court which would enable the parties to authorize it to go beyond its purely judicial function and to exercise a semi-legislative function, that is, to create new law binding upon the parties and modifying their existing legal relations out of which the dispute has arisen? The Court alone can answer these questions, and it has never had the opportunity, because the parties to a dispute have never given their consent, in pursuance of paragraph 2 quoted above, to the exercise by the Court of this power. It is more likely that the expression *ex aequo et bono* means merely that the Court, while exercising a truly judicial function, can be authorized by the parties to mitigate the rigidity of the law. It may be, on the other hand, that it enables the parties to confer upon the Court a wider function. However that may be, the failure by litigating States to avail themselves of this power during a period of thirty-five years is significant.

There is nothing to prevent two States from referring to arbitration a dispute which requires for its solution the application of extra-legal or non-legal considerations such as political or economic or financial factors, but in fact this is very rarely done. It is interesting to ask ourselves why. There is the fact, as I have pointed out, that the Statute of the International Court permits the Court, with the consent of the parties, to adjudicate *ex aequo et bono,* and that although this provision has been in existence for some thirty-five years no use has ever been made of it. Why is this? I think the answer is that before two persons or two governments are willing to refer a dispute to settlement by any tribunal they wish to feel that there exists a body of accepted principles and rules which will guide the tribunal in giving judgment upon that dispute. It is only in this way that these two persons or two governments can obtain competent expert advice upon the prospects of their success, and so the reasonable predictability of what a tribunal will do is an essential element. Of course no person embarking on litigation can be sure of success, but at any rate he wishes to be in a position to obtain expert advice as to his prospects of success. Such advice is reasonably possible in the case of a legal dispute because there exists a body of rules and principles reasonably well established, though always developing, upon the basis of which legal experts can advise. When, however, one passes outside the field of legal disputes and has to deal with a dispute turning upon political or economic or financial or religious factors one is completely at sea because in these spheres of action there are no such agreed bodies of rules and principles which would be likely to guide a tribunal in coming to a decision.

It will be remembered that the first Lord Davies, a deeply respected man who devoted a very large part of his energies and his means towards improving interstate relations and interstate machinery for the solution of disputes, was a strong advocate of something that was called an "Equity Tribunal." I have always felt that the consideration to which I have referred, namely, the lack of settled rules and principles outside the sphere of law, is the real obstacle in the way of the establishment of an 'Equity Tribunal' for international purposes. Let us first of all concentrate upon the international legal tribunals which are already available and help them to develop existing rules of international law. When the day comes at which legal disputes between States will, in default of settlement by negotiation, automatically go to an international tribunal, it will be time enough to consider whether anything can be done for adjudication upon non-legal disputes. Meanwhile it seems to me that the proper method of dealing with them, failing success by negotiation between the parties, is either by invoking the mediation of some other State or group of States, or by bringing the matter before some international organ such as the Security Council of the United Nations.

The second point concerned with the intrinsic nature of the judicial or arbitral process is this. I have pointed out that the essence of this process is to declare the law, including reasonable developments of it, and to state the existing rights and duties of the parties. To change the law and the existing rights and duties of the parties for the purpose of settling a dispute is foreign to the judicial or arbitral process, and involves quite different functions, namely, the legislative or the executive function, or a combination of both. Accordingly, one must not expect legal tribunals to depart from their true function and set up as legislators.

I now turn to the *personal limitations* upon the use of the judicial or arbitral process, by which I mean limits determined by the legal personality of the litigants. International justice in the strict sense is the administration of justice between States. The Hague Court of Permanent Arbitration, established in 1900, is available to States, not to individuals. Article 24 of the Hague Convention which established it makes it clear that it is available "for the settlement of a difference which has arisen between" the signatory powers, and all the cases that have been decided by arbitration within the framework of this Court have been cases between States. Again, the Statute of the International Court of Justice is explicit on this point. Paragraph 1 of Article 34 is as follows: "Only States may be parties in cases before the Court." That is the strict and normal scope of the administration of international justice. (The corresponding article in the Statute of the Permanent Court of International Justice contained the expression "Only States or *Members of the League of Nations*," which was probably due, at any rate in part, to the necessity of including the British Self-governing Dominions which were Members of the League of Nations but then hardly recognized as "States.")

But several qualifications must be made.

(a) In practice international tribunals such as the Hague Permanent Court of Arbitration and the present International Court of Justice, and tribunals of arbitration specially created by the parties for the purpose of settling a dispute, are often found dealing with claims by individuals against foreign States, because every Government has a right of protection over its subjects and in the exercise of this right it is entitled to adopt and espouse the claim of its subject, when it is of the opinion that the claim is a good one, and put it forward to the foreign Government on the international plane. . . .

These are real contests between States, and a Government which has adopted its subject's claim and put it forward on the international level is in full control of that claim and could indeed discontinue the proceedings if it thought fit.

This adoption by Governments of the claims of their subjects with a view to converting them into interstate claims is not confined to proceedings before the Hague Court of Arbitration or the International Court of Justice and constantly occurs in the case of arbitration tribunals which are constituted by two States for the express purpose of adjudicating upon a particular claim . . .

(b) From time to time when two Governments find that a number of claims by the subjects of one against the other Government have accumulated they establish what is called a "Claims Commission" or a "Mixed Arbitral Tribunal," usually comprising one arbitrator nominated by each Government and an umpire nominated by the two arbitrators and coming from a third or, as it is often called, a "neutral" State. These commissions or tribunals, often sitting for many years, decide these claims with the aid of counsel upon the basis of international law either customary or conventional, that is, arising from treaties and other agreements. Amongst other examples I may mention several British-American Claims Commissions, the American-Mexican Claims Commission, the American-Venezuelan Commission, the British-Mexican Commission, etc. At the end of the First World War a large number of Mixed Arbitral Tribunals were established between pairs of opposing belligerents for the purpose of adjudicating upon disputes either between their respective subjects or between the subjects of the one and the Government of the other. One of the main sources of the law administered consisted of the provisions of the peace treaties relating to private property, contracts, concessions, etc.

(c) In addition there are many disputes and arbitrations thereof which can be called international in the popular sense of the word but which are not truly interstate disputes and arbitrations. There are many concessions and other contracts, made between large corporations such as construction companies, oil companies, public utility companies, on the one hand, and foreign Governments, on the other, which contain an arbitration clause providing for the reference to arbitration of any disputes which arise between the parties to the concession or contract. I merely mention this as a means of settling disputes which might otherwise become interstate disputes by reason of the Government responsible for the corporation adopting its case and putting it forward on the international level. In many of these private and non-official arbitrations rules of international law are invoked by the parties. . . .

I now come to the *jurisdictional factor* which limits recourse to international tribunals. It is this. The present international society consists of independent States. I use the word "independent" in preference to "sovereign," because "sovereign" is a term of political science rather than of law. The terms "sovereign" and "sovereignty" are apt to lead to confusion and frequently raise the blood pressure. It is a fundamental rule of law that no State can be compelled to litigate against its will either before an international court or before any foreign court, except that in some countries a foreign State can be forced to come in and litigate in respect of what are regarded as its commercial and non-sovereign activities. Thus consent is the basis of the jurisdiction of any international tribunal. That is fundamental. There are various ways in which this consent may be manifested, of which the following are the principal:

(a) Which is very common, especially in non-political matters—by a clause contained in a treaty whereby the parties agree to refer all disputes as to the application and interpretation of the treaty which they cannot settle by negotiation to the International Court of Justice or some other tribunal; hundreds of such treaties exist.

(b) The jurisdiction of the International Court of Justice is not *ipso facto* compulsory, but Article 36 of its Statute contains provisions whereby States may file with the Court a declaration of acceptance of the jurisdiction of the Court for the purpose of all legal disputes, or certain categories of legal disputes, upon a basis of reciprocity, whereupon it becomes compulsory to that extent. That requires explanation. Between thirty and forty States have filed some kind of declaration of acceptance, but they vary greatly and only apply upon a basis of reciprocity, that is to say, only when the particular dispute in question falls within the scope of the declarations of acceptance filed by both parties—the claimant and the respondent States. For instance, some declarations of acceptance exclude disputes arising before a certain date, or arising out of war or hostilities, or arising between two Members of the British Commonwealth, or which are essentially within the domestic jurisdiction of the State making the declaration of acceptance. The variety is great. What is essential is reciprocity in relation to a category of disputes which comprises the dispute in question. . . .

Membership of the United Nations and, in consequence, of the International Court, its principal judicial organ, does not automatically involve the acceptance of the jurisdiction of the Court. For that purpose, acceptance of the jurisdiction must be established by one of the three methods which we are now discussing.

(c) The third method is adopted when two States go hand in hand to the International Court or to some other tribunal and ask it to decide a dispute between them, or when they themselves create a special tribunal of arbitration by means of an agreement and thereby refer a dispute to it and agree to accept its award. . . .

Such are the principal methods by which States consent to the jurisdiction of the International Court of Justice or of other international tribunals and thereby subject themselves to the jurisdiction and agree to carry out the judgment or award. Nevertheless, it very frequently happens that a respondent State which is called upon to appear and litigate raises, and vigorously contests, the point that the particular claim made against it does not fall within the ambit of its consent to the jurisdiction. The result is that Objections to the Jurisdiction are frequent and are usually tried and disposed of as a separate and preliminary issue, for obviously there is no point in the Court examining what are called "the merits" unless and until it is satisfied that it possesses jurisdiction. How remote all this is from British or any national jurisdiction where, by virtue of the power of the Crown or its equivalent in a foreign State, jurisdiction is compulsory, certainly upon persons who reside or carry on business within the local jurisdiction and in some cases upon persons outside the local jurisdiction!

AN INTRODUCTION TO THE
ISLAMIC LAW OF NATIONS*

Majid Khadduri

It has been observed throughout the various civilizations so far known to us that the population of each civilization, in the absence of a vital external threat, tended to develop within itself a community of political entities, that is, a "family of nations," rather than a single nation. This is indicated by the fact that there existed, or coexisted, several families of nations in such areas as the ancient Near East, Greece and Rome, China, Islam and Western Christendom where at least one distinct civilization had developed in each one of them. Within each civilization a body of rules and practices developed for the purpose of regulating the conduct of states in peace and war. "The mere fact of neighborly cohabitation," says Baron Korff, "creates moral and legal obligations, which in the course of time crystalize into a system of international law." Even among primitive people such rules seem to have existed as part of the mores before they developed into a rational system among civilized groups.

Such systems of international rules and practices, however, were not truly *international,* in the modern sense of the term, since each system was primarily concerned with the relations within a limited area and within one (though often more than one) civilization and thus failed to be worldwide. Further, each system of international law was entirely exclusive since it did not recognize the principle of legal equality among nations which is inherent in the modern system of international law. It was for this very reason that there was no possibility of integrating one system with another. Though each freely borrowed from the others without acknowledgment, each system claimed an exclusive superiority over others. Consequently, each system of international law disappeared with the disappearance of the civilization (or civilizations) under which it flourished.

* Majid Khadduri, "International Law," in Majid Khadduri and Herbert J. Liebesny, eds., *Law in the Middle East* (Washington, D.C.: Middle East Institute, 1955), I, 349–372. Reprinted by permission. Majid Khadduri is Professor of Middle East Studies, School of Advanced International Studies, Johns Hopkins University; author of *War and Peace in the Law of Islam* (1955), *Independent Iraq, 1932–1958* (1960), and *Modern Libya* (1962); and coeditor of *Law in the Middle East* (1955).

The rise of Islam, with its universal appeal to all people, inevitably raised for the Islamic State the problem as to how it would conduct its relations with the non-Islamic states and with the tolerated religious communities within its territory. The jurist-theologians developed a special branch of the sharī'a, known as the siyar (based on the same sources as the sharī'a) which was the Law of Nations for the Muslims. In theory the siyar was designed to be only a temporary institution, until the Islamic State would correspond to the then known world, but failure to achieve this end inevitably rendered the siyar an elaborate and permanent part of Islamic law.

Theories

The modern law of nations presupposes the existence of a Family of Nations composed of a community of states enjoying full sovereign rights and equality of status. Islamic law recognizes no other nation than its own since the aim of Islam was the subordination of the whole world to one system of law and religion, to be enforced by the supreme authority of the caliph. Similar to Medieval Christian international law, the Islamic law of nations was based on the theory of a universal state. Both Christendom and Islam assumed mankind to constitute one community, bound by one law and governed by one ruler. The character of such a state is entirely exclusive; it does not recognize, by definition, the existence of a second world state. The aim of both these states was the proselytization of the whole of mankind. Their rules of foreign relations, accordingly, were the rules of an imperial state which would not grant an equal status to the other party (or parties) with whom it happened to fight or negotiate. It follows that the binding force of such a law of nations was not based on mutual consent or interest; it was merely a self-imposed system of law binding on its adherents, even though the rules often ran against their interests, because the sanction of the law was moral or religious.

In theory the Muslim world had to deal only temporarily with non-Islamic state communities, but the failure of Islam to convert the whole world made such dealings a permanent problem. The world accordingly was sharply divided, under Muslim law, into the dār al-Islam (abode of Islam) and the dār al-ḥarb (abode of war). The first corresponded to the areas under Islamic rule. Its inhabitants were Muslims, by birth or conversion, and all the people of the "tolerated" religions who preferred to remain Christians, Jews, Sabians, and Magians (Zoroastrians) at the sacrifice of paying a poll tax. The Muslims enjoyed full rights of "citizenship"; the members of the tolerated religions enjoyed only partial rights, and submitted to Muslim control in accordance with special rules regulating their relations with the Muslims. The dār al-ḥarb consisted of all states and communities outside the World of Islam. Its inhabitants were often called infidels, or, more accurately, unbelievers.

On the assumption that the aim of Islam was the world, the dār al-Islam was always, in theory, at war with the dār al-ḥarb. The Muslims were required to preach Islam by persuasion, and the caliph, or his commanders in the field, to offer Islam as an alternative to paying the poll tax or fighting; but the Islamic state was under legal obligation to recognize no other authority than its own and to enforce Islamic law and supersede any other authority even though non-Islamic communities had willingly accepted the faith of Islam without fighting. Failure to accept Islam or the poll tax (jizya) by non-Muslims made it incumbent on the Islamic state to declare a jihād (holy war) upon the recalcitrant individuals and communities. Thus the jihād, as an alternative to paying the jizya, was the State's instrument of transforming the dār al-ḥarb into the dār al-Islam. But the jihād was not the only legal means of dealing with the unbelievers since peaceful methods (negotiation, arbitration, and treaty making) were applied in regulating the relations of the believers with unbelievers when actual fighting ceased. The Islamic law of nations was, accordingly, the product of the contact of an ever expanding state with its neighbors which led to the development of a body of rules and practices followed by the Muslims in war and peace. The mores followed by the Arabs before Islam in their intertribal warfare were regarded by Islam as too ungodly and brutal; thus Islam abolished all war except the jihād, and the jurist-theologians consciously formulated rules to subordinate all other considerations to *raison d'état* based on religous sanction.

Nature and Sources of Law

The Islamic law of nations, as part of the sharī'a, may be regarded as an effort to rationalize the relations of a society with the outside world in which chaos and conflict predominated. The aspiration was order. In the same way that natural law was regarded as the ideal legal order consisting of the general maxims of right and justice, so was Islamic law looked upon as the ideal system designed by God, the author of nature, for the Muslims. Man cannot make law, for the sharī'a, as a divine law, tolerates no other law than its own. Just as natural law exists in nature, to be discovered by reason, so the sharī'a, as an Islamic natural law, was revealed to, or "discovered" by, the Prophet Muḥammad. On the basis of Muḥammad's revelations and Traditions the law was later developed by the jurist-theologians who made use of analogy and consensus for the interpretation and elaboration, if not for the "discovery," of derivative laws. In theory the sole source of law is Allah, the head of the Islamic State, who alone is the fountain of right and justice. Man can only obey, and in his attempt to consummate his obedience to law he realizes his religious ideal. Divine law is infallible. It includes dogma as well as social and political rules, for in the Islamic State the religious and the political are not separate aspects of life. Law has the character of a religious obligation; at the same time it constitutes a political sanction of religion.

The divine law, it is held, existed in a complete heavenly book which was revealed piecemeal to the Prophet Muḥammad. But this flow of divine legislation was not possible after Muhammad's death, since the caliphs were not entitled to communicate with the Divine Legislator. The need for further legislation, however, was pressing as the Islamic State was rapidly expanding and new situations necessarily arose. New sources of law had to be used, if the state was to continue its relations with the outside world. The Muslim jurist-theologians undertook the matter and developed the so-called fiqh, or Muslim jurisprudence. The doctors of fiqh did not, in theory, make new law; they only developed a system which enabled them to deduce derivative laws from the Qur'ān, the sunna, and such other sources as analogy and consensus which were accepted by the various schools of law. In the early conduct of the Islamic State opinions of the caliphs as well as their practices were often followed as rules of international law; but such rules were regarded valid as law only after they were sanctioned by tradition, analogy, or consensus.

Analyzed in terms of the modern law of nations, the sources of the Islamic law of nations conform to the categories defined by modern jurists and the statute of the International Court of Justice, namely, agreement, custom, reason, and authority. The Qur'ān represent the authoritative source of law; the sunna is equivalent to custom; rules expressed in treaties with non-Muslims fall in the category of agreement; and the opinions of the caliphs and jurists, based on legal deduction and analogy, may be regarded as reason. Such opinions, "fatwas," or decisions had great influence in the development of the law. . . .

The Law of Peace

The doctrine of the jihād presupposed the condition of war as normal between the Islamic State and the outside world. But this war condition, in theory, was only temporary until the whole world be transformed into the Islamic State. We may argue therefore that war was not considered a permanent condition in the Islamic society, but merely a means to achieve ultimate peace under Islam. If that end was ever achieved, the *raison d'être* of the jihād would come to an end.

The impossibility of universalizing Islam and the failure to set up a world state divided the world into the *world of Islam* and the *world of war*. It is true that this division, in Muslim theory, was only transitory; yet in practice it persisted throughout the life of the Islamic State. The relations between these two worlds were normally unpeaceful; each world was legally at war with the other. But this state of war should not be construed as a state of actual hostilities, for the Muslims concluded treaties of peace with the enemies on more than one occasion. This state of war was rather in practice equivalent to what is termed "nonrecognition," that is, the incapacity of the world of war to possess a legal status under Muslim law so long as it lacked the essential elements of the true faith. This nonrecognition did not imply, as in modern international law, the impossibility of concluding treaties or initiating official relations, for such actions were not considered to imply equality between the two contracting parties, and were only temporary.

This state of affairs induced a few jurists ... to devise a third "temporary" division of the world called dār al-ṣulḥ (world of peace) or dār al-'ahd (world of covenant). Its relations with the world of Islam were defined by treaties of peace which were never, in theory, to last long. Other jurists, however, especially the Ḥanafīs, never recognized the existence of a third division of the world. Abū Ḥanīfa argued that if the inhabitants of a territory concluded a treaty of peace (and agreed to pay the *jizya*) they were considered as dhimmīs and their territory as part of the world of Islam since otherwise it would be a part of the world of war. Peace accordingly was not a definite term to mean entirely normal relations under Muslim law. Certain Qur'ānic rules, it is true, emphasize the tendency towards peace, but the jurists' interpretations do not stress this tendency and they even hold that the imām should not resort to peace unless he were under necessity....

Treaties

The treaty-making power in Islam rested in the hands of the head of the State who, as the person charged with the duties of prosecuting the jihād, was *ipso facto* the ultimate authority who would decide when the jihād was to be relaxed and a peace treaty signed. This power was often delegated to the commanders in the field. During the early Muslim conquests, they were empowered to negotiate treaties with the inhabitants of the occupied territories regarding their paying the jizya as an alternative to acceptance of Islam.

While the Muslim jurists did not stress the tendency towards establishing peaceful relations with their enemies, the caliphs in practice were often forced to come to terms with them, justifying their action by the force of "necessity" and by the precedent established by the Prophet Muhammad in coming to terms with the non-Muslims of Mecca.

The model treaty which later the caliphs and the jurists often cited from the Prophet's tradition is the so-called Hudaybiya treaty which, in its form, procedure of negotiation, and duration, supplied a precedent (if not indeed a source for the law of treaty-making) which was followed by the Muslims.

After a bitter struggle between the Prophet in Medina and the stubborn pagan Arabs of Mecca (e.g., Quraysh) who resisted his mission, the two parties were ready for peace. For Muhammad such a peace was necessary, even though by no means permanent, to accomplish the pilgrimage to Mecca. He sent 'Uthmān, the future third caliph, to carry the peace message of Muhammad to the people of Mecca. The Meccans accepted and sent Suhayl, their representative, to negotiate a peace treaty. 'Alī, the future fourth caliph, acted as a secretary, while a number of persons from both sides were brought who swore to observe the terms of the treaty. The text of the treaty follows:

In your name, O Allah;
This is what Muhammad ibn 'Abdullah has agreed upon peacefully with Suhayl ibn 'Amr;
They agreed peacefully to postpone war for a period of ten years. People shall be secured and guaranteed [from attack] by each other;
If anyone from the Quraysh wishes to join Muhammad without authorization of his walī [protector] he should be sent back; if any one of Muhammad's followers wishes to join Quraysh, he will not be refused;
Unbecoming acts between each of us are prohibited; and that there should not be between us defection, nor treason;
Those [people] who want to join Muhammad's alliance and his pact may do so; those who want to join Quraysh's alliance and its pact may do so.

This treaty, which stipulated that the duration of peace was to last for ten years, supplied a precedent for the jurists that no peace treaty with the enemies should last longer than that. But its violation within less than two years renewed hostilities and offered the Muslims justification for taking Mecca by force. The reason for the violation was the attack of Quraysh on Muhammad's adherents. Negotiations were conducted to resume peaceful relations but to no avail since the Muslims disliked the violation of the treaty. The Meccans, it seems, were very weak at this time and Muhammad captured the city without difficulty.

The treaties which the Prophet Muhammad concluded with the non-Muslims were models which the caliphs followed after his death. With the exception of those treaties which the caliphs (or their representatives) had concluded with the peoples of the occupied territories, all Muslim treaties were concluded for a limited period to fulfill certain specific functions. . . .

Once a treaty had been signed by the Muslims, though the Muslims were reluctant to come to terms with the non-Muslims, the terms of the treaty were strictly observed. This is urged not only by the Qur'ānic injunctions, but also by the ḥadīths and supported by practice. The Qur'ān urges the Muslims "not to break oaths after making them," and if the non-Muslims did not break them, then "fulfill their agreement to the end of their term."

The following may be regarded as general characteristics of the treaties which the Muslims concluded with the non-Muslims:

(1) The texts of the treaties were, on the whole, brief and general. The phraseology was simple and even, at times, vague due to the brevity of the text. The content of the treaties dealt with certain specific issues rather than principles of law.

(2) The form of the treaties was simple; it included the preamble, the content of the treaty, and ended by stating the names of the witnesses who swore to observe its terms. The preamble consisted of the so-called basmala (i.e., the name of Allah, etc.) and the names of the representatives of the two parties.

(3) The terms of the Muslim treaties we possess, as reported by the Muslim publicists, show in most of the cases that they were pledges by one party to the other rather than contracts between equals. This is particularly true of the Muslim treaties with the people of occupied territories who agreed to live in the Muslim state. This is evidenced by the terms which demanded security of lives, property, and religion in lieu of submission of the people (the dhimmīs), and their payment of the jizya. Further, the treaties bore the names of the Muslim witnesses but not the names of the dhimmīs. This special type of treaty had the character of constitutional guarantees to the people of the annexed countries rather than an agreement between "independent" countries.

(4) The duration of a treaty was specified by Muslim jurists. The Shāfi'ī school held that a peace treaty with the enemy should not exceed the term of ten years, that is, the term of the Hudaybiya treaty which the Prophet Muḥammad concluded with the Meccans. The Ḥanafī and Mālikī schools maintained that the Hudaybiya peace did not last ten years and argued that no peace treaty should last for more than three or four years. (The treaties with the dhimmīs, which were in the nature of "charters" to guarantee their rights so long as they resided in the Islamic State, were indefinite.)

(5) Finally, the system of taking human rahā'in (hostages) to insure the

sanctity of treaties was followed by the Muslims. If the treaty were violated, however, the Muslims did not kill the hostages. If the Muslims
started the war, the hostages were sent back home, but if war was started
by the other party, then the hostages were kept.

Arbitrations

Arbitration was practiced among the Arabs before Islam. The Prophet
Muḥammad respected this tradition and himself acted as an arbitrator.
The Qur'ān refers to arbitrations in the following verse:

O you who believe! Obey Allah, and the Apostle and those in authority
among you; if you differ, bring it before Allah and the Apostle, if you believe
in Allah and in the last day. . . .

Conclusion

The political ascendancy of Islam was followed by a period of stagnation and decline which was paralleled in the West by far-reaching development. Thus the Islamic international law was abandoned by the
Islamic States when the European Powers, in their contact with the Islamic
countries, gradually began to recognize these states and to conduct their
foreign relations on the basis of Islamic law. This naturally meant that
the European system of international law, which originally had developed
as a European and Christian law, had to undergo certain changes in its
character in order to include non-European and non-Christian countries.
At the opening of the nineteenth century the European system had already changed in scope and nature to meet the new circumstances of the
world. The emergence of the United States and the South American re-
publics changed its scope from a regional to a world-wide system; the
participation of the Ottoman Empire in the Concert of Europe and the
emergence of Japan as a Great Power rendered it no longer Christian in
character.

The development of the European system of international law from a
continental into a world-wide system might have helped to integrate the
various systems of the law of nations of Islam, India, and the Far East.
But the disintegration of these Eastern societies had already gone too
far to enable them to deal on a par with the European Powers. In the
circumstances, the contact of Europe with the East, the domination of
the latter by the former, helped to set in motion the slow but disruptive
process of the Westernization movement—a movement which almost
caused the destruction of the older legal systems of the East, including
their traditional systems for the conduct of foreign relations.

The modern system of international law, however, is far from being complete or satisfactory to meet the needs of a rapidly changing World Community. Not only the last two World Wars, which have rendered the Law of War almost completely obsolete, but also the urgent need for an effective World Government require the further development of a truly world-wide international law. Further, the participation of Eastern and Islamic peoples in the new World Order has given these people an opportunity to make their influence felt in the development of modern international law. The Statute of the International Court of Justice permits the adoption of new maxims of law from the legal systems of "civilized nations." This possibility of using non-European sources of law opens the way for the Eastern and Islamic nations to make their contributions to the development of modern international law.

INTERNATIONAL LAW IN THE MISSILE AGE*

Oliver J. Lissitzyn

Impact of Cultural Traditions

Does the non-Western cultural background of the Asian and African states tend to make them adopt attitudes toward international law different from those of the Western nations? Some Western and non-Western writers have suggested that, in Asia at least, the basic cultural tradition is to favor mediation and conciliation rather than the strict application of law as a means of settling disputes, and to regard law as a set of broad and flexible principles permitting of adjustment and compromise rather than as a body of rigid technical rules. But generalizations about "Asia" or "Africa" are dangerous, for they tend to overlook the large variety of cultures and traditions that exist within those continents.

So far as attitudes toward specific norms of international law are concerned, all the evidence points to the conclusion that present interest,

* Oliver J. Lissitzyn, "International Law in a Divided World," *International Conciliation,* No. 542 (March 1963), pp. 57–69. Reprinted by permission of the Carnegie Endowment for International Peace. Mr. Lissitzyn is Professor of Public Law, Columbia University; author of *International Air Transport and National Policy* (1942) and *The International Court of Justice* (1951); and coauthor of *Creation of Rights of Sovereignty* (1938) and *International Organization* (1955).

rightly or wrongly understood, rather than cultural tradition has been the immediately decisive factor. Differences in the levels of economic and political development lie behind the more extreme differences between legal institutions. Much of Western law, including international law, has developed in response to the requirements of the Western business civilization. As non-Western countries have moved toward fuller participation in present-day economic and political life, they have come to realize that many of their legal traditions are no longer adequate to their needs. Most of these countries are adopting, in varying degrees, modern institutions, largely derived from those of the West. In some, reception of Western law has already reached an advanced stage. In the West itself law does not stand still. The effects on law of greater state participation in economic life and the rise of the "welfare state" are likely to be worldwide. In the long run, this factor should serve to reduce differences in attitudes toward international law.

Cultural factors, however, may influence a nation's attitude toward international law in various ways. They may have a role in determining the level of a country's development and thus, indirectly, its specific interests with respect to particular norms of international law. They may enter into the very definition of "the national interest." A nation's attitude toward the role of law in world affairs may reflect, however subtly, the role that domestic law plays in the life of the nation and the extent to which international law is known and understood within its ruling elite. Among the less developed nations, there are wide differences. In some of the newly independent countries where an educated elite has just begun to form, there is a critical shortage of all kinds of specialists, including persons trained in international law. In others there are a substantial number of lawyers, civil servants, and university professors who are in varying degrees familiar with international law. These countries are contributing significantly to the literature of international law. All of the newly independent nations, however, suffer in varying degrees not only from a lack of resources such as libraries, but also from the fact that during the colonial regime their elite were given few, if any, opportunities to participate actively in the handling of foreign affairs, and had little reason, therefore, to acquire a knowledge of international law. At the seventeenth General Assembly in 1962, many of the less developed nations acknowledged the importance of removing deficiencies in international law training; they strongly supported a resolution requesting the Secretary-General to study and report on the possibilities of technical assistance to promote the teaching, study, dissemination, and wider appreciation of international law.

It is tempting to ascribe to non-Western cultural factors the attraction international legal slogans of great generality seem to have for a number of the less developed countries, particularly for the newly independent nations. In the absence of definitive comparative studies of traditional attitudes toward law in various parts of the world, the possibility of such a relationship can be neither categorically denied nor affirmed. But those who emphasize the effect of cultural heritage on attitudes toward international law tend to overlook the diversity of approaches to law that exist in the West as well as in the non-Western parts of the world. The recent trend in the West, particularly in the United States, is toward a less technical view of the law. The increasingly influential school of international law created by Myres S. McDougal of Yale University regards law as a process of decision into which all relevant factors, and not merely technical norms, enter. It virtually identifies law with policy and calls the study of law "a policy science." While this rather extreme position is not yet widely accepted in the West, it points up the danger of wholly identifying the West with a rigid, technical conception of law that neglects broad principles of justice and overlooks the necessity for adjustment and compromise.

Furthermore, the Western cultural tradition is no guarantee of adherence to "the rule of law" in either domestic or international affairs. Western commentators tend to forget all too easily that in the twentieth century one of the most arrogantly nihilistic challenges to the traditional principles of law and morality came from a highly developed and educated nation in the heart of Europe with an impeccably Western ethnic and cultural pedigree—Nazi Germany.

Some diversity in attitudes toward law is bound to remain in the non-Western world, as in the West. But as the process of reception of modern law continues, there should be less and less reason to fear that differences of cultural heritage have produced an unbridgeable gap between Western and non-Western attitudes toward law in general and international law in particular. The long-term trend is toward greater uniformity of legal systems and traditions.

Although the less developed nations tend to question some of the content of customary international law, they are showing awareness of the role of international law in modern life by signing treaties, becoming parties to multilateral conventions, and joining international organizations. Indeed, the Western commentators who speak of a "crisis" in international law seem to overlook the increasing role that treaties and organizations are playing in the process of international regulation of the conduct of states. Customary international law, it is true, provides the essential framework within which treaties operate and organizations function. In this sense, custom may still be regarded as the primary source of international law. But the norms regulating the conduct of states that are laid down in multilateral and bilateral treaties, or prescribed by international organs acting within the scope of powers conferred upon them by treaties, are today far greater in number and, in the main, more specific than those found in customary international law. Since treaties generally bind only those states parties to them, treaty law is not "universal"; it is, nevertheless, of steadily growing importance in the life of nations.

The less developed nations, including the newly independent states, have become parties to multilateral treaties, such as the Universal Postal Convention and the International Civil Aviation Convention, for their obvious practical advantages. Their adhesion to treaties that prescribe social and humanitarian standards for primarily domestic application may be motivated by prestige considerations and may be less indicative of willingness to become bound by international regulation. Non-compliance with treaties of the former kind is likely to be quickly noted and to bring protests from the other parties. Yet the newly independent states become parties in large numbers to this kind of treaty.

Particularly significant is the willingness of many less developed nations to participate in organizations and treaties, such as the International Monetary Fund (IMF) and the General Agreement on Tariffs and Trade (GATT), which involve some regulation of international economic relations. Among the members of IMF are most of the leading countries of Asia and Africa and all the Latin American states. A considerable number of newly independent nations have become parties to GATT. Eighteen African states are becoming associated with the European Economic Community. Considerations of sovereignty thus do not prevent the less developed nations from entering into complex economic and financial arrangements that limit their freedom of action when such arrangements offer significant advantages. The readiness of the newly independent nations to join international organizations is due at least in part to the desire to benefit from technical assistance and other aid programs.

A Western jurist has drawn a strikingly imaginative parallel between the emergence of less developed nations into a position of greater political influence and the rise of the working classes to power in the West. In both cases, there has been a process of democratization of the legal community. The previously submerged classes have demanded fuller participation in the law-making process and revision of the legal systems developed by the older ruling classes. They have also pressed for welfare legislation. At times, the spokesmen for the emergent classes have seemed uncouth and dangerously radical. In the Western democracies, the result has been a compromise. The continuity of the legal system has not been destroyed; much of the old law has remained. Nor have the old ruling classes been completely dispossessed, although they have lost most of the exclusive privileges they once enjoyed. There has emerged the modern democratic "welfare" state in which the previously submerged classes have obtained substantially what they wanted. It was only when the old ruling classes stubbornly refused to heed the demands of the masses or were too slow in adjusting to them that violent upheavals swept away the old order completely.

The Outlook

The sense of a "crisis" in international law experienced by many observers today is a product of the acceleration of the processes of change in the international community that is characteristic of our era. The factors that have caused this acceleration are well known. They include rapid technological progress; the rise of new ideologies and systems of public order, including militant communism; decolonization, itself spurred on by the Communist challenge to the West; the appearance of many new states of widely different cultural backgrounds and levels of development; rising demands for social reform; the fear of war and the growing reluctance of the more advanced states to protect their interests by coercive means; and the increase in the number and functions of international organizations. The processes of change have, on the one hand, tended to limit the operation or decrease the relevance of some traditional legal norms and, on the other hand, have created new areas of need for legal regulation. What then are the prospects for the future of international law in a divided, rapidly changing world?

At first glance, there appear to be many disturbing similarities between the attitudes of the Communist elites and those of the less developed nations, particularly the newly independent states, toward international law. Both the Communist elites and the less developed nations emphasize, for example, self-determination, anti-colonialism, equality, non-intervention, and invalidity of "unequal" treaties. The latter, like the Communist governments, tend to manipulate such highly general principles without much regard for consistency or reciprocity. Spokesmen for the newly independent nations, like those for the Soviet Union, tend to reject the traditional doctrine that norms of general international law are automatically binding on new states (and on states ruled by new governments) and claim freedom to decide by which of the old norms they will be bound. On the specific issues of "the international standard" and the three-mile width of the territorial sea, many of the less developed na-

tions have ranged themselves with the Soviet bloc in opposing the traditional norms favored by the West and Japan.

Yet, on closer examination, the danger that the Communist elites and
the less developed nations might form a coalition is seen to be illusory.
The aims and motivations of most of the less developed countries diverge
widely from those of the Communist elites. A large number of these nations have not supported Communist proposals on expropriation of foreign investments and the width of the territorial sea. Nor have they supported the Soviet bloc on the issue of sovereign immunity. The posture of
these nations toward judicial settlement of international disputes, despite considerable reluctance to accept the compulsory jurisdiction of the
International Court, is by no means identical with the basic Communist
hostility to such settlement—as the submission of several cases to the
Court by Latin American, African, and Asian states indicates. The
Soviet Union has failed to gain the solid support of these countries for
its position in the United Nations on many important political issues
such as Korea, Hungary, Tibet, and the Congo. Furthermore, the less
developed nations have been far more willing than the Soviet bloc to
participate in international regulatory organizations and arrangements
such as ICAO, IMF, and GATT.

Some of the attitudes of the less developed nations, particularly those
related to the real or fancied vestiges of colonialism, will continue to
trouble the West for a long time to come. The relatively low level of
economic development of most of the non-Western and Latin American
states, and the continued dependence of these states on the industrial
nations for capital and technical assistance, will tend to prolong feelings
of inferiority and to breed suspicion that the more advanced nations are
using their superior position to dominate the poorer countries. To mini-
mize resentment, the colonial powers should not exact, at the time of the
granting of independence or subsequently, agreements that the less developed states are likely to regard as burdensome, unfair, and inconsistent with their best interests. The West cannot—and does not—disregard
either the distinctive viewpoints of the less developed nations, or their
claim to full participation in the international law-making process. Experience indicates that even on the seemingly most intractable of issues
—that of protection of foreign investments—adjustment, compromise, and
settlement on mutually acceptable terms will continue to be possible, at
least so long as nations do not choose the path of complete elimination of
private enterprise from their economic life.

It would be a mistake to discount as mere verbiage the often expressed
concern of the less developed nations for the strengthening and development of international law. Weak in material power, these nations must

seek protection and assistance in international law and organization. This does not mean, of course, that the less developed nations will have no distinctive points of view or will not attempt—as all nations have done—to use international law to promote their own real or fancied interests. Moreover, the less developed countries will insist on having their voices heard in the formulation and development of the law, and will utilize their collective numerical strength to maximize their influence in this process.

Customary international law has at times developed with considerable speed to provide for the regulation of new transnational needs and activities. The twentieth century has witnessed, for example, the rapid development of the doctrines of air sovereignty and the continental shelf. Nevertheless, the acceleration of the processes of change in the international community and the detailed nature of the regulation required for many new activities render custom an inadequate instrument for the formation of legal norms in response to all the new needs and expectations.

The less developed nations may be expected to use their influence to strengthen the trend toward law-making by multilateral treaties, particularly on subjects of special interest to them, such as racial discrimination. Nations with a close community of interest or with similar attitudes and institutions will continue, as in the past, to devise special norms to regulate their mutual relations. The network of multilateral and bilateral treaties will continue to increase in complexity. Regional legal institutions, such as those of Europe, will continue to be created by states with special common interests.

The conclusion of treaties embracing limited numbers of states may seem to be a further impairment of the "universality" of international law. But such treaties continue to be made and to operate within the framework of the more basic and general rules that constitute "universal" international law. Among these general rules, those of the law of treaties— the rules concerning the conclusion, validity, interpretation, performance, revision, and termination of treaties—will continue to be of fundamental and perhaps increasing importance.

There will be sustained efforts to formulate and develop the basic customary rules in negotiated conventions similar to those on the law of the sea and on diplomatic intercourse and immunities.

Here, again, the fact that such conventions deal with general norms which in principle are "universal" and yet are unlikely to be adhered to by all states—and thus formally to bind all states—might indicate a further breakdown in the universality of international law. Nevertheless, the necessities of international life will continue to demand a large measure of uniformity of basic rules, and many, if not all, of the rules formulated in the conventions may be expected to be universally accepted in practice.

The numerical strength of the less developed nations may also lead them to favor efforts to formulate and develop the law by declarations, adopted as resolutions by the General Assembly. Such declarations are not formally binding. However, they have the appearance of expressing a world consensus and cannot be totally disregarded by national and international decision-makers. They may be employed to confirm and strengthen existing precedents and trends in international law, or to initiate new trends. General Assembly resolutions have already been so used. The actual effect of such declarations depends, of course, on several factors, including the extent to which they express a real consensus, the number and importance of the states supporting and opposing them, and the degree to which they correspond to the requirements of international life. There are many indications that the less developed nations are becoming aware of the fact that a resolution opposed by the more powerful states, or by some of them, does not carry as much weight as one that is not so opposed. The influence of the more advanced states may be expected to continue to offset, in some measure, the numerical preponderance of the less developed nations in the General Assembly, thus preventing the appearance of too large a gap between the purported content of the law and the realities of material power.

Thus, international law will continue to be "universal" in the sense that there will be a substantial number of concepts and norms understood, invoked, and followed—despite occasional violation—by all states. The scope and complexity of international law, furthermore, will continue to expand, especially in the form of treaties, in keeping with the expansion in the number and complexity of transnational activities and interactions in a shrinking world.

International law will still be viewed by many observers as inadequate and fragmentary, since it will not constitute, for a long time to come, a comprehensive order in which the most important aspects of the relations between states—including resort to violent forms of coercion—are effectively regulated by law. But legal institutions can never guarantee lasting peace and security. Even in the best organized national societies, they are often ineffective in resolving major conflicts of interest and power. In the United States, the federal Constitution and the Supreme Court did not prevent civil war a hundred years ago. The excellent British legal system did not make impossible a twentieth century civil war in Ireland. Contemporary international law, of course, is not nearly as adequate or effective as the national legal systems of well-organized states. But its role in world affairs, although not as important as the role of national law in most states, is far from negligible. In fact, it is an essential framework for many aspects of international relations, as shown by the measure of its acceptance in practice even by the Communist states.

The absolutist dichotomy between the presence and absence of worldwide agreement on values is false. In the world community, as in national societies, there is a broad spectrum of values and of degrees of consensus on them. A large measure of agreement on values does, of course, strengthen the cohesiveness of a community and the efficacy of its legal order. But it is not a question of all or nothing.

A black-and-white contrast between a world in which common ideological values prevail and in which peace rests securely on law, on one hand, and a world in which lawlessness and naked force rule, on the other, is out of place here. These are but non-existent extremes of a continuum in which, as history suggests, international law will play varying roles in different periods and in relations between states with different interests and systems of public order.

Side by side with conflicting values and interests are many common or mutual interests. It is the existence of the latter that makes possible the regulation and adjustment of the conflicts of interest by law. Virtually all human beings agree on the importance of such basic material needs as survival, health, food, clothing, and shelter. Even antagonistic systems of public order such as "socialist" and "capitalist" have a common stake, for example, in the avoidance of general war, the maintenance of diplomatic relations and of facilities for international transport and communication, the conservation of certain natural resources, and the exchange of certain goods and services on a mutually advantageous basis. In the relations between the advanced and the less developed nations, the number of common or mutual interests is even greater.

As already indicated, the conflicts of interest—and particularly those caused or reinforced by the Communist ideology and system of public order—today prevent a rapid expansion of the role of law in international affairs. The more exacting demands addressed to international law are not likely to be fully satisfied in the immediate future. A world public order comparable in scope and effectiveness to the public order of a well-organized nation is still far away. In the international community there are, as yet, no formally established special institutions for orderly modification of the law and of existing legal rights without the consent of the states concerned. But the conflicts of interest do not prevent mutually acceptable regulation of transnational activities in the areas of international relations where there is some community of interest, however limited. Since all states engage in such activities, there is a basis for the existence of "universal" international law in the sense of a number of concepts and norms understood, invoked, and honored by all states, as well as of "particular" international law—norms that apply to some but not all states. Both universal and particular international law may be expected to grow in scope and complexity as the volume and variety of transnational activities increase. Universal agreement on ideological goals and ethical values is not a prerequisite for the existence—or even the growth—of international law.

PART FOUR

THE GREAT DEBATE IN INTER-STATE AND INTERNATIONAL RELATIONS

CHAPTER SEVEN

Realism versus Idealism

Since the days of the Greek city-states, Western political leaders and philosophers have engaged in a great debate concerning the ends and means of foreign affairs.[1] The realist school maintains that personal standards of right and wrong are inapplicable when deciding or evaluating questions of international relations. The national interest of the state, its adherents argue, is and must be of paramount importance in determining the proper course of action. The idealist or utopian school insists that man's rationality and moral capacity must be reflected in the affairs of state. For the idealists, the practical approach toward achieving world peace is to proceed deliberately and as speedily as possible toward giving up national quests for power. At the heart of the lengthy dialogue between these two positions is the question whether national power and hegemony should prevail over international law, collective security, and notions of a future world community. The great debate, therefore, involves fundamentals in the theory of international relations and is deeply concerned with ethics.

The policies that the United States followed (or did not follow) in the World War I period accelerated the tempo of the general discussion. In the thirties, the American academic community began its still-continuing search for a theory of international relations, for a conceptual analysis to provide an explanation for state action. Innumerable publications have appeared since that time. Positions that originally were stated in black-and-white terms subsequently have been modified or altogether abandoned.

Arnold Wolfers' essay "The Pole of Power and the Pole of Indifference" offers a systematic exposition of the current beliefs of both schools

---

[1] See, for example, Coleman Phillipson, *The International Law and Custom of Ancient Greece and Rome* (London: Macmillan & Co. Ltd., 1911), I, 90–101.

of thought. As Professor Wolfers makes clear, each faction views the nation-state quite differently. To the realists, "states are conceived as the sole actors in the international arena." The basic propositions of the idealists, on the other hand, "deal not with states, but with individuals, with people or with mankind." In his proposed reconciliation between realism and idealism, Wolfers advocates considering the goals or ends of foreign policy a more enlightened approach than continuing the great debate. His selection presents a provocative scheme for understanding and evaluating international politics at the same time that it provides some focus and organization for the field.

Previous essays in this book have shown how power oriented early Hindu statesmen were, and we include here a portion of the *Mahābhārata* to illustrate how closely the politically realistic philosophy of this epic resembles the *Prince*. In this selection, Kanika's advice recalls John Morley's well-known description of the realism of Machiavellian foreign policy:

Test there is no, save reason of State. We should never condemn a man for extra-ordinary acts to which he has been compelled to resort in establishing his empire or founding a republic. In a case where the safety of a country is concerned whether it be princedom or republic, no regard is to be paid to justice or injustice, to pity or severity, to glory or shame; every other consideration firmly thrust aside, that course alone is to be followed which may preserve to the country its existence and freedom. Diderot pithily put the superficial impression of all of this when he said that you might head these chapters as 'the circumstances under which it is right for a Prince to be a scoundrel.'[2]

The second article dealing with Hindu realism is a comparison between Indian and Western theories of power politics. D. Mackenzie Brown concludes that the East has had its ruthless advocates of political opportunism, but that it also is heir to a spiritual outlook, an idealistic, non-materialistic point of view that is quite unlike any political philosophy found in the West. His selection emphasizes the divergent natures of Hindu and Western political thought. But more important is the fact that both civilizations have had their realists and their idealists, each school continually attempting to prevail.

[2] John Viscount Morley, *Politics and History* (London: Macmillan & Co. Ltd., 1923), pp. 129–130.

THE POLE OF POWER AND THE
POLE OF INDIFFERENCE*

Arnold Wolfers

In international relations, two opposing schools of thought have fought each other throughout the modern age. Ever since Machiavelli published the *Prince*, his "realistic" views have shocked "idealist" thinkers. As a battle of the mind, fought by and large outside the political arena, the dispute between the two schools was of great concern to philosophers and moralists; but not until Woodrow Wilson set out to bring Utopia down to earth did it become a political issue of the first magnitude. For the first time, the responsible head of one of the leading powers acted as though the world were on the verge of crossing the threshold from sordid "power politics" to a "new era" in which the admonitions of the idealist philosophers would suddenly become the political order of the day.

No amount of disillusionment has been able to wipe out the deep marks left by the outburst of idealist enthusiasm which Woodrow Wilson's leadership evoked. Today more than ever American statesmen and the American public find themselves torn between the conflicting pulls of idealist and realist thought. Often the same event ... is interpreted simultaneously in terms of both schools, as an incident in the age-old struggle for power on the one hand, as a great venture in community action against an aggressor on the other.

This puts the theoretical analyst in something of a predicament. When interest in a theory of international politics became alive in the United States in the mid-thirties, it did so as part and parcel of a reaction which set in at the time against the prevailing optimistic Wilsonian school. Machiavelli rather than Wilson became the patron saint of the new venture. But, today, the "realist" engaged in theoretical pursuits finds himself

* Arnold Wolfers, "The Pole of Power and the Pole of Indifference," *World Politics*, IV, No. 1 (October 1951), 39–63. Reprinted by permission. Mr. Wolfers is Sterling Professor Emeritus of International Relations, Yale University, and Director of Washington Center of Foreign Policy Research, School of Advanced International Studies, Johns Hopkins University. He is author of *Britain and France between Two Wars* (1940) and coauthor of *The Anglo-American Tradition in Foreign Affairs* (1956).

swimming against the stream, and a powerful stream it is when leaders of both political parties insist that American foreign policy centers on the United Nations and collective security. . . .

The realist image of the world has been presented in its essential features by a number of authors concerned with the theory of international politics. In its pure form it is based on the proposition that "states seek to enhance their power." In this brief statement are implicit the major assumptions of realist thought.

States are conceived as the sole actors in the international arena. Operating as a group of sovereign entities, they constitute a multistate system. The analogy of a set of billiard balls or chess figures comes to mind. All the units of the system behave essentially in the same manner; their goal is to enhance if not to maximize their power. This means that each of them must be acting with a single mind and single will; in this respect they resemble the Princes of the Renaissance about whom Machiavelli wrote. Like them, too, they are completely separate from each other, with no affinities or bonds of community interfering with their egotistical pursuit of power. They are competitors for power, engaged in a continuous and inescapable struggle for survival. This makes them all potential if not actual enemies; there can be no amity between them, unless it be an alignment against a common foe.

Under these conditions the expectation of violence and even of annihilation is ever present. To forget it and thus to fail in the concern for enhanced power spells the doom of a state. This does not mean constant open warfare; expansion of power at the expense of others will not take place if there is enough counter-power to deter or to stop states from undertaking it. Though no state is interested in a mere balance of power, the efforts of all states to maximize power may lead to equilibrium. If and when that happens, there is "peace" or, more exactly, a condition of stalemate or truce. Under the conditions described here, this balancing of power process is the only available "peace" strategy.

While few would deny that the picture presented in these sweeping generalizations resembles the world we are living in at this time, it would not have passed for more than a caricature at other times. International relations within the Western world in the twenties or within the inter-American system today cannot be fully understood in terms either of balanced power or an all-out struggle for survival. This does not preclude the possibility that the "pure power model" of the realists can render service at least as an initial working hypothesis. The actual world might never fully comply with the postulates of the model, yet to the extent to which it did, consequences deduced within its context would apply to the real world. Countries engaged in a race to enhance their power could, for example, be expected to align themselves in disrespect of earlier "friendships" or ideological affinities; expansion would be sure to take place wherever a power vacuum existed.

Of course, no such approximation of reality to "pure power conditions" can be taken for granted. It presupposes that the basic "realist" contention about state behavior is truly realistic. If an insatiable quest for power were not the rule, but represented instead an abnormality or marginal case, developments in the world might deviate drastically from those which the model leads one to expect. Peace strategies other than the balancing process might have a chance of success.

Realist scholars have sought to explain why it is that states do in fact behave as postulated or why they are compelled to do so. They have offered two different explanations. According to the first, human nature is such that men, as individuals and as nations, act like beasts of prey, driven by an insatiable lust for power or *animus dominandi*. Their will to power, moreover, when transferred from small and frustrated individuals to the collectivity of the state, takes on greater dimensions and generates an all-round struggle for survival.

According to the second explanation, which is gaining adherents, the quest for power is due not to any desire for power as such, but to a general human craving for security. The insecurity of an anarchical system of multiple sovereignty places the actors under compulsion to seek maximum power even though it run counter to their real desires. By a tragic irony, then, all actors find themselves compelled to do for the sake of security what, in bringing about an all-round struggle for survival, leads to greater insecurity. This "vicious circle theory" makes statesmen and people look less vicious than the *animus dominandi* theory; what it does is to substitute tragedy for evil and to replace the "mad Caesar," as Lasswell calls the *homo politicus* of the pure power model, by the "hysterical Caesar" who, haunted by fear, pursues the will-o'-the-wisp of absolute security.

The validity of these explanations of an alleged uniform behavior of states toward power need not be discussed here, because the realist scholars who started out with the assumption of such uniformity have not stuck to it after descending from the high level of abstraction of their initial propositions to the lower levels where the shape of actual things can be apprehended. All of them have found it necessary to "deviate" from their original assumption to the point of distinguishing between at least two categories of states with different attitudes toward power.

Few have stated more emphatically than Morgenthau that in international relations "power is pitted against power for survival and supremacy." But more recently he has drawn a sharp distinction between two types of states, the "status quo powers" and the "imperialist powers." Of the former, he says that their policy tends "toward keeping power and not toward changing the distribution of power"; of the latter, that they aim "at acquiring more power." Similarly, Frederick Schumann starts out with the assertion that in international politics "power is sought as an end in itself," but then goes on to differentiate between "satiated" and "unsatiated" states. His statements that "each state left to itself tends to extend its power over as wide a field as possible" and that "enhancement of state power is always the goal" are contradicted, it would seem, by his subsequent contention that states which benefit from the established status quo naturally seek "to preserve that from which they benefit," in contrast to those "which feel humiliated, hampered and oppressed by the status quo." The authors of another recent text, Strausz-Hupé and Possony, follow a similar line. After stating at the outset that "foreign policy aims at the acquisition of optimum—and sometimes of maximum—power," the optimum remaining undefined, they go on to define, as a special type, the "natural aggressors" who in contrast to other states are "driven by a particularly pronounced dynamism, i.e., urge toward power accumulation." Finally, Spykman, who did much to introduce the pure power hypothesis into the contemporary American discussion, deviates from his opening statement, according to which "the improvement of the relative power position becomes the primary objective of the . . . external policy of states," by speaking of the "dynamic state" which, as he puts it, "rarely sets modest limits to its power aims." This implies that non-dynamic states, on the contrary, do set such "modest limits."

One consequence of distinctions such as these is worth mentioning. They rob theory of the determinate and predictive character that seemed to give the pure power hypothesis its peculiar value. It can now no longer be said of the actual world, e.g., that a power vacuum cannot exist for any length of time; a vacuum surrounded by "satiated" or "status quo" states would remain as it is unless its existence were to change the character of these states and put them in the category of "imperialist," "unsatiated," or "dynamic" states.

The idealist model, if such there be, cannot be as easily derived from writings or statements of exponents of the idealist school itself. This school has been anything but theory-minded. Its attention has been focused on peace strategy and on blueprints for a better world. However, it would have made no sense for idealists to proffer advice on policy if they had held no general views about the existing world which permitted them to regard as practical the policies they sought to promote. As a matter of fact, Woodrow Wilson himself, with his predilection for broad generalizations, has expressed on one occasion or another all the main tenets of the "Wilsonian" school.

One feature of the idealist image strikes the eye because of its contrast to the realist view. Here the basic propositions deal not with states, but with individuals, with peoples or with mankind. The idealist seems to be looking out not on a multistate system with its separate national entities, but on a nascent world community and the people who make it up. This precludes from the start that the emphasis be placed on national quests for power or on the struggle for power among nations. Instead, the accent is either on the "common purpose of enlightened mankind" or on the common values which men hold as individuals. Because the vast majority of men are assumed to value the same things—such as individual freedom, the right to govern themselves, the safety of their homeland, and above all the absence of violence—it is concluded that there can exist no basic conflict between them even as nations. If it were not for extraneous interference—and a remediable measure of ignorance and misunderstanding—there would be harmony, peace, and a complete absence of concern for national power. "I sometimes think," said Wilson, "that . . . no people ever went to war with another people." But he goes on to say that "governments have gone to war" with one another, thereby pointing to the darker side of the idealist picture.

Only a dreamer could mistake for the existing order the vision of a world of independent nations in which there is no conflict, nor any drives for power. The idealist school does not do so. It not only fully recognizes the continued presence or threat of "power politics," but considers this discrepancy between "what is" and "what should and will be" as the crucial moral and political issue of international relations. The explanation for it is believed to lie in the operation of evil forces which violate the peace and law of the community.

There is no doubt about the character of these forces. They are conceived as anachronistic remnants of an age—now coming to an end—in which autocratic rulers rather than the peoples themselves controlled the destiny of nations. It was these rulers who were "playing the game of power," as Woodrow Wilson puts it; their ambitions, not the interests of their peoples, were in conflict and plunged the world into power politics and the struggle for survival. Whenever and wherever such autocracy asserts itself—or reasserts itself through a relapse into a bygone age—the community of peace-loving nations falls victim to the onslaught of aggressive power and violence.

One might suspect that when such aggression occurs, the world would return to conditions very much like those portrayed by the pure power model. The only difference would seem to be that now the power of aggressors would be pitted against the collective power of peace-loving nations. The idealist denounces such a comparison as superficial and dangerously misleading. It would be no less inappropriate, he maintains, to speak of a struggle for power or a balancing of power process when describing the defense of international peace and lawfulness than it would be to apply these same terms to the actions of a national police force engaged in fighting individual criminals.

According to idealist thought, then, the quest for collective international police power has taken the place of the obsolete quest for national power as far as the majority of the actors is concerned. One would be tempted, by way of contrast, to call this idealist image by some such name as the "pure solidarity model" were it not for the emphasis placed on the continued threat or presence of aggressive antisolidarity forces.

The idealist school has been taken to task by its critics for the illusory character of much of its interpretation of the existing world, especially for its *a priori* optimistic assumptions concerning human nature and the harmony of interest, as well as for its narrow explanation of the phenomenon which it terms aggression. The validity of such criticism should become clearer, at least by implication, from what will be said later. It is more important, here, to point to some of the insights which the idealist approach suggests to the theoretical analyst.

By distinguishing from the outset between two types of behavior toward power, rather than introducing discrimination as an afterthought or deviation, the idealist has been more aware of the problems arising from this lack of uniformity.—If anything, he may be too much inclined to take the lack of uniformity for granted, for example, when asserting categorically that democracies behave differently in foreign affairs than dictatorships.—Because of the important role he assigns to individuals and their values as well as to bonds of community transcending national boundaries, he has an eye for aspects of reality—such as the relative ease with which the English-speaking world has learned to collaborate— which are hard to reconcile with the image of a "billiard ball world." ...

The two schools are obviously far apart, if not diametrically opposed on many issues. Yet, despite striking differences, their views are closely related to each other, at least in one significant respect. Both approach international politics on the same level—which might briefly be called the power level—though they approach it from opposite ends. By way of simplification, it can be said that while the realist is primarily interested in the quest for power—and its culmination in the resort to violence—as the essence of all politics among nations, the idealist is concerned above all with its elimination. On this level there can be no meeting of the minds. ...

Normally, power is a means to other ends and not an end in itself. . . . to treat the quest for power, positively or negatively, outside the context of ends and purposes which it is expected to serve, robs it of any intelligible meaning and, by the way, also makes it impossible to judge its appropriateness or excessiveness. . . .

One gets a very different picture if one considers first the values and purposes for the sake of which policy-makers seek to accumulate or use national power, as they may also seek alternative or supplementary means.

This suggests beginning with a "theory of ends" and proceeding from there to the analysis of the quest for power as it develops in conjunction with and under the impact of the ends it is meant to promote. It must be kept in mind, however, that one is not dealing with a simple cause-and-effect relationship. The degree to which power is available or attainable frequently affects the choice of ends. Prudent policy-makers will keep their ends and aspirations safely within the power which their country possesses or is ready and willing to muster. Statesmen with a respect for moral principles, or under pressure from people who have such respect, may hesitate to pursue goals which demand the sacrifice of these principles or of other values in the process of power accumulation or use.

There is little reason to expect that all actors on the international stage will orientate themselves uniformly toward one and the same goal, whether it be peace, security, or "power as an end in itself." However, the possibility will have to be considered that they may be operating under some form of "compulsion" which may force them in the long run to fall in line with each other. . . .

The idealist school is correct in stressing the value which men in general place on peace and in insisting that such evaluations can affect the decisions of policy-makers. Whether of their own volition or under pressures from more peace-minded groups of the population, statesmen under certain circumstances will desist from pressing national demands through means of power or will limit their demands. Realists would not be so eager—as was Machiavelli himself—to impress their governments with the "necessity" of playing the game of power politics as consistently as their opponents, were it not for fear that these governments might act otherwise.

However, the idealists refuse to recognize that while peace-loving peoples wish for peace, they also wish to preserve what in the past they as individual nations have acquired or helped to establish. When their valued possessions come to include a wide circle of values reaching far beyond the national boundaries, as they do in the days of ideological or religious conflict, the occasions for power competition and violence are further enhanced.

Idealists are right in stressing that policy goals transcending the "national interest"—as traditionally interpreted—and affinities transcending national boundaries not only exist, but can be promoted by suitable policies. Nations defending common values and interests may come to form such bonds of friendship that their relationship ceases to be merely that of a temporary and expedient alliance in a balancing of power process; in the end they may merge or federate. However, if this process of amalgamation—clearly not compatible with the image of a world of billiard balls—takes place, as it usually does, in the context of a common conflict with an "out-group," such national self-abnegation within the "in-group" does not diminish the intensity of power politics in the world at large; it may increase it. Thus, if the "Free World" or the North Atlantic group of powers or Western Europe were drawn ever more closely together and learned to act as an organized community in accord with commonly accepted laws, it would still depend on the intensity of the East-West struggle how deeply the nations of the world were engaged in "power politics."

The extent to which there is a struggle for power is decided, then, by what might be called the "relationship of major tension," not by the attitude which nations not engaged in conflict take toward each other. In the same sense, it can be said that the degree of power competition and the expectation of violence rest not upon the behavior of countries concerned with self-preservation, but upon that of the "initiator." Idealist optimism in regard to the elimination of "power politics" is out of place, therefore, as long as the trend toward major tensions and toward the eruption of new and ambitious demands for self-extension is not reversed.

The drastic change which has taken place over the last fifteen-odd years in the attitude toward peace strategy of the idealist school itself bears witness to the deterioration in the prospects for enduring peace. While earlier the emphasis was on conciliation and disarmament, it has come to be placed almost exclusively on "force behind the law" and "enforcement of peace." This means a swing to the realist view that counterpower and counterforce alone—though it be the collective power and force of the peace-loving community acting under the rules of an international organization—can safeguard the peace. This is the old idea of the balance of power, if within a new institutional frame. The change of attitude has gone so far that other means of peace strategy, such as the negotiation of concessions to satisfy demands of potential "initiators," are now often condemned without qualification as "imperialist deals," "appeasement," or "rewards for aggression." This is not said in a critical vein. The idealist school may prove itself realistic in recognizing that we are caught at present in a situation of such extreme tension and incompatibility of goals that anything except the display of adequate defensive force on our part will merely serve to encourage offensive resort to violence on the part of others.

The realist school has merited its name for having appreciated the role which the quest for power plays in international politics, though it has devoted little attention to the policy goals from which this quest for power springs. It has recognized that a multistate system—a term which still properly designates the outstanding feature of contemporary international politics—is heavily slanted toward struggles for power. Lying somewhere within a continuum which stretches from the pole of an "all-out struggle for power" to the pole of an "all-round indifference to power," the actual world tends to be pulled more strongly toward the former. This is true, whether the realist *a priori* assumptions concerning a universal human hunger for power or of a "security dilemma" arising from *la condition humaine* are correct or not. The main reason lies in the ever-recurring new incentives to demands for change and the equally strong incentives to throw power in the path of such change. By a curious irony, the same readiness to resist through power which is the prerequisite of any competition for power may, if strong, quick-moving, and determined enough, prevent the struggle from degenerating into violence. This is what the realists have in mind when placing their hopes for peace on the balance of power.

It is quite possible that most of the great drives toward national and revolutionary self-extension which at intervals have thrown the world into struggles of sheer survival could not have been prevented by any means available to man. One can hardly escape a sense of fatalism if one asks oneself retrospectively whether the rise and aggressions of a Hitler could have been avoided. But this does not mean—as realist thought would seem to imply—that no influence can be brought to bear on policymakers which would serve the interests of peace. Anything that bears on their value patterns and preferences, on their estimates of gains and deprivations, or on the scope of their identifications will, in principle, be able to affect the course of policy upon which they decide to embark.

It may be Utopian to expect that the causes accounting for resorts to power and power competition could ever be wholly eliminated—as it is Utopian to believe that defensive counterforce could be consistently held at sufficient strength to prevent the actual resort to violence; but there need be no resigned acceptance of the "enormity" of a continuous all-round struggle for survival. Through suitable policies, pressures, and appeals designed to attack the causes of intensive drives for enhanced power, the pulls toward the pole of all-round indifference to power can be strengthened. The main task of those engaged in developing a realistic theory of peace strategy is to discover policies and practices which offer most promise of turning nations away from goals that point toward power competition and violence.

HINDU AND WESTERN REALISM: KANIKA'S ADVICE*

The Mahābhārata

Then summoning unto his side Kanika—that foremost of ministers— well-versed in the science of politics and expert in counsels, the king said, "... the Pandavas are daily over-shadowing the earth. I am exceedingly jealous of them. Should I have peace or war with them? O Kanika, advise me truly, for I shall do as thou biddest!"

"Listen to me, O sinless king, as I answer thee! ... Kings should ever be ready with uplifted maces (to strike when necessary), and they should ever extend their prowess. Carefully avoiding all flaws themselves, they should ceaselessly watch for the flaws of their foes and take advantage of them. If the king is always ready to strike, everybody feareth him. Therefore should the king ever have recourse to chastisement in all he doeth. He should so conduct himself that his foe may not detect any flaw in him. But by means of the weakness he detecteth in his foe he should pursue him (to destruction). He should always conceal, like the tortoise hiding its body, his means and ends, and he should always conceal his own weaknesses from the sight of others. And having begun a particular act, he should ever accomplish it completely. Behold, a thorn, if not extracted wholly, produceth a festering sore! The slaughter of a foe who doeth thee evil is always praiseworthy. If the foe be one of great prowess, one should always watch for the hour of his disaster and then slay him without any scruples. If he should happen to be a great warrior, his hour of disaster also should be watched and he should then be induced to fly. O, father, an enemy should never be scorned however con-

---

* The *Mahābhārata*, trans. by Protap Chandra Roy (Calcutta: Bharata Press, 1893), pp. 416–423. The *Mahābhārata* was composed between 200 B.C. and A.D. 200, and is traditionally ascribed to Vyasa.

temptible. A spark of fire is capable of consuming an extensive forest if only it can spread from one object to another in proximity. Kings should sometimes feign blindness and deafness, for if impotent to chastise they should pretend not to notice the faults that call for chastisement. On occasions such as these let them regard their bows as made of straw. But they should be always alert like a herd of deer sleeping in the woods. When thy foe is in thy power destroy him by every means open or secret. Do not show him any mercy although he seeketh thy protection. A foe or one that hath once injured thee should be destroyed by lavishing money if necessary, for by killing him thou mayst be at your ease. The dead can never inspire fear. Thou must destroy the three, five and seven (resources) of thy foes. Thou must destroy thy foes, completely tearing them up by their roots. Then shouldst thou destroy their allies and partisans. The allies and partisans can never exist if the principals are destroyed. If the root of the tree is torn up the branches and twigs can never exist as before. Carefully concealing thy own means and ends, thou shouldst always watch thy foes, always seeking their flaws. Thou shouldst, O king, rule thy kingdom always anxiously watching thy foes. By maintaining the perpetual fire, by sacrifices, by brown cloths, by matted locks, and by hides of animals for thy bedding, shouldst thou at first gain the confidence of thy foes, and when thou hast gained it thou shouldst then spring upon them like a wolf. For it hath been said that in the acquisition of wealth even the garb of holiness might be employed as a hooked staff to bend down a branch in order to pluck the fruits that are ripe. The method followed in the plucking of fruits should be the method in destroying foes, for thou shouldst proceed by the principle of selection. Bear thou thy foe upon thy shoulders till the time cometh when thou canst throw him down, breaking him into pieces like an earthen pot thrown with violence upon a stony surface. The foe must never be let off even though he addresseth thee most piteously. No pity shouldst thou shew him but slay him at once. By the arts of conciliation or the expenditure of money should the foe be slain. By producing disunion amongst his allies or by the employment of force, indeed, by every means in thy power shouldst thou destroy thy foe." . . .

Kanika continued, "If thy son, friend, brother, father, or even spiritual preceptor, becometh thy foe, thou shouldst, if desirous of prosperity, slay him without scruples. By curses and incantations, by gift of wealth, by poison, or by deception, the foe should be slain. He should never be neglected from disdain. If both the parties be equal and success uncertain, then he that acteth with diligence groweth in prosperity. If the spiritual preceptor himself be vain, ignorant of what should be done and what left undone, and vicious in his ways, even he should be chastised. If thou art angry, show thyself as if thou art not so, speaking even then with smiles on thy lips. Never reprove any one with indications of anger (in thy speech). And, O Bharata, speak soft words before thou smiteth and even while thou art smiting! After the smiting is over, pity the victim, and grieve for him, and even shed tears. Comforting thy foe by conciliation, by gift of wealth, and smooth behaviour, thou must smite him when he walketh not aright. Thou shouldst equally smite the heinous offender who hath since been living in the practice of virtue, for the garb of virtue simply covereth his offences like black clouds covering the mountains. Thou shouldst burn the house of that person whom thou punishest with death. And thou shouldst never permit beggars and atheists and thieves to dwell in thy kingdom. By a sudden sally or pitched battle, by poison or by corrupting his allies, by gift of wealth, by any means in thy power, thou shouldst destroy thy foe. Thou mayst act with the greatest cruelty. Thou shouldst make thy teeth sharp to bite with fatal effect. And thou shouldst ever smite so effectually that thy foe may not again raise his head. Thou shouldst ever stand in fear of even one from whom there is no fear, not to speak of him from whom there is fear. For if the first be ever powerful he may destroy thee to the roots (for thy unpreparedness). Thou shouldst never trust the faithless, nor trust too much those that are faithful, for if those in whom thou confidest prove thy foes, thou art certain to be annihilated. After testing their faithfulness thou shouldst employ spies in thy own kingdom and in the kingdoms of others. . . . In speech thou shouldst ever be humble, but let thy heart be ever sharp as the razor. And when thou art engaged in doing even a very cruel and terrible act, thou shouldst talk with smiles on thy lips. If desirous of prosperity, thou shouldst adopt all arts—humility, oath, conciliation, worshipping the feet of others by lowering thy head, inspiring hope, and the like. A person conversant with the rules of policy is like a tree decked with flowers but bearing no fruits; or, if bearing fruits, these must be at a great height not easily attainable from the ground; and if any of these fruits seem to be ripe, care must be taken to make them appear as raw. Conducting himself in such a way, he shall never fade. . . . He who having concluded a treaty with an enemy reposeth at ease as if he hath nothing more to do, is very like a person who awaketh having fallen down from the top of a tree whereon he had slept. A king should ever conceal his counsels without fear of calumny, and while beholding everything with the eyes of his spies, he should take care to conceal his own emotions before the spies of his enemies. Like a fisherman who becometh prosperous by catching and killing fish, a king can never grow prosperous without tearing the vitals of his enemy and without doing some violent deeds. The might of thy foe, as represented by his armed force, should ever be completely destroyed, by ploughing it up (like weeds) and mowing it down and otherwise afflicting it by disease, starvation, and want of drink. A person in want never approacheth (from love) one in affluence; and when one's purpose hath been accomplished he hath no need to approach him whom he had hitherto looked to for its accomplishment. Therefore when thou dost anything never do it completely, but ever leave something to be desired for by others (whose services thou mayst need). One who is desirous of prosperity should with diligence seek allies and means, and carefully conduct his wars. His exertions in these respects should always be guided by prudence. A prudent king should ever act in such a way that friends and foes may never know his intent before the commencement of his acts. Let them know all when the act hath been commenced or ended. As long as danger doth not come so long only shalt thou act as if thou art afraid, but when it hath overtaken thee, thou must grapple with it courageously. He who trusteth in a foe who hath been brought under subjection by force, summoneth his own death as a she-mule by her act of conception. Thou shouldst always reckon the act that is future as already arrived (and concert measures for meeting it), else, from want of calmness caused by haste, thou mayst even overlook an important point in meeting it when it is before thee. . . . If the foe is insignificant, he should not yet be despised, for he may soon grow like a palm tree extending its roots, or like a spark of fire in the deep woods that may soon flame up into an extensive conflagration. As a little fire gradually fed with faggots soon becometh capable of consuming even the biggest blocks, so the person who increaseth his power by making alliances and friendships soon becometh capable of subjugating even the most formidable foe. The hope thou givest unto thy foe should be long deferred in the filling; and when the time cometh for its fulfilment, invent some pretext for deferring it still. Let that pretext be shown as founded upon some reason, and let that reason itself be made to appear as founded on some other reason. Kings should, in the matter of destroying their foes, ever resemble razors in every particular: unpitying as these are sharp, hiding their intents as these are concealed in their leathern cases, striking when the opportunity cometh as these are used on proper occasions, sweeping off their foes with all allies and dependents as these shave the head or the chin without leaving a single hair. . . ."

HINDU AND WESTERN REALISM:
A STUDY OF CONTRASTS*

D. Mackenzie Brown

[D]oes not India possess a system of cold realism in the Arthashastra literature as brutal and animalistic as, say, the Western Machiavelli? No doubt, all cultures possess both spiritual and material value systems and one must be careful to avoid a one-sided approach. With this in mind, let us examine briefly the writings of the political realists.

Machiavelli's evil counsel has long been deplored: "There are two methods of fighting, the one by law, the other by force—the first method is that of men, the second of beasts; but as the first method is often insufficient, one must have recourse to the second. It is therefore necessary for a ruler to know well how to be both the beast and the man ... to know well how to act as the fox and the lion ... It is not necessary for a ruler to have (good) qualities, but it is very necessary to seem to have them. Thus it is well to seem merciful, faithful, humane, sincere, religious ... But it must be understood that a ruler cannot observe all those things which are considered good in men, being often obliged, in order to maintain the state, to act against faith, against charity, against humanity, and against religion ... A ruler must take great care that nothing goes out of his mouth which is not full of the above named five good qualities, and, to see and hear him, he should *seem* to be all mercy, faith, integrity, humanity, and religions. And nothing is more necessary than to seem to have this last quality."

On the face of it, at least, it would be difficult to conceive a more complete cynicism and ruthless opportunism than that contained in this Western treatise on government. Yet India's writers are not without their own opportunism. We find in Kautilya: "A ruler who is situated between two powerful rulers may seek protection from the stronger of the two;

* D. Mackenzie Brown, "Indian and Western Realism," *Indian Journal of Political Science*, XV, No. 4 (October–December 1954), 265–272. Reprinted by permission of the author. Mr. Brown is Professor of Political Science, University of California, Santa Barbara, and author of *China Trade Days* (1947), *The White Umbrella* (1953), and *Indian Political Thought from Ranade to Bhave* (1961).

... or he may make peace with both of them on equal terms. Then he may begin to set one of them against the other by telling each that the other is a tyrant ... and thus cause dissension between them. When they are divided, he may put down each by secret or covert means ... or pretending to be a close friend of one of them, he may strike the other at the latter's weak point. ... When the enemy is in the habit of paying frequent visits to monks, temples, sacred shrines, and images, spies hidden in underground passages or inside the walls may strike him down." And again, we find: "The ruler who is desirous of achieving prosperity should join hands, swear, use sweet words, worship by bending down his head, and shed tears. One should bear one's foe on one's shoulders as long as time is unfavorable. When, however, the opportunity has come, one should break him into fragments like an earthen jar on a stone."

Up to this point there is little to choose between Machiavelli and Kautilya insofar as standards of political behaviour are concerned. On the other hand, if it be claimed that Kautilya's ruthless advice is tempered by warnings against personal corruption in government, we can point to similar and parallel warnings in Machiavelli. Thus we find in Kautilya: "Ignorance and absence of discipline are the causes of a man's troubles. An untrained man does not perceive the injuries rising from vices. ... Rulers given to anger have fallen a prey to popular fury. Rulers addicted to pleasures have perished. ... The bad effects of drinking are loss of money, insanity, ill health, loss of knowledge of the Vedas, disassociation with the good, suffering, etc." Machiavelli, in his turn, echoes the warnings of the Greek Polybius on the dangers of license and tyranny: "The children of former rulers quickly degenerate from their fathers; and instead of trying to equal their father's virtues they consider that a ruler has nothing else to do than to excel all the rest in luxury, indulgence, and every other variety of pleasure. The ruler consequently draws upon himself the general hatred."

If, in both Eastern and Western Realism, we find the same ruthlessness and the same frank recognition of the dangers of personal corruption on the part of the wielder of the scepter of political sovereignty, how can it be said that in India we have a spiritual outlook that respects the "Rule of Higher Law" while we have in the West a materialism that recognizes only animal values in a secular world? It would be wisest at the outset to recognize that there are to be found both idealism and cynical realism in East as well as West. Kautilya and Vyasa offer sufficient cold realism in the East and Aquinas and others give us a considerable measure of idealism in the West. Nevertheless, insofar as the active tradition of the Western world is concerned (especially since Machiavelli and the

Renaissance) there is a basic element of contrast between its political theory and that of India.

This contrast begins with the tendency of Western thinkers to make the State an end in itself. With certain exceptions to be found in Plato, for instance, the Greeks had largely looked upon the State as the terminus of human development—an end to be achieved beyond the lower developments of family and community. Machiavelli and later Western writers generally take the State for granted as a necessary and desirable human goal—much of *The Prince,* for instance, comprising a manual of the rules for getting, holding, and enlarging the petty State of sixteenth century Italy. Indian writers, on the contrary, have recognized the State, not as an end in itself but as a means to man's ultimate spiritual goals and have related State policy and political values to a higher set of values—*i.e.,* to a "morally valid philosophy of life."

This can be demonstrated even in the writings of the most ruthless of the Indian "Realists," Kautilya, Vyasa, and Shukra. We find in Kautilya: "Harmlessness, truthfulness, purity, freedom from spite, abstinence from cruelty, and forgiveness are duties common to all. The observance of duty leads one to *Svarga* and infinite bliss. When it is violated, the world will come to an end ... Hence the ruler shall never allow the people to swerve from their duties; for whoever upholds his own duty, will surely be happy both here and hereafter. For the world, when maintained in accordance with injunctions of the triple Vedas, will surely progress, but never perish." Thus, even for Kautilya, there is a higher law to which state policy is subordinate. Vyasa, having earlier made clear the spiritual goals of humanity, warns us (after advising rulers how to engage in cynical power politics) that "a ruler should not always act in this way; this course of conduct should be pursued only in seasons of distress." Vyasa also points out that the Kshatriya ruler need practice but three fourths of the high virtue required of the Brahman, presumably because there existed a graduated scale of virtue among the four castes and among the orders with ultimate spiritual standards which few individuals could approach. Vyasa realizes that human motivation determines political morality and that conduct must be viewed from "considerations connected with the gods," that what may appear virtue may under circumstances be sin and vice versa. Thus, untruth, killing, and taking property may be virtues (*i.e.,* the son may lie to protect his father from robbers; the policeman may kill a murderer to protect a child; the ruler may tax the landholder). Shukra also relates State policy to a higher level. He says: "The ruler who is virtuous is a part of the gods. He who is otherwise is a part of the demons, an enemy of religion and oppressor of subjects. The ruler is made out of the permanent elements of Indra, Vayu, Yama, Sun, Fire,

Varuna, Moon and Kuvera, and is the lord of both the immovable and movable worlds. As Yama is the God who punishes human beings after death, so also the ruler is the punisher of offenses in this world."

Western political theorists, on the other hand, have generally viewed morality and religion not as keys to man's ultimate salvation and his relation to the powers of the universe, but rather as tools to obtain secular success in the material world. Thus Machiavelli pays tribute to the ancient Roman religion as follows: "Whoever reads Roman history attentively will see in how great a degree religion served in the command of the armies, in uniting the people and keeping them well conducted ... There are many good laws, the importance of which is known to the sagacious lawgiver, but the reasons for which are not sufficiently evident to enable him to persuade others to submit to them; and therefore do wise men, *for the purpose of removing this difficulty*, resort to divine authority.... Considering then, all these things, I conclude that the religion introduced by Numa into Rome was one of the chief causes of the prosperity of that city; for this religion gave rise to good laws, and good laws bring good fortune, and from good fortune results happy success in all enterprises.... And therefore everything that tends to favor religion, *even though it were believed to be* false, should be received and availed of to strengthen it." (Italics mine.) The Greek Polybius had commented upon the same phenomena seventeen centuries before Machiavelli. In *The Histories* we find: "The quality in which the Roman commonwealth is most distinctly superior is, in my opinion, the nature of their religious convictions. I believe that it is the very thing which among other peoples is an object of reproach, I mean superstition, which maintains the cohesion of the Roman State.... As every multitude is fickle, full of lawless desires, unreasoned passion, and violent anger, the multitude must be held in by invisible terrors and suchlike pageantry. For this reason I think, not that the ancients acted rashly and at haphazard in introducing among the people notions concerning the Gods and beliefs in the terrors of hell, but that the moderns are most rash and foolish in banishing such beliefs."

Commenting upon the false spirituality of this same Roman power, Aurobindo Ghose remarks, "The spiritual and cultural is the only enduring unity, and it is by a persistent mind and spirit much more than by an enduring physical body and outward organization that the soul of a people survives. This is a truth the positive Western mind may be unwilling to understand or concede, and yet its proofs are written across the whole story of the ages. The ancient nations, contemporaries of India, and many younger born than she are dead and only their monuments are left behind them. Rome imposed a political and a purely outward cultural unity on the Mediterranean peoples, but their living spiritual and cultural oneness she could not create, and therefore the East broke away from the West. . . . But India still lives and keeps the continuity of her inner mind and soul and spirit with the India of the ages." Dr. Radhakrishnan also believes that an "essentially spiritual" attitude has been a basic factor in the political survival of the Indian state through the centuries. Thus, "External invasions and internal dissensions came very near crushing India's civilization many times in its history. The Greek and the Scythian, the Persian and the Mogul, the French and the English have by turn attempted to suppress it, and yet it has its head held high. India has not been finally subdued, and its old flame of spirit is still burning."

There is much evidence to indicate that to the Western political theorist Religion was simply a means to his ultimate human goal—the successful State; to the Indian political theorist the State was merely a means to his ultimate human goal—*Moksha* or salvation.

Although in the earlier phases of Western political development we can find exceptions to the general trend (in the works of the Stoic writers, the Church Fathers, the Medieval scholastics, and especially in the monumental work of Aquinas), the Western tradition that has come down to us is basically materialist-humanist. After the Renaissance this is especially so. Ever since the modern Western theory of law emerged (with Grotius and others conceiving of it as grounded in human nature as against divine order), we have observed a continuing flux of legal theory which finally resulted in the separation of "pure law" from its ethical and moral context. Jellinek's declaration that the legality of an action depends upon its *form* and not its *content* is far removed from the traditional Indian concept of political Dharma. This is illustrated in the well known passage from Manu: "For the man who obeys the law prescribed in the revealed texts and in the sacred tradition, gains fame in this world and after death unsurpassable bliss." . . . While the Dharmashastras are founded squarely on the idea of the stability of the supreme law or Dharma, the outlook developed by Grotius, Jellinek, Austin and Kelsen has finally stressed mere legal form and has depended upon legal norms or customs or current statutes in determining the content of the law. It is precisely the stability and fundamental character of supreme law that Western political thought has now rejected. In the words of Laband, "There is no idea which could not become a law." In the broadest sense today we find the traditions of Indian and Western political thought divergent at the source, for the Indian holds the state to be the product of law, the other holds it to be the source of law!

SELECTED BIBLIOGRAPHY

PART I. GENERAL

Bozeman, Adda B., *Politics and Culture in International History*. Princeton, N.J.: Princeton University Press, 1960.

Hoffmann, Stanley H., ed., *Contemporary Theory in International Relations*. Englewood Cliffs, N.J.: Prentice-Hall, Inc., 1960. See Part III.

Kahin, George McT., Guy J. Pauker, and Lucian Pye, "Comparative Politics of Non-Western Countries," *American Political Science Review*, XLIX, No. 4 (December 1955), 1022–1041.

Modelski, George, "Agraria and Industria: Two Models of the International System," *World Politics*, XIV, No. 1 (October 1961), 118–143.

——, "Comparative International Systems," *World Politics*, XIV, No. 4 (July 1962), 662–674.

Northrop, F. S. C., *The Meeting of East and West*. New York: Macmillan Co., 1946.

——, *The Taming of Nations*. New York: Macmillan Co., 1952.

Russell, Frank M., *Theories of International Relations*. New York: Appleton-Century-Crofts, Inc., 1936.

PART II. CHINA

Bodde, Derk, *China's Cultural Tradition*. New York: Holt, Rinehart and Winston, Inc., 1957.

DeBary, Wm. Theodore, Jr., *Sources of Chinese Tradition*. New York: Columbia University Press, 1960.

Goodrich, Luther C., *A Short History of the Chinese People*, rev. ed. New York: Harper & Row, Publishers, Inc., 1959.

Grousset, René, *The Rise and Splendour of the Chinese Empire*. Berkeley: University of California Press, 1953.

Latourette, Kenneth Scott, *The Chinese, Their History and Culture*, 3rd ed. rev. New York: Macmillan Co., 1946.

Linebarger, Paul M. A., Djang Chu, and Ardath W. Burks, *Far Eastern Governments and Politics*, 2nd ed. New York: D. Van Nostrand Co., Inc., 1954.

Reischauer, Edwin O., and John K. Fairbank, *East Asia: The Great Tradition*. Boston: Houghton Mifflin Co., 1958.

PART III. INDIA

Dreckmeier, Charles, *Kingship and Community in Early India*. Stanford, Calif.: Stanford University Press, 1962.

Ghoshal, U. N., *A History of Indian Political Ideas*. New York: Oxford University Press, 1959.

Sarkar, Benoy Kumar, *The Political Institutions and Theories of the Hindus:*

A Study in Comparative Politics. Leipzig: Verlag von Markert und Petters, 1922.

Smith, Vincent, *The Early History of India from 600* B.C. *to the Muhammadan Conquest.* New York: Oxford University Press, 1924.

———, *The Oxford History of India,* 3rd ed. rev. by Percival Spear. New York: Oxford University Press, 1960.

PART IV. ISLAM

Brockelmann, Carl, *History of the Islamic Peoples.* New York: G. P. Putnam's Sons, 1960.

Gibb, Hamilton A. R., *Mohammedanism,* 2nd ed. New York: Oxford University Press, 1953.

Gibb, Hamilton A. R., and Harold Bowen, *Islamic Society and the West.* New York: Oxford University Press, 1957.

Hitti, Philip, *History of the Arabs,* 7th ed. rev. New York: St. Martin's Press, Inc., 1961.

Kirk, George E., *A Short History of the Middle East,* 5th ed. New York: Frederick A. Praeger, Inc., 1959.

Lewis, Bernard, *The Arabs in History.* New York: Harper & Row, Publishers, Inc., 1960.

Smith, Wilfred C., *Islam in Modern History.* Princeton, N.J.: Princeton University Press, 1957.

Von Grunebaum, Gustave E., ed., *Unity and Variety in Muslim Civilization.* Chicago: University of Chicago Press, 1955.

INDEX OF AUTHORS